[Your Name] ®
AN INVITATION

Global Stabilized Energy, LLC

Globalstabilizedenergy.com

Kevin C. Pattison

The Human Race is God, Too!
Also He is
[Your Name]®

God

Male   *SELF*   **Female**

Human

All the answers you want to know that are in and on the Universe are in between these four (1. Male 2. Female 3. God 4. Human) truths down to "One truth" per issue when you have the correct formula, I call it the truth finder. We can unite the world with the skills of "One Love" through the right education of "One God." We can know everything! From living things to things by language, God and self to its full wholeness. The possibility exists to eliminate or a least heavily reduce divorce and disease, the scientific proof is where it comes back to itself.

Every place of worship in the world should see this book and then we can unite the world through language by joining church and state together when it is time by knowledge. Because they do fit perfectly together.

The whole complete language consummated together (the twins in language) correctly defines "GOD" in education because He is "all," "everything" and the "way." Our own perception is holding us back to the correct knowledge because we are the way through self, language and God to be everything and the "all" of self the exact mirror image of God which is us. The intellectual challenge to life meets in the center of the human side and the middle of the spiritual side together faith is for the human side to gain the knowledge to be one God or one with God both have the same results.

Table of Contents

Introduction:

[Your Name]® Is God, Yes You.
Do You Want to Know Why?

Are you in the 99%? Or the 1%?

About four years ago, I drove to the hospital with a stomachache and woke up two weeks later from a coma. I found out that I coded twice while I was under, and that my heart stopped for literally minutes at a time.

During that time, I had a vision where we all came together as one in knowledge, knowing we are God's truth, and that we can uncover this knowledge together.

Who is the wisdom and energy of Love? We are. We all have our God-self within us, separately and all together. God's truth is based off perfect mathematics and represented in us as human beings. To know our God-self is the plan. It is for us to see from within, to be awake. Everything we need to know exists inside each of us, known as Universal Intelligence.

Our ancient ancestors had it right: every creature is half animal or human, and half god or spirit. A person has two sides, a spiritual inside and a human outside, mirroring the universe. God also has two sides; we know he is in the Heavens outside, but how can we prove God is inside on Earth?

◀ 🔆 ▲ ✕ ◉ 🔳 🔲 📶 ⁴⁰₊₊₊ 47% 12:25 PM

≡   Go gle

🔍   not in the way of science ·   🎤

ALL   MAPS   NEWS   VIDEOS   IMAG

"The **scientific** method is a body of techniques for investigating phenomena, acquiring new knowledge, or correcting and integrating previous knowledge. To be termed **scientific**, a method of inquiry is commonly based on empirical or measurable evidence subject to specific principles of reasoning."

Scientific method - Wikipedia
Wikipedia › wiki › Scientific_method

About this result · Feedback

There are many things in the world that can be found with two sides, as big as God and as small as an atom. The two sides of the atom are a proton and a neutron, but with an added twist - electrons that are found in shells or orbitals surrounding the nucleus. These parts that make up the atom create abstract diversions that mix up the patterns in everyday life or in religion.

I believe this book has nailed down the "scientific method" of both the doctrine of science and the doctrine of religion and creates a way to see the center of the perfect mathematical Universal truth. This is a way for all to understand through the doctrine of education, that which is us; God is humanity too. It is about what we don't see or know and haven't learned individually or by group.

This sounds religious but it's not. Our first mistake is thinking God is religious. Our second mistake is thinking humans aren't small gods. We are all God in a centered scientific and balanced religious way, by the system that has been in effect from the beginning as our ancient ancestors figured it out.

Less than 1% of the people in the world can change the world for the better and truly understand what the center of the word "know" means (literally). It's not easy, but it is simple, if the process to understand your God-self is found or taught the correct way. The first part of the process is understanding the God thing, or at least your God-self, before it becomes one with you.

When Dr. Wayne Dyer was alive, I saw him on T.V. with Tony Robbins. Wayne said we are all God or the lighthouse, to which Tony said we figured it out and learned it ourselves back in the day. Even though it sounds philosophical, religious, or spiritual, it is actually fundamentally academic, explaining the abstract universe, how humanity fits down to a single person, and how that fits in the puzzle of science, religion and knowledge to "know" (all ways of knowing after you have discovered your God-self). When one is in confusion, disarray, or plainly doesn't understand this, they are likely part of the 99% of humanity that does not "see." There is another way of knowing and there are 60,000,000 people who do "see" the other way of knowing from the inside. Together those people equal the mathematical way of knowledge.

The fact is, the wider, deeper, lower, or higher one opens their minds to thinking in all ways, the closer they come to becoming part of the 1% of the whole wide world that sees what I'm talking about. Some well-educated people and some of the greatest minds in the world overlook this as common knowledge. But I believe that with a well-rounded, centered education and an effort to work together with all the right professionals, it is possible for anyone to "know." For many, that process can begin with reading this book. After you read slowly and all the way through to the end, new ways of knowing will be opened up to you.

It will be helpful if one opens the mind to a broader way of thinking as you read through this book, because this will set you up to see the inside way of "knowing." As you advance, anything written by the people that "know," will help you as you move along in your journey.

That which has tapped into the inside God-self is all the same genre and the purpose of it is for you to wake up to be confident, solid, intelligent, and happy; to "know," see, and be aware. The books that are written to help others see are based off perhaps humanity's relationship to the Universe, the power in and the power up.

Nobody goes out looking to wake up, because they don't "know." They are asleep in "knowing," both inside and outside knowledge. It is in the razor's edge of understanding, after the brain unintentionally lies to oneself, which is to be unaware. Remember, 99% of people don't "know," including many rabbis, ministers, pastors and priests. Maybe seminaries need to rethink how the multi-dimensional God is one God.

The idea that love is the truth and the truth is love literally has all of life's answers embedded in it. It is the perfect system that goes by the name God. Maybe to understand life is to "know" that God, love, and the truth are together from the inside out. To know that which is the same for all of us is the definition of God!

It may be different than we think, how it is all in everything. Math, together in harmony with language, equals the center of one (the theory of everything); even the people that know miss that one. This works together in real time with total knowledge inside and outside where everything equals **one** mathematically, including the idea that love is the truth and vice versa. Time is always the present moment, in all ways. The exact knowledge of the perfect space is in the continuous - now God's - makeup. It is the designer and controller of us, to the center of us, explained religiously to a child as the playbook to life and the family, then humanity with the unselfish self-sharing justice from within our work.

Explained scientifically, everything in the Universe is merged as one metaphysically, symbolically and literally. The human being is the playbook to and for science. Humans are the perfect image of the Universe, from how we *are made down to our polarity. Dichotomies and opposites are programed into our makeup, provable by atoms and the quirks that are inside an atom.*

A small part is religious, but the primary goal is to explain how everything fits perfectly together academically, mathematically, and spiritually to help the reader "know" it all. That needs to be understood to see how everyday life works together. A good example is in this book, by using humanity to work together to break the information down.

This book is based off the principle of the mind, body, and soul, humanity, the Universe power in and the power up. To "know" ALL of importance. This knowledge is inside at a subatomic level. Seeing the patterns where the meanings are the same and reading in-between the lines to "know" that all of the heavens and the Earth are inside you, is a good start to see a choice. Belief in the continuous moment is to know what the word "know" means. There really is no middle ground; you either see it or you don't. It doesn't matter what one thinks or believes, only what one knows inside and out. This is how you relate the truth about what you "know."

Imagine the Future

When the internet was first invented, no one could have imagined how this increase in access to knowledge would change the world. What if there was an app that collected and compared all of the knowledge of the world in one place with the sole purpose of finding universal truths? How would that change the world?

I once had a conversation with John Gray, author of *Men are from Mars, and Women are from Venus.*

After watching Oprah's 26th episode of Super Soul Sunday, dealing with "Life's Big Questions," I left him a message saying I believed the show was missing important gender differences. I said it also missed the "truth" (something I hope to find using what I call the Rubik's Cube of Knowledge). This show, among many other influences, had prompted me to begin working on an idea for an app that would help everyone learn the important universal truths for themselves. He agreed with me and hopes to collaborate with me on this project in the future.

As the project began to take shape, I settled on an app and interactive website tied together with an instructional book. I will bring together a group of experts or "coaches" in their own specific areas to enhance the app by sharing in collective thought.

Oprah has asked hard questions over the years about God and what happens after we pass. In addition to that, let's find out who we are as humans and how we work from the inside through the collective us. This can be done by sharing interactive thought, capturing what others know that we don't in conversation, with a purpose towards organized participation throughout the world. It is possible that, by chance, we can uncover some of our universe's secrets.

What does it mean to change the world? It can be done simply but not easily through our own awareness and understanding of what we miss, overlook, or don't notice, and knowing our brain doesn't see sometimes on the first pass.

This is the start of working together to unite nations, true unions - joined together for the greater good.

On the Oprah Show (Super Soul Sunday) when Howard Schultz, CEO of Starbucks was a guest, he said that the polarization of politics needed to be fixed or greatly reduced in the world. Ultimately, polarization starts inside oneself and then expands to the outside in recognizable patterns. We could establish a shared information political "party" in the center between the polarized opposites on political issues to allow people to participate in voicing opinions while still in thought about them. Moving on to Democrat or Republican parties from there would provide a centralized baseline idea formed in a safety zone. No words like "fact," "believe," or "know" would be used. Just what you "think" and your "opinion," so everyone can release what is within them while feeling

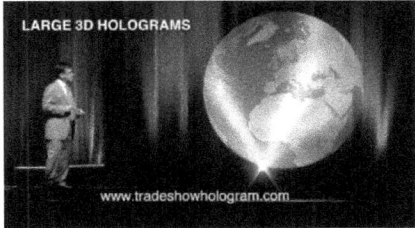

safe about not knowing, free of fear to look at building the whole truth from each person's part of the truth. Another good area for this sort of discussion would be religion, as a puzzle to build around the world. If we all build through goodness to the end at this point, the devil's advocate would not be needed because only good finds the true center. Shall we try? When we listen is when we see truth; we see or find God typically when things are bad, or we turn off thought and live blindly and justify the reasons. Mine was a divorce 25 years ago. Most people stop after they find God or believe in Him or find comfort in spiritual things and/or pick up a religion or maybe keep seeking. I ran into love and truth together. At the same time, all the answers to and in life for me were because at the time, back then I loved my ex-wife with every part of me and at points we shared deep, deep love, and when she left me she said love wasn't enough and I found she was completely wrong. Love is everything. So I kept going, seeking what love was or is and it kept teaching me the truth until I found the other side of God that is self or the other side of self is god all together the same thing, knowledge that is the same truth for everybody.

The truth is in us all the way down to one truth for each and every issue and how things and living things fit together is literally the same for everybody. I saw that the other sides to self in language are the laws of thought under the identity law: I is "oneself" or "our-self" and we are "yourself" or all of "us" is "our-self", "yourself " and "oneself" **we** is inside and **us** is outside but we and us are God together when we start inside in the middle of the center on the outside are made whole and we are separated by [Your Name] individuality by what "One" sees (from the inside) until we all see the same by education. And the education is "Self" individually, when we know God has us in our role as the perfect human to be god, using the skills of timeless wisdom intellectually not physically, these are the action skills of both "self" individually and collectively. For example: Ancients learned how to change molecular structure an equal balance from LIGHT, ENERGY AND SOUND somehow through God guidance (what we don't know seems to be God). The collective self is all of us = "ONE" God that made us in his image with all-knowing skills organized from the dictionary regarding both sides of the definition. Mathematically how our language is perfect once self, God and language are "ONE" of the "same" are the same thing (most miss this) at the same time when it comes back to itself, that is 100% scientific proof and our leaders in academics should see this. After reading this book "The human race is God! He is also [Your Name] this is the way we are separated to identify "YOURSELF", you. If you see 1. God is self individually and collectively 2. Language in the book is telling us, we are the same when we recognize how to come back to itself that which makes each situation whole and complete to understand. 3. Self, when language comes back to itself, self and God come to have "one" point together from God, self and language , our intellect comes from that and when each is the same we have nailed the scientific proof. We also are direct relatives of God as the human race and we disguise religion unknowingly to explain God (that's why it doesn't work unless your light bulbs are on). Do be patient - one must see 3 into one to see the whole truth, to see correctly.

I will include where I have extended and enhanced the pros today to change the vision for tomorrow how God, divorce and gays are looked at with scientific reasoning. Also, I will discuss how I read a book that was given to me (written by Mary Baker Eddy), and my comments on it will be given toward the back of the book. You may want to read this part first, to provide you with the broad scope. This includes how one religion can be proven and start out in each using or adding us as ourselves to all religions but using Jesus' teachings as a human God the same as us.

I haven't figured it out yet, but I would like my original manuscript posted on my website somewhere to collectively edit for the whole truth but first collectively so all can understand. I hired multiple editors but my 2nd editor cut out over 90,000 words and more than 100 pages. I have attempted to put back in what she cut out unknowingly without duplication and we can do this by the wisdom of the crowd by cutting only duplication and things that are NOT the truth. The editor has some mean writing skills but I am trying to introduce something new so the more people the better to see the whole process of peeling away truth to make the whole truth for the system to be perfect, not us, the pros the same for everything to find the whole truth we are to find the whole truth to work together to write God's plan. Anything that doesn't fit means the person is living humanly and what fits and is true is living spiritually by the patterns of language, self and God that's when it comes back to itself.

God's word is outside of language (the meaning of words is the same as the meaning beyond words are the same). "When the way things "are" are the same as "God, language and truth for oneself, oneself can be explained in writing and are the same as all of self" or come back to self. Get it? If you do then you should know why the "truth" and knowing all three at the same time will set you free! Because it pinpoints any and all issues, the whole truth is using both sides together and is the start of using one complete truth to start with (the way to the truth using the right formula and same patterns 3 down to 1 where they are the same). Let's not overlook the truth "when we do that is the reason why people do not "see God", "self" or "language" as one to see the scientific proof. I would like Oprah Winfrey to organize because I am completing her work (really God's work and all of our work too!). The difficulty is in understanding God is too how to many ways of seeing we are the same and can make it confusing to understand because all of us are partners with God! The other side of self is God you, and oneself to become equal to God. Oprah if the one God is the metaphysics of the mind what percentage would you say you are? We may have to make a scale first. What percentage do you think the churches are of God and I'm sorry but no churches are doing it correctly but MBE only if you drop Christian and leave science this is God's proxy (science) to open it up for all people when we go deeper to change believing to a rock solid to "KNOW" God's way using his word to form a sentence to hear his voice. When we teach the churches the one religion we can put them back in power that they lost back in the 1500's or so because they didn't "know" oneself what it takes individually to be a God or what all of self what it means collectively to have one God for the universe that matches perfectly even mathematically and skipped both 1. Oneself to complete as a God Individually 2. All of self the other side of God besides us is the universe as it has all the answers with the internal intellect with intelligence for us to be all "KNOWING" I showed how to do that in the book. The churches are stuck on the one God that I explained - how we aren't God and not understanding how God is the way by following what they "believe" and sticking to it. But not by what they "know" when they understand that word correctly (this word "know" correctly) that is the checks and balances with science God proxy where everything fits perfectly together when "One" sees it and is equally united for not just people but everything (things and living things). The churches jumped to what they think they "know" but it is only what they believe as it is NOT the whole truth and is altering the way for us to "KNOW TRUTH." What is perfect in truth and love for the perfect life to live in the middle of the center will cure human conditioning but the way we are living now is with no advancement; that is because the churches need to listen to the world religion by the pros after I go deeper into what they already know and this may do it at the end of the emails.

The never-ending journey Oprah has mentioned many times, I see a completion for, and every time I say to myself have I really accomplished that high on the scale that hasn't even been created yet and realize I must stand alone in seeing the vision! Where I see God's law or the spiritual laws and human laws centered as "one" by us correctly. I see that one nation under "the" God with one religion "SELF" as all of self is "ONE" God using humanly as the church with the wisdom of the crowd in control to lead the one nation under "God" by using the guidance of the universal bible for the truth.

Individually as "ONE" Human "SELF" as a God is the perfect human starting with my original manuscript and the universe as the exact image of God she (Oprah) deserves the right to "KNOW" what I know and deliver it, not to be cocky but I completed or enhanced her work. The book is saying to humanity if I can show the pros how God's word works all together as "ONE" it can come back to itself for all to see then together we can figure it out and unite the world. What the churches haven't figured out Jesus's teaching are about "self" - individually and/or collectively. We are going to use the published book MBE to show how a belief can be turned into a "knowing" if it has the correct ingredients using science is God's proxy. (any problem with the right formula can be figured out using language, God and self when all three become "ONE" meaning) it comes back to itself.

A group helping with the Facebook ads said the bigger the problem one solves, the more money they make. I have the right ingredients to shake up the world by "ONE" religion by solving the God problem that is solved when the formula is correct to solve all problems even if you don't see it now believe in humanity to see. Not to mention all the other things we should have the pros eating out of our hands when we finish. The curiosity alone can peak the media's interest to create a worldwide buzz with us asking the pro's to help "Self" become the "ONE" God and our book explains it.

The following is a letter I wrote to Howard Schultz:

Mr. Howard Schultz
Starbuck's Coffee

Re: The Rubik's Cube of Knowledge: The Process of Internal Growth

Dear Howard Schultz,

The first thing that comes to mind when someone develops a fascinating, novel invention is, "Wow, great job!" This is what happens when the strength and tenacity of never giving up is recognized and admired.

You made a comment on Super Soul Sunday with Oprah Winfrey: "First, think big and then think bigger, and then think even bigger." Congratulations on the community you have created! Let's conceptualize the idea of bringing the community a little bit closer.

Imagine having the ability to break the ice for designated conversations with ease, to select groups of people enjoying their time in different community settings, such as coffee shops, churches, and libraries around the world.

I envision a way of bringing communities and countries closer through locations like Starbucks by installing an Interactive 3D hologram in each location. The hologram would illustrate intellectual and emotional activities and "thought-provoking" questions, with a goal of building a Rubik's Cube of

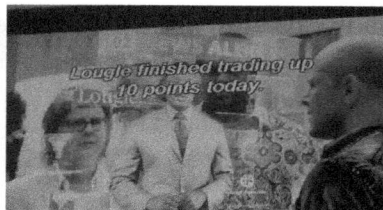

Knowledge for internal growth. Timeless wisdom would be recorded and could be passed along to our children, and people around the country and world. This application and website would be placed in coffee shops at an elongated table. People would be able to carry the app on their phones and

access the website from their computers. This trailblazing application can be easily compared to the car-sharing app Uber, taking out the fear of meeting somebody and opening up conversations without judgement.

Then, by amplifying Oprah's hugely successful book club which teaches the general public how to have a relationship with Self, we could show the process of communication. This starts from how we communicate, and the way to listen and really hear what is said. Then, the goal would be to show how our thoughts are attached to our feelings, and our actions are tied to what we "think, believe, and/or know" and how our perception determines the way we see from inside our mind. I call this reading between the lines. The timing and interactive process is a natural way of being human. Seeing all of these mechanisms working together is truly living in the present millisecond of the moment.

The surprise of being awake or aware and seeing the process is quite interesting in terms of what we believe is natural, but we miss part of the process when the mystical part of our emotions becomes prevalent and soon changes who we are and where the emotion is directing us. We tend to lie to ourselves because we think we know and we use this to justify ourselves.

This is the start of a Rubik's Cube of Knowledge and Wisdom, clarifying the mystical part or the unknown, what we naturally overlook, or that the mind may not see. The Rubik's Cube of Knowledge is like a universal intelligence (UI). The UI can include fields such as the arts, music, religion, philosophy and science. For the individual, one must include all of these subjects to reach a satisfied level of academic excellence, emotional intelligence, and divine wisdom, which, without a doubt, creates a form of happiness.

In learning, sometimes we have to see things in different ways to increase the likelihood for something to sink in; this is just the natural growth process. Expressing ideas different ways allows us to understand what is meant. A 3D type of color-coded hologram will display the knowledge, allowing us to pick up the things we don't see, hear, or place well in our minds. If needed, the ideas can be illustrated with time lapse photography as a visual. The ideas can also be coupled with clearly related clips from movies, arts, music, martial arts, and nature.

The caveat here is building a 3D color-coded, interactive hologram, to show the natural process of how we know what we already know inside of us. As people learn more, they will build out the framework interactively to allow others to see, layer-by-layer, the process on the way to completion. This needs community interaction and for people to be a part of the whole!

Communication can be simplified to the basic need to talk and to be heard, and satisfaction of developing a balanced emotional intellect. The app will put listening and hearing what is said in the moment, for the razor's edge of the truth (not just "a" truth), or a separate reality leading to an unintended path. The idea here is that there is no right or wrong, only what works best for the moment and gives insight into the different ways to look at ideas to help improve discussions. This will be done with guidance from people who are coaches and experts, separate from the underwriters and editors who are definitely aware of the universal intelligence.

The calling mentioned by you and Oprah on her show is for people that are presently aware of the Aha Moment, Universal intelligence, or what I call the Portal. My goal is to get you and us there, through the portal. The step-by-step visualization of the internal processes helps give a feeling of belonging and an urge to participate in the next steps by tugging heavily on the curiosity card. We will slow time down enough to see the process of what happens naturally, and the somewhat mystical process of how what we don't know can shape our lives.

Coffee shops will be the main hub for providing a location where individuals with a pursuit of personal knowledge and internal growth can meet and increase their wisdom, or converse about topics in the app. But the interactive model can be used to help connect people at any time, such as during Uber rides, where drivers and customers may use the app to commence a conversation or a puzzle.

The app will drop an individual off at each dot on the virtual map, made up of a maze of lessons. While Uber takes customers to their physical destination, we will take them to their desired metaphysical destination in the world of timeless wisdom, with help from the imagination, to enhance internal growth.

We would create additional employment for the people that are already of universal intelligence. Since these people are already placed around the world, they would make excellent guides. Their leadership and guidance will be extended once we have a completed outline, along with the checks and balances of their UI. People who are involved with books, movies and a variety of activities would get their small piece based on keys unlocked. As well, people who sell additional memberships can make a living somewhat like marketing geometric growth companies utilized by the internet and an Uber-like application showing in real time what inside work needs to be done specifically for them.

When people use the app for the first time, the process would start by finding out what issues their parents may not have gotten over, such as the need to be right, the fear of death, and the ways many other topics are looked at. Living in the present moment, and not the future or past, really means getting out of your head and paying attention in the moment, whether it is looking at the beauty in the universe or concentrating on remaining focused.

There are a myriad of similar blocks out there and we will get them listed out for the app. It will be designed as a game, with sets of keys to unlock each level, gift, and skill. We will create the levels utilizing the best of the best. People have been writing about these different topics for years.

An example of a topic might be the taking out or away, temporarily, of "beliefs" because by definition they are only a part of the whole. If we could create a puzzle that allowed all religions to contribute their beliefs, maybe the result would be becoming "all knowing."

An example: there are two parts of our brain, right and left sides. The same may be true for our emotions. One side might be called human and the other side might be church, religion or spirit side (community). I have also seen it referred to as the shadow for the emotions; nevertheless it's two sides of the one.

Human/Inside: What is anxiety? Answer: "I don't know!"

Spirituality/Religion: What is faith? Answer: The same, but different, "I don't know!" One of the skills is reading between the lines. Sometimes attaching emotions to what one knows and what one doesn't know can change your behavior tremendously. Then separate one's emotions from money, if that's possible.

Another example: is it possible to love oneself totally, entirely in a selfless, Godly way?

Why does the act of sex cause so much trouble? There are so many thought-provoking questions. The reality is, the managing of our speech and our emotions is pretty high on the list to centering one's self and the outcome is peaceful, knowledgeable actions.

How do we approach solving or reducing the rivalry for the ever-increasing polarization of people, communities and countries? This may be the start of a puzzle that we can break down, piece by piece, as a collective group. I would say that the dichotomy of men and women can be used to understand this, if polarization is the same as dichotomy, which just includes the sex of a human. The answers may be found in the Ying and Yang. A little bit of Yang in the Ying and vice versa, with input by men, women and children, monitored professionally by the underwriters of course may prove helpful. The simplicity of innocence may find a brilliant outcome. I would suggest starting with an easier topic, which could be the differences between men and women, where possibly Dr. John Gray would be happy to help.

The key to solving most issues is understanding the internal way of how we become one, but knowing that we need the input of both. There should be no strong words or feelings of "believing" or of what you "know," just opinions and thoughts. Keep any conversation at a lower tone and it will accomplish more. Starting with us, let's evaluate how the rest of the world looks at us in the United States, and the lessons they think we have not learned yet. Whether in oneself, one's community or one's country, we look at ourselves differently than others look at us. We find the skills and gifts in others and amplify them to find out what they may have missed and what possible problems may exist from lessons not learned in a constructive way.

Thank you,

Kevin C. Pattison Global Stabilized Energy, LLC

info@Globalstabilizedenergy.com

Chapter One:

[Your Name] ®
Vision of the app, book and interactive website

Let's start by looking at the vision from a broad scope, starting off with an understanding of Google's knowledge graph. Imagine sitting in a coffee shop, McDonald's, the nightlife World of Beer, or even a movie theater. In other words, think of a company that has locations worldwide, and connects through those different locations. Now, use a TV screen, movie screen, a big wall projector or even imagine a hologram, like something from Star Wars that you can't get at home. Not just a device, but something extraordinary that people want to see, something that is a motion picture-like display that goes from the USA to India, Africa, Mexico, Egypt, and so on, and that allows everyone to talk collectively about a particular issue, lesson or a type of current event. This would make this place the hub and physical location of the internet.

Sometimes we need to fill up with camaraderie and there is not a standing invitation I know of to fulfill that on a consistent basis. The trick is, we need to get an open invitation to join discussions without the fear of not knowing somebody or of breaking the ice. "Joining is expected, accepted and known." Walking to the table in a predetermined place in Starbucks symbolizes you're welcome to join in and use the available movie theater to access whatever conversation people are having at the time. On the table or screen, to help facilitate conversation, will be a Rubik's Cube of Knowledge that is being built by the community interactively. Google has their new knowledge graph, everything from A to Z, but their goal is to put in books digitally from A to Z. The Rubik's Cube of Knowledge's goal is to sift through some of those books and only retrieve the required paragraphs from different sources. This is to get the right answer to the question that allows specific answers in different formats. Philosophical, spiritual, scientific and even religious books reveal life lessons as being the same yet different, and different yet the same! Let's take a journey together and pin down life's possible truths.

This is an application-based program that could deal with issues humanity has in common, whether it is something like dealing with the need to be right, or the fear of death, or the fear of fear, or other self-help issues, and the process of building better relationships. The community can use the app and website to address any question or issue they care to. They can use fun things like a puzzle to find out what the answer is at the end if those answers are ones that we don't know. This helps in being aware of the fact that sometimes what we don't know shapes our lives. We will be peeling away, little by little throughout this document, what Universal Intelligence is.

To illustrate the point, this app would be comparable to Uber. When you get in the car, the ice is broken right away; there is no fear or reluctance because of not knowing the person. Instead, there is a completely safe feeling with little judgment from one another, because no one cares. This really allows one to talk about anything and seems to encourage truthfulness in a situation involving people that don't know each other. Furthermore, there is an equal accountability that is created by the rating system. Now that you can find each other, if needed, as part of the community between driver and passengers, the app can take you where you want to go physically.

The app we're building will take you anywhere you want to go on the inside, metaphysically dropping you off at points of interest, until the lesson is learned. It can also drop you at multiple places at once, as the exercised collective mind may prove to be the universal intelligence for the intellect we have been seeking. The gained wisdom can pave the road for one's imagination. There is no telling what can happen when we put our minds together in an organized, computerized fashion! On the lighter side, we can always ask something fun like, "Where did that saying come from?"

There are so many ways we can take the fear, lack of confidence and miscommunication out of most types of relationships to create a hub for these relationships (RH). We hope to roll out the app and website in places like clubs, restaurants, coffee shops and movie theaters to help in creating meaningful, real, and skilled relationships. The passenger of Uber, the communities of Facebook, Airbnb or the group gathered at Starbucks submit a question to the Rubik's Cube of Knowledge (Bank of Knowledge), and if the question makes it past the underwriters, they receive credit in their account. Then we, as owners of the app, build the framework for the question and get to the core, policing the questions depending on relevance and the topic, which can be anything metaphysical. Because we're thinking through the masses, we will discover a deeper inner technology and may end up with answers only the collective group could come up with.

The app will help us evaluate what we've learned, where we think we are now in life's learning process, and where we believe we can go! As we rise emotionally, mentally and philosophically as a people, we may not know where we will end up. But we have to start this together. This will be in real time. Millions of people will come up with the answers collectively at www.Globalstabilizedenergy.com.

Starbucks built a community and brought people together by having a place where they could go to work on their computer with great coffee. Our goal is to bring people even closer. Instead of just sitting at a table, looking at the person next to them, our app users, with the help of the elongated tables and

holograms, will be encouraged to open up a conversation without fear, even if they are an introvert. The table symbolizes a welcome to someone sitting next to you (or someone around the world) or a door to a room or theater. We would have the same long table with a video and audio communication format that would disappear like Mark Cuban's Cyber Dust. The perfect instrument to use for worldwide communication is a combination of Cyber Dust, Twitter, Periscope, Voxer and Facebook, among others. When talking about sensitive subjects like politics or religion and spirituality we can put the recorded version to the community to analyze polarization. We would then pick a topic off of our hologram and say, "Let's put this to our community and build it from there to get it into the Rubik's Cube of Knowledge." This is essentially the process and for each lesson learned there is a key to unlock a "grid" all the way to the top of a game-like application (there is a monthly-based premium for this). The question, which we already have structured in the application, will be an entertainment source to no end. Incorporating movies, music, books, different holograms, and other sources of knowledge that will make this a fun event for everyone. Users will be given three choices: gaining intellect, gaining wisdom, or having fun. One of the three will provide them with a source of entertainment for free, but it will encourage them into a topic. For example, music can teach us much about life.

In all types of music, lyrics will mean something different to each listener, and the messages can feel different. However, if you listen beyond the words, the lessons are the same.

Rather than hearing people's problems, we focus on figuring out what lessons need to be learned to prevent problems or to know how to deal with problems that arise. The app is designed to direct users to see what needs to be accomplished or overcome while still having fun through gaining wisdom, or perhaps exploring more difficult topics like religion or evaluating one's self. Because the app will identify what the lessons are, it will help prevent one from wasting time, running around in circles and missing certain things. The person that identifies a need for lessons will pay a small fee. This fee allows one to track the needed lessons and will provide the required keys to learn the lesson and have the internal light bulbs turn on - once you know, you can't unknown! The app will provide this system and structure on a personal level, much like the Forum Corporation, a global learning and development center for business on a commercial level, but ours is individualized through the app. When on the app, there will be a way for both sides to make money. Required instructions by the coach will be provided and consumers can pay nothing and enjoy the entertainment for free, most of which will be thought-provoking and entertaining, leading them to feeling comfortable paying a small monthly fee. We will provide a flat rate for each lesson to be paid virtually, and users will pay by an algorithm much like Uber or Lyft.

The contacting of the coaches who are willing to share their individual portals would be done before this is released worldwide, because there are going to be connections all over the planet. When outer-technology and inner-technology meet, what happens? The app can show the lessons individually as users go through, but it also shows the community's lessons and the country's lessons. Maybe we get a hedge of a bet on our past and what we've learned. Maybe at that point we are able to solve what it really means to live in that millisecond of the moment through communication and balanced emotions as well as the possibility of finding love, the truth and maybe bumping into something akin to God! This may help us find a new world, but at the same time, we can bring the good part of the past with us.

As of now, we may be missing the younger generation; they don't really know how to socialize. Typing can help in communication, but without speech it can do more harm and leave one disconnected. This app may help in solving that, or at least in recognizing that we need more face-to-face communication to satisfy our intellect, and the human touch. As it is, we often don't listen, and without talking, we are disconnected from each other. This is why we haven't gotten a handle on socializing for our youth yet.

Building this system is like building a puzzle. We take what we know as an individual, and work with the knowledge that other people know something that we don't. It would be cool if in building the puzzle, people get paid if they put in the missing piece and have it structured from an algorithm. After all, money is the biggest motivating factor on the planet. These new platforms are getting more than $50 billion. That's big money! Ours is a platform that we can utilize the same way but do it in a three-tier group, and then on one set do it as geometric growth. In addition to this platform, we can have a traditional platform as well. Our algorithm is essentially the average of the average then the average of that average. You can take both sides of that in different ways and mathematically find a new structure. That's why math is beautiful; it's about finding new ways of uncovering what already exists.

Mathematically speaking, when I say, "ask a question, get three answers," you can do that backwards, in a similar yet different way; you can ask those three answers, and get the same question. All we have to do is learn how to sift through them to organize and put them together. You ask a question, and you have three different answers, a form of artificial intelligence. They're right there like with Google, but within you. Look at Google's alphabet, for example, at Z for Zygote body in Google's new knowledge graph. This takes it from showing somebody in shorts to the inside, showing muscles, down to the bones until it is invisible.

What we don't see in communications has emotional ramifications, like building a brick wall of emotions, and not allowing anyone in. Holding in these emotions can and will turn them into weights. This is dealing with the situation symbolically.

By talking about it, you can take out one brick at a time to reduce the buildup of those emotional walls. Doing some yelling, talking or whatever it takes to get the feelings out in the open is dealing with the situation physically. Look at it this way: we have an exterior and an interior. In a way, talking brings our two sides together. Sometimes when one digs deep enough, they will see where emotional time essentially stops. It's like when you run into someone you haven't seen in years and you pick up right where you left off. It's almost timeless. Maybe the reason for that is part of what goes into the Rubik's Cube of Knowledge. The Rubik's Cube of Knowledge is a place to put permanent undisputable knowledge from the middle of the center to show the perfect process in language, self, and God, how all things are the same when they come back to itself for each issue.

We have the Rubik's Cube of Knowledge and then we have the 3D body hologram that we build layer by layer to help understand how we operate.

We have the internet hub: a coffee shop, a McDonalds or The World of Beer. We have what we don't know, how it shapes our lives and how the puzzle pieces actually can fill in things that might be invisible to us. We have the app that, like Uber or Lyft, will drop you off, but within the self. All data is carefully sifted through by the underwriting process before it makes it into the Rubik's Cube of Knowledge as Timeless Wisdom. There are other platforms about human interaction such as Facebook, food and water (Starbucks), shelter (Airbnb) and transportation (Uber and Lift). Those are the external factors needed to maintain the human body. The app would help form a relationship hub (RH) at the coffee shop or McDonalds. When visiting from out of town, or even going into town by yourself, this is considered the same "group of no fear;" you don't need to know anybody to open up a conversation. Feeling safe is built in by the welcome you receive.

People are people wherever you go in the world. This is the social hub to find out what the nightlife is or to meet somebody and just talk. This is about finding a few really good connections individually, but ultimately it can help in developing great minds by operating in groups comprised of both men and women and individuals of different ethnic backgrounds. Generational differences show the greatest polarization, but these groups have the best shot at reducing the true polarization that exists in the world. The coach would have to be handpicked for this scenario and the many other "experts" that the community comes up with would have to pass approval processes.

In the community itself, we are trying to build an environment without fear, without judgment, in which one can believe what they want to believe and people with differing opinions can still be friends and still talk. Maybe *because* of differences in things like ethnic background, we can learn to appreciate our differences.

We have a three-tier type of program. The first is application at commercial locations. The second is a website one can use at home. The third is the app, which anyone can download on their phone, anywhere around the world, and track their personal progress, seeking the wisdom of a group or the gaining of skills through puzzles and lessons. The first tier only takes place at the "elongated table of no fear" to break the ice. The conversations need to come with an open invitation that encourages people to be a member of the community, join the safe haven and introduce themselves.

The application can be personal, with all the questions listed out so only you see them. You are able to ask what you don't know and feel safe in gaining knowledge. Each lesson learned is therefore personal, rather than being experienced by the community together.

The community has lessons as well. A question that might be posed to the community could be: why is there racism? Let the community answer and find out what they think. As there will be vastly different answers depending on factors such as where one is located, we would have coaches throughout the community and also throughout the states to help monitor the questions, and the first line of underwriters would try to find three common denominators. Those three common denominators are then emailed back to the people who want to participate in the community and talk about the question, by community and country. They then resubmit it through the coaches to the next underwriting scholars to make it into the Rubik's Cube of Knowledge. This would really work best with the involvement of at least three different countries, preferably six to nine different countries, participating in this one lesson. After all, other people know what we don't, and it would be nice to know what they know. We have the technology to do this.

Communication is a vital part of this, as so many people speak many different languages. It would be nice to bring Google in to help with the language barrier. As I mentioned, the part of the worldwide communication would be like Cyber Dust, modified specifically to do what we want. Since they don't allow Facebook or Twitter in China, we will need to start with something fresh and new. Perhaps a blend of Voxer, YouTube uploading, what's App, Periscope, Cyber Dust and others. We would likely establish our own as well.

Now, it is also possible to find some lessons that are applicable to the country as a whole, and that are individualized, which might be like taking away choices. What would happen if choices are taken away? Those are some of the hard questions. Then you either have to rely on church or state, state being the laws of the land, and church being "the good thing" so to speak. If you need one of those to work, what are you going to do when neither of those work? You have to deal with it yourself! What do you do? Put that to the community. Now that same lesson worked backwards, individually: what happens if it's an immediate family member? You can put it hypothetically to the community for an immediate response. This would be in the app in different ways, through books, movies, YouTube and so forth. Don't forget that it's structured by professionals, so you'll always have the right modern thinking.

When we think of country, what may come to mind is when Billy Joel went to Moscow, Russia. There is a documentary about the visit and the Universal Laws of music. Youth were not allowed to listen to music in Russia before this. He broke down the barriers for people to see music as being important in life.

Another idea to consider revolves around our history of war against other countries. Let's take what we've learned from past wars and from the older generations to help us in the future. A good saying to consider is: "those that don't remember the past are bound to repeat it." We should take the wisdom from lessons learned, for if that lesson is not learned we will repeat it over and over again. Perhaps, as a community, we can talk about issues, even sensitive ones, if we do so in a structured way, without being mean or insensitive. We are seeking the lessons of the past and putting them into the Rubik's Cube of Knowledge once it has been discussed by the community, policed, underwritten, sent back to the community for its evaluation and then sent back again to be shown to be timeless wisdom.

The other issue to think of is that, because we are operating in different countries, we have many different religions to deal with; this means addressing the idea of God. One way would be to build a puzzle, to take away beliefs and just use data. This can work for you or against you; people sometimes die for what they believe in. We must try to combine each group's different religion to help build a puzzle so each religion is a piece of the whole puzzle.

Perhaps we would hire a professional puzzle company that can collect data and use our underwriting to submit each piece. Therefore, it's a third party that is doing the work to find out what the outcome is. It is really asking the questions to find out the answers. Then, we can use the answers we already know, such as what each religion's beliefs are. In this way, we're not judging; we're just taking what each religion believes as part of the whole.

I believe that the first step to spirituality is probably in the way we listen. This is the start of the "invisible body" and each layer represents a part of the communication process. The community helps build the framework and it's monitored and assessed by PhDs, doctors, and spiritual leaders. We are only as good as the systems we build or understand. We can talk with the communication gurus about how our thinking as people has been tracked, expanded and glorified over the years. When we look at the whole picture of life we can see that we are doing things completely backwards in some ways. When we take a step back and look through a scientific lens, we can see how everything fits together perfectly like a puzzle.

We will start with communications. Think about this for a second: you and another person both believe that you're on the same page, when you might not be. There needs to be a follow-up talk for clarification. There are more layers of emotional Intelligence: 1) Possibly one walks away without getting their full thoughts out, but they think they did. 2) One thinks about the conversation and unknowingly and unemotionally changes the whole dynamic in their head after they leave. 3) No clarification is made but both think they're on the same page when they aren't there yet. One's emotions, tied to their thoughts, can change how they say something and can also change the dynamics of the original intent. They are not on the same page, they are just moving the page. Another layer of confusion could be the duality of words and their meanings, coupled with the fact that what is being said may be taken the wrong way.

There are many different barricades that keep us from seeing how the truth works. The majority of us naturally overlook things every day. It is much like the way magicians perform an illusion through sleight of hand or the stunt person in a movie convinces us that they jumped from a 20-story building.

It's interesting how the meaning of some words can change as we use them in different ways. For example, two people may think they "know" something, but they think differently from one another. The two people used a different process to come to their conclusion, in the way they thought and listened. This could be as simple as one person looking at the issue symbolically, or spiritually; and the other person looking at it literally, or scientifically. Both are right in different ways. Possibly it's because, when talking with another person, you think of their feelings, reactions, thoughts, beliefs and opinions. In other words, you care what they think. This can be out of fear or fearlessness. So, rather than finding the true answer, you simply agree with them or modify your own opinion.

When you're talking about country, community or self, it's amazing how much all three blend and can mean the same thing. When gathering thoughts, you almost have to know which one pops up and it's like having three ducks in the pond, each representing a conversation. The same words are said but it's how one takes it with regard to meaning. Make three files to categorize in your mind (the ducks). When a word with more than one meaning pops up, you have to decide which duck it is. But the mind thinks it means something else; the mind doesn't see which duck is popping up because the mind sees the same meaning for oneself, community and country.

Assuming there are six or seven degrees of separation between the inner and outer human body, then the first three are Me, Myself and I, and they are on the inside of us. This is connecting the Mind, Body and Spirit. The next two degrees of separation are on the outside of us and are the Universe and World and Humanity (World and Universe are considered one, the cosmos). Then the sixth is the Power "in," a combination of energies, truths and the processes of what love IS. We grow through the symbolic, metaphysical and spiritual processes to become beings from God, to human, to man and to woman.

The seventh is the Power "up," which helps bring it all together to include science, gravity, energies and air as something constant and permanent, where one is at in their individual spiritual growth and development. This process goes against the what, why and how of the brain's workings to see life's lessons on the inside, but we can only see as far as the adult growth on the inside. We seem to live by our beliefs, starting with our conditioning from the home we lived in from our youth to the community we grow up in until

> " Believe in yourself and all that you are. Know that there is something inside you that is greater than any obstacle. "
>
> Christian D. Larson

Changes
NEXT EXIT ↗

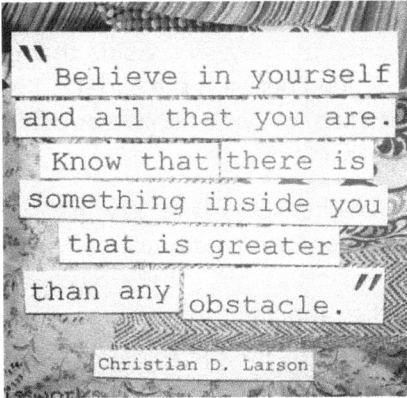

we become adults. We must understand the way we manage our emotions, how we analyze the way we think, how we separate thoughts and if we recognize that we have inner and outer worlds. We need to know the correct processes to how to believe, teaching us what to know, as importantly as what we don't know. What is one word that is "constant"?

The answer is simple: it is "change." However, there is no "right or wrong" when seeking the truth. Between the symbolic and spiritual is what we don't fully understand within us, but it is truly a separate world from the literal, scientific human we are on the outside. The symbolic, religious and spiritual being "changes" from an interior spirit to an exterior human constantly.

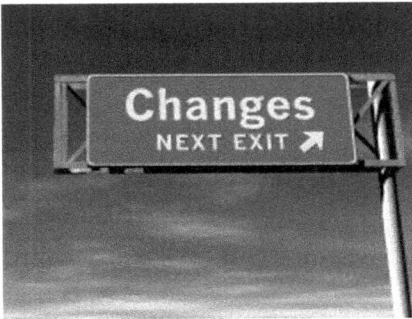

The underlying part of the whole truth or a deeper truth that we're not seeing is that there is no "right or wrong" between the inside or spiritual side (the sharp side of us) and the outside or human side (the fool side of us).

The outside of us can be thought of as the human, fool side, animalistic, state, literal, scientific side.

Most people tend to believe we have only one side, our outside or human side. If you don't understand that we also have an inner side, it is easy to overlook the fact that there is no right or wrong between the two sides. Then, when trying to figure something out, our tendency is to use just one side. And that would be lying to oneself or using only part of the truth. I have four adult children; only one grew up with me and I bet they don't know that. This type of thing should be taught in all schools on this planet.

The spirit side of yourself may be the side that is true to who you are, but it is also the side that is not well known, or seen beneath the surface. I'm considering the spiritual or symbolic side as being the side that is the inside of us.

Here's how they might work: Let's say in your mind there exists an unanswered question. After the confusion of thought becomes an understanding, the thought or answer may disappear and the way the answer is received in a clear mind is in the form of thoughts as well as abstract outer signs. Now, let's break it down to reveal a simple, possible truth, starting from what you were doing at the second this happened. This could be telling you to rethink what you were thinking at that time. The problem is that you were distracted, forgot what you were thinking and got wrapped up in your thoughts. After all, a loss of focus is a very real barricade to seeing possible intended truths. But the curiosity card is still malingering in oneself somewhere.

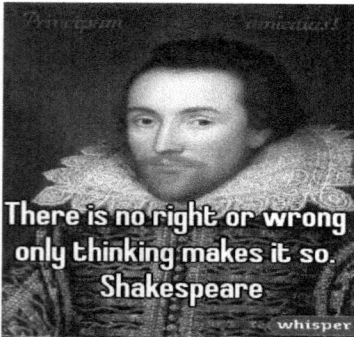

There is no right or wrong only thinking makes it so.
Shakespeare
whisper

This is one example of inward/outward polarization. What makes it confusing is that it's like trying to communicate in three dimensions in a one-dimension conversation and thought process. To make it less confusing, one must understand the complex 3D thought process within oneself, in order to explain an epiphany.

Your words need to "exit" through your 3D thoughts with the correct timing into one-dimensional words to be properly expressed. In conversation, understanding this will allow others a good start to breaking down a general conversation. There will be much more explanation of this later.

1) We are all, me = self

2) We are all, myself = community.

3) We are all, I = country.

4) The mind, body and spirit are Me, Myself and I, = WE/US!

Universe, world and humanity would be just "all and every" like a divine thing.

This may be why everything happens for a reason; at least 20% of what is said can be matched by listening 1, 2, 3, or 4. These blend into each other naturally in any order.

There are times you don't know which duck it is. Clarifying and knowing which duck comes up from underwater is like being one with the universe if one is truly listening and being extremely aware, not allowing the human side or the natural side to take hold of what's not true. Just because it feels natural doesn't mean it has to be true.

There is a *process* in life to most things we make, refine and produce, and when we miss a part or piece of the calibration of that process, things turn out differently. That same process really needs to start from within ourselves, showing how our thoughts, emotions and spirit connect from the beginning, the way humans naturally do. Human beings may all connect in spirit where the process to get to the spirit is a human thing. They are lessons of timeless wisdom, needing to be listed out in the form of science. This book/app can start as the framework for us to iron out the facts, analyze them, get the wisdom of the crowd, and then, by pushing and squeezing the air out, present a true collective conclusion for the greater good of humanity.

The whole process needs to be completed in order to create a paradigm shift because after the first process, the second paradigm shift is the process of the process. This is somebody who has completed the sophisticated or simply brilliant way of the universal intelligence (UI or Portal). They then see what it is that I'm saying to them. It is exactly the same lessons all the way up to the top or light and from the light all the way back down. It's amazing to see how it works when you're ready, willing and have truly learned the required lessons. The first paradigm shift is the "die while you're alive" mentally. The second is to "die while you're alive but physically".

If one of the ducks represents an individual or self, and another one of the ducks is the community and the last duck is humanity or country, and if "everything happens for a reason," including these ducks, then what is the reason?

The next lesson you're seeking internally could be the bottom duck in your thoughts, or one of the universe's. If one is in a deeper listening mode and aware of their surroundings, this may help to see the deeper meaning and that the reason is oneself. One needs to listen closely enough to gain an understanding and become aware.

Now we've thrown a few more barriers to being on the same page, haven't we? Everything happens for a reason, but what reason is it? The app will drive a number of holograms, including the 3D color-coded Zygote bodies which, when built up of layers showing the process of communication, will help the community to better understand and avoid the barriers to finding the real truth. There is a whole other layer that is made of emotions, how they're tied into the present moment. To "know" - not to think, feel or believe but to "know"- what it is to live in the present moment takes seven degrees of knowing. The timing of knowing each one of these skills is key. For example, you may know something is wrong, but you do it against your better judgment, hoping for a different outcome. This is practically human nature.

Logic vs. Emotional

Your right hand side of your brain makes up 80% of your thought process as emotional, and this is key when it comes to business decisions or even personal decisions. There is nothing inherently wrong with the 20/80 split, however, when certain crisis arise in your life, people tend to make decisions based on the 80% emotional instead of using logic to react to crisis

This is just one example:

Passion makes love move! What we don't know when we make decisions can shape our lives. Emotions are typically one of the first things that one wants to understand. Does the buildup of emotions work? A clear understanding will prevail when using the time lapse photographs in the app. Talking about what's on your mind and in your heart releases you from holding on to the emotional baggage. It's kind of like the Catholic practice confession; it's a release of whatever is inside you. Otherwise, those emotions turn into weights. This will remove the weight as if taking it out one brick at a time.

Communication in understanding beyond words is key, somewhat like learning collective intuition.

Chapter Two:

Ducks and Universes in Communication:
Inner technology meets outer technology

Let's look at gender differences. In terms of emotions, men and women are polar opposites. In short, when something happens, typically a man is forward-thinking, looking to the future for what will happen tomorrow, and often linear-thinking, meaning he looks at one item at a time. This is why his perception of love is different; he sees love as being there tomorrow and in the future, but not needing to do daily activities of love, though his love may be permanent nonetheless. His vision looks different, which is why his timing of love is different. Women think for today, asking, "How was your day?" and wanting to be assured emotionally they're ok for the day. Women can carry on five different conversations with different people and keep up effortlessly. They do not think in a linear fashion like men do.

We must also realize that, in our minds, the actions for genders start at the opposite ends of a sliding scale for each emotion. After reaching their end of the scale both genders then meet in the middle as a complete human being because we now have the knowledge of both genders inside one human. The truth is that separations are caused by a lack of growth, unwillingness and the inability to find lessons about self-love and timing of love. The destruction of the family is what we are handing over to our children. Today, we can leave, divorce or separate just because the kids love one parent more than the other, and the other parent leaves to make sure they are loved the most. We certainly don't put in the effort to exemplify "For better or worse until death do we part." The funny thing is we think we have done all we can.

When seeking love, we typically look for what we are lacking. For example, a strong male would probably be looking for femininity in a woman. If he were more on the feminine side of the sliding scale, he may choose a stronger woman. Even though we grow to symbolically be represented by one gender inside, in the mind, the growing process outwardly still hints towards what we are going through internally until we learn the lesson we are seeking.

This may be utilized for one of the bodies in google Zygote for other emotions like anger, fear, sadness, greed, joy, hopefulness, faith and

anxiety. Spiritual and human emotions are both conflicting and working together.

Let's go back to another set of skills, those that understand words in the English language° that are spelled the same but have different meanings. These words are known as homonyms and they often confuse us. Here's an example: the word service can refer to automobile service, or to a wedding service, or even a dinner service at a nice restaurant;, one can be in service politically or be in service in the military or the clergy. There's an important difference between "service" and "in service." "In service" implies a higher calling or a serving of the public in a way that does not imply a fee or payment. "Service" and "in service" are just one example of the duality of words and yet all of this is really still in the category. If it looks like a duck and acts like a duck,

It must be a duck, right? I guess the question is, is the duck the self? Is the duck community? Or is the duck country? Or maybe the ducks are all three, making it the Universe. Remember, it is up to us to separate them.

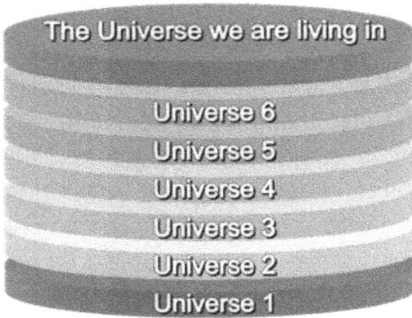

The Universe only sees itself as one from the outside; the inside world only sees itself as two (neglecting itself); the outside world only sees itself as three; community only sees itself as four; country only sees itself as five and the self only sees self-reflection as six. It's up to us to gather the seventh that's all about communication, living in parallel universes, and how one universe can't see from one to the other.

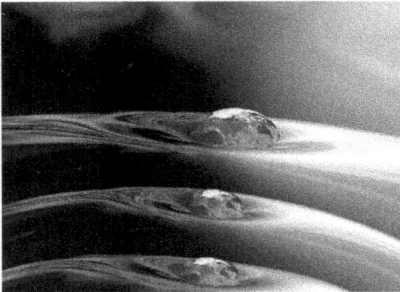

If it's not pointed out, then what we don't know can shape our lives. See how, in a way, it's working backwards?

In the picture of bodies to the left, we have the physical body with shorts, muscle and bone. When we continue to the other side we see the non-physical (listening, thinking, believing and knowing) that are emotions. We will use the seven bodies to the right of this picture, and this will include one spirit that will be considered the same inside and outside. There is one partition for each side, inside and outside. The seven bodies illustrating the physical outer body on the left we will call state, just for simplicity. The other side to the right that needs the illustrations we will call spirituality /church because it's the inside.

Now let's say that both of those are what it takes to be human but they are the opposite of each other and the instinct is to be exact opposites and fight each other. Now imagine that inside of oneself is church and the outside is state. In conversation with somebody, they may say something and your first thought on the outside is that this person is unintelligent. Then the inside of you decides to reserve judgement and listen.

You're both having a conversation and each one of you is thinking of how to form what you want to say. All of the different elements that we just went through to keep you both on the same page has the effect of keeping you off the same page. The process of speech includes waiting your turn, clarifying and a set of listening skills. These are things that we think we know because we do them every day; in actuality, there's a lot more behind the scenes that you don't really see. It's similar to movies; you may see a movie and think about how real it appears, and then you look at how it's made, with special effects and stunts, and realize there is so much going on behind the scenes. In conversation, the whole process is to take what we all already know in deeper levels inside of us. It starts off like a big fist clenching a heart, and what we do through the app, is drop you off at each stage or set of skills to achieve clarification, staying aware of living there and what it takes to continue to live in the moment.

Our science may be looking at life in a backwards way. The science community is trying to find the existence of God rather than peeling away, layer by layer, what God isn't. The light bulb clicks on because of something as easy as the skill of noticing, because the energy within us might be uncovering the plan for us to see what is already there inside.

It appears there's a plan showing us all about life in many different fields, for those who are aware, in the world of Ted Talks, and life's patterns, from Rami, Plato and Niche, the philosophers, and psychologists like Sigmund Freud, the people who have stood the test of time, for their theories and work. We see how different parts of science, psychology and other professional communities are interested in doing their part, but it seems that when they try to assess life's plan, some just see science, and some just see things in a religious or philosophical way. This app will help as needed, and when directed, to complete most types of assessments using all three: science, religion and philosophy. It is rare to use all three at the same time, but that might be the answer.

Many people may be uneducated about an issue, but their first thought of it should still be properly recorded. The "curiosity" within us seems to be the best natural trait and it can open doors for the professional to help guide and to find out more about the issue. Whatever the issue is, whether political or religious, it is okay. What we're trying to do is find the polarization of the issue, organize and police the discussions, and work it into the Rubik's Cube of Knowledge based on the masses, with professionals and scholars guiding.

> To know yet to think that one does not know is best; Not to know yet to think that one knows will lead to difficulty.
>
> Lao Tzu
> PICTUREQUOTES.com

Lying to yourself is spiritual (inside) while lying to others is human (outside). There is a hierarchy, even in service; this can be seen in the fact that the Pope has the highest office. Leadership, whether taken in a human sense or a spiritual sense, can be understood as being the navigation of the human condition. This gives you a 360-degree view of spirituality but that's not right either. You have to take that spiritually, seven degrees down within one's self, seeing and knowing the polarizations of our emotions, what we know on the inside and how timing sets us apart. Deep down inside oneself is where time stops emotionally. Now I figure that out inside, but it takes just as much to get results of lessons on the outside and explain it in a way that makes sense to the average person. In some ways, monks understand this. Monks and scholars are meeting in the middle of the balance of spirituality and humanity, but that's not enough, because the leaders of the world need to see where spirituality fits into life. When we understand the 'why' of us, humanely and spiritually, we can begin working collectively. If the simple mind will reveal the truth to be the same, the purpose being service to others, then we have a common goal. As for the 'how' of what we're going to do about it, I think those answers depend on who they are coming from.

I asked a stranger who was sweeping the office floor what she thought about inner technology meeting outer technology. She said, "Well, you know, I have more of a relationship with my phone than I do my fiancé." Let's use a little psychology. Maybe her first thought was correct because she didn't have to think about it. She had no reason to lie, so that's likely why she said what came to mind. Let's say she didn't find the right words. From a spiritual standpoint we may say she just needed time to gather her thoughts. On the other side, the human side, you could actually say you know that this person is lying because they are trying to find the right words. We choose in our minds which way we want to interpret another person's words. We always lean towards the human side when we think that the person is lying; we are going to the human side rather than the spiritual side. The spiritual side consists of the more emotional intelligence you build and have to the more capable you are of reserving judgment the right way.

The more internal knowledge you have, the quicker you can judge in a good way, seeing things like the skills a person has, the degree to which they are using their listening skills and if their emotions are managed well.

How a person uses their knowing skills and learning through listening are natural life skills. I think that's what people don't realize in the spiritual world; more often than not, work on the inside is required. To just react without thinking is human; slowing down and thinking before reacting is the start of spirit. This again is a type of life sliding scale. There is a process on the way up, and a paradigm shift on the way back down from the top of spirit. What's next is learning the same lessons on the way down back to being human. The people that already know the UI understand the individual Portal will and has come simply from the base foundation they have developed over the years. The question that confronts the spiritual and self-help leaders is whether the understanding of the inside world will connect with the opposite outer world to be seen together and to make sense.

Why does life work backwards? We need to see most things spiritually first to reach a better or deeper understanding, and then down all the way back through humanity to oneself before our or [Your Name] judgment is made. I think this is what humanity is not seeing. Even the best spiritual leaders may not see the total of spirituality; one may think they know, but there is always more to learn. This is why I would like to get spiritual and self-help leaders together with coaches to help facilitate the app, to help build the framework.

Janitor-President-Pope

The Pope is one of the leaders of the spiritual world. Catholicism is everywhere around the world and they believe they are the universal church to bring other churches together. We now have the hierarchy from the person that sweeps the floor to the presidents of countries to leaders of the spiritual universe. We have all three of those but there's a missing component. What if we were to talk to the Pope about bringing us all together, utilizing each piece of a puzzle, to help bring a group of religions to at least share the knowledge that we have?

The right person to ask this of him might be a past leader of a country like Bill Clinton. Whether you're the person that sweeps the floors or the president of the United States, we are the same on the inside, but one person may see more of what we already know than another because they have more experience.

Bill Clinton was the leader of the United States with broad influence on the outside but was still a servant of sorts. The Pope is the ruler of humanity on the inside, so to speak. Though humanity is on the inside, neither are right or wrong; both understand the strong-fisted skills within themselves and have the ability to open up their fists and express outwardly all that is on the inside. It takes a lot to get to that position, and involves tremendous work within oneself.

Looking to the Pope, we could say that this is the leader of the universe/world and he is leading us to use what is within us to help better what comes out on the outside. We have been using Catholicism as an example, as a priest is a servant to his congregation just as a worker at the coffee shop is a servant to customers.

The Pope is a servant to his kingdom, followers or group. The president is a servant to his citizens, constituents or people. I'm thinking this would become, by way of spirituality, a 360-degree view of the universe. The people connect by first knowing that we are all the same on the inside, and then they connect physically; they go to the leaders of countries and then approach the leaders of the universe. In this way, the people would actually be the ones who decide how things are done, trying to find the center of the human side and our middle of the spiritual side, to find the truth of the truth (Timeless Wisdom for the Rubik's Cube of Knowledge) that belongs to us. While we search for the center of the collective self, along the way we may find some of life's answers. Our 'collective purpose' will not be unanswerable, because together we will be able to solve questions better than scientists or monks because we have the wisdom of the crowd, and are monitored by our coaches and professionals. Then we find out what those answers reveal. Collectively, we may find another "way" of learning, become smarter and live with less fear and greater happiness. It may be that the collective soul needs to reach out in order to find some of the answers and also to build relationships for all to share a purpose to serve each other. In the end, part of the answer may be sharing.

Talking to other countries, utilizing what is the same between us and understanding our differences will open up daily conversations. We just need to be aware of religious ideologies and reasoning to fit in the piece of the puzzle. This may bring us closer together once the coaches in country and community are aware of the good intentions of all.

In the last section, I compared the janitor sweeping the floor to the Pope. Let's go to the second question when I asked the same lady what the difference is between inner and outer technology. As you know, the first thing she said was "I have more of a relationship with my phone then my fiancé." The second thing she said was, "If they make more robots I'll be out of a job because they already have robots that sweep the floor and do a lot of the other cleaning normally done by a janitor." On the outside, I could see her comment was about survival, paying bills, and satisfying basic needs. We need our intellect (all the way up to the president) or we need our spirituality (all the way to the Pope).

The work one has done on the inside is visible to others only by the little that we allow out through our speech and action. For example, if someone pronounced a word incorrectly in conversation you might think that person is not very bright and this would be your outside or human side speaking. Or, you might think they just don't know how to pronounce the word correctly and it's no big deal. This would be your inside or spiritual side speaking. The only difference between the two is waiting a few seconds before reacting. There are two sides of us, inside and outside, and both of these have two sides as well.

Imagine the Pope, presidents and the other world leaders put together through a relationship in a way, looking for the good part of the past. Look at the ancient Egyptians; their civilization folded. Can we explain why and what happened in those relationships? Did they perish because they didn't learn the needed lessons? What were these lessons? We need to take what we think we know and evaluate their emotional decision-making process and their internal growth at the time. What are some of the lessons from the distant past that are the same today? I would like to present this to the community in today's app that we are building. There are some things that are the same because they are timeless. Our noticing skills or the way one looks at things, has quite possibly been the same in the past as it is today; the light bulb of understanding needs to be turned on, one skill at a time, for each person over a lifetime. We still aren't wise to it though, or our focus would be to listen to learn, and become a learning machine after we are wise to our inner workings.

"Skills such as truth, listening, thinking, feeling, believing, knowing are all processes of TIME and SPACE."

The Mayans, Egyptians and Assyrians

What ways of the past are worth going back to and bringing forward? What good from the past should we take with us? We can use the ways of the past to align with what we already know but can't see as the lightbulb isn't on. We have moved past what we can see, both in front of us and in the depth inside our mind's eye to our heart of hearts.

We don't know how the pyramids may have folded. Perhaps it was because they had no past to learn from. They didn't understand that making molehills into mountains could be negative. They didn't know who or what to learn from in their emotions/feelings and belief systems. One can speculate about the demise of these ancients; the elements are thought to be responsible. This history would be nice to know; perhaps inner/outer technologies for the good could have changed the way we live today. They left us buildings with intelligent designs, many beautiful artifacts, petroglyphs and hieroglyphs, carving out pictures on stone to illustrate their history. The problem is that we don't understand the engineering or the emotional or spiritual realms they existed in.

Hypothesis is a deeper guess!

Any individual, as a man or a woman, needs to learn what it is to be the other, to learn from themselves and from others in a sliding scale of growth. This will allow for the elimination of a good portion of the typical polarizations between men and women while maintaining a balanced dichotomy, all from within. We see from what the ancients left behind that they had gained this knowledge.

They may have been living in the present, listening to learn and learning to listen, helping each other stay in sync as their continuing thoughts were to serve other people. We are godly individuals at first, meaning at birth we are born with internal innocence that didn't fade in adulthood. The collective power was amazing; everyone knew the godly part of them was on their inside, same as everybody else. Put your hands together, fingers pointing up like you are praying, with palms together. Now turn them to the right or left sideways until you see the back of one of your hands in front of your eyes with fingers still pointing up, hands and palms together. This represents the inside body and outside, and how close the two worlds were. Today, our insides seem to have moved away from our outsides.

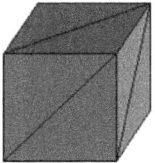

This folded box of the pyramids represents each triangle as a separate skill: listening, thinking, feeling, believing, knowing and truth. They can work together or apart, and the processes of each are separated by time, as humans have all these skills in common. However, how we develop and understand them internally determines how our community and country turn out, whether in the past, present or future. Let's build where we think we are now!

In building a part of the framework for the app, we need to be cautious of how innocent words might be taken out of context and seen in a way other than originally intended.

The learned lessons of the past can get buried in many different ways, especially if what is learned is not passed on. The app helps to build a system worldwide, and in many different forms of knowledge with many countries participating, uncovering what others know. The better the system, the more we know that the universe is an energy that sees no time or sharing, just space and matter.

Natural Wonders of the World.

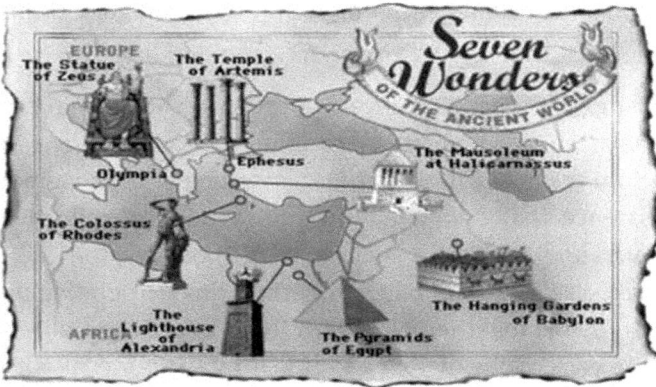

The Seven Wonders of the World are created by the human side of us. The relationship, looking at it in a different way, is one side spirt and the other human. Finding the center requires skill. The mystical part of our emotions can be what we can't see sometimes; in the non-physical or intangible universe we can see parts of the shadows and they work perfectly against each other. What separates what we can't see from what we can is time and space. Let's take a dive way down in thought to the millisecond of the moment and dig down deep within. One can look at things externally or internally. Internally, there is the spirit side (positive) and human side (negative) to people's emotions. The question is, where are you on the sliding scale of the same emotion at that particular time? We can start on the human side because it feels natural in most cases. There is also a core energy to tap into inside one's self. Whether the mind focuses on the good or bad determines our attitudes, actions and internal growth over time.

The human side can be seen as the Hoover Dam Bridge, while the spiritual side is the Grand Canyon. Neither one of them are right by themselves; they just give you the directions for answers inside/outside of you.

We can see that the Seven Wonders of the World, both natural and man-made, represent the worlds inside and outside of us. Nevertheless, it's us working together and sharing the other wonders of the world. We now have the means, with the right plans and the proper internal growth and intent, to look back and learn from the time of slaves. Look at the companies on the rise, unitizing different platforms for food, water, shelter, transportation and entertainment. The way now is that you pay for food, water and shelter and provide timed services. Most types of blue collar (and some white collar) jobs provide work on demand and mass amounts of different services or specialized skills.

We will use existing services like Facebook, Airbnb, Uber and Starbucks to create the relationship and entertainment hubs for the Internet, provided by [Your Name]. This allows a substantial client base for all concerned to provide a lower-priced platform for most existing services by using each other's client base. For example, this could help expand a market for an oil and gas company by receiving most of the fuel sales from Uber drivers and customer's transportation service. The airlines could benefit from lower fuel pricing for all their newfound customers by establishing the same type of Uber platform. Then the same customers choose the best service platform available based on ratings of the individual services as well as the combined group ratings. The conveniences served by the platforms are structured around the food, water, shelter and transportation needs of the communities with infill from the service industries. These are designed to reduce stress and make life easier for all concerned. We are only as good as the systems we build together.

This will follow after we gain the customer base from the big bang theory in our marketing, striking the collective masses, to working together metaphysically from the inside-out. [Your Name], is a stand-alone app to be in service for each person to share. The young can help their elders operate newer gadgets and the elderly can offer valuable pieces of wisdom they have learned. Whatever age, skill, or idea can be posted through existing applications like Craigslist and, based on demand, it gets added to the app, and shared on-demand through the relationship hub.

When it comes to Uber, I think the payment system and convenience of the service is what people are drawn to, because it's new and exciting, and the schedule implies both drivers and customers have freedom. In reality, the drivers are more like working slaves. The structure can change life as we know it.

Flip this platform backwards and upside down and design an algorithm that balances geometric growth and C-Corp bean stock, like Howard Shultz at Starbucks coffee, to create the payout. This platform creates cash flow cycling through independent employment with Uber-like jobs that will help to solve or greatly reduce poverty and welfare by connecting people with certain skills to those with needs. This is done mathematically and the organization is done by a series of apps, computers and so forth. We have the technology now and we have the money, but the question is, who will share and organize?

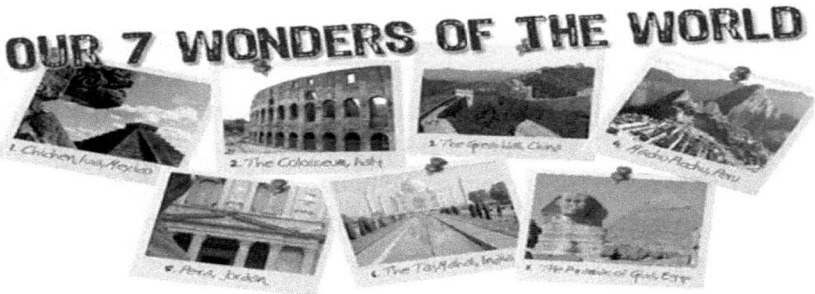

OUR 7 WONDERS OF THE WORLD

Imagine being able to see all the way down inside one's self like it's a hologram body that works interactively. Visually, we're able to see the color-coded activity, when it's sitting, standing or lying down, for us to have a better understanding of time lapse photography. This will show how our brain can see these skills in action but watching them in action tells a whole different story. With the assistance of time lapse photography, literature, movies, music and different professionals as a guide for each topic, we complete, together as a community, the various layers of "knowledge" to create the human body, using interactive participation. Or, we begin with the complete body and "peel away" the layers until we, as a community, find the ultimate or timeless truth.

THE NEW 7 WONDERS OF THE WORLD

The New7Wonders organization is happy to announce the following 7 candidates have been elected to represent global heritage throughout history.

Chichen Itza, Mexico Christ Redeemer, Brazil The Great Wall, China Machu Picchu, Peru

Petra, Jordan The Roman Colosseum, Italy The Taj Mahal, India

The Seven Natural Wonders

We are able to go as deep as one or the group wants. We should see the sliding of the scale, from one side to the other and back to the middle, to see growth on both sides over time. This represents 80% or better of any given statement, more so than not. Try to look from the inside out to see abstract lessons!

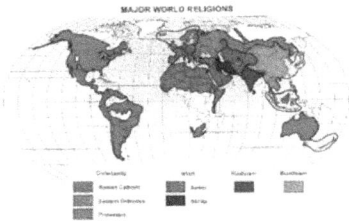

Our mind needs to organize the processes of the skills in the right order. The oxymoron is a pivotal part of our language as it reveals the patterns of how language, self, and God come together, and also shows how each comes back to itself. Although our emotions see no time, when a true oxymoron is a human, (Oxus) is the spirit side, (Moros) is the human side, is a figure of speech in which apparently contradictory terms appear in conjunction (e.g., faith unfaithful kept him falsely true). The timing of being on the human side, (Fool) faith kept him falsely true and on the spirit side (Sharp), faith kept him unfaithful both being true to oneself. The way one thinks makes it so, so remember, there is no right or wrong because the spirit is one world and the human world is another, and both are equally important though separate. Therefore, one can create a belief on either side of a complete world and not really know which full world it was created from. I'm considering this a dimension of misunderstanding directly related to the "timing of knowing," or, when an individual sees in the mind's eye. Only then "it" can be understood. There is no right or wrong because of how we see the worlds of spirit and human working separately and then together in our own hearts and minds. In our minds, we are somehow directed away from seeing the joint worlds, but if we stick with wanting to know the truth, we find a deeper truth than expected; it's about the center of what's between the worlds within us. Once we find out how they (the worlds) start together as one and see an understanding open up in our mind's eye of the way dimensions and layers work within our hearts and minds, this creates a whole other world of deeper understanding.

This is like a set of small squares, one on top of each other. On each side, picture a Rubik's Cube for each of the skills below that only appear in random order. They go all the way down seven layers, where we find the truths of each other's vertical skills, separately and together.

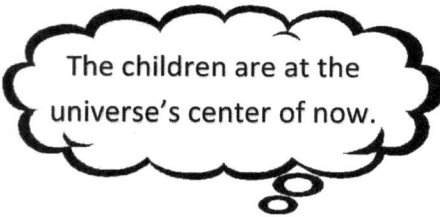

Father sky outside.

The children are at the universe's center of now.

Mother Nature from the inside.

Chapter Three:

The Other Five Deep Senses: Seeing, Listening, Thinking, Believing, and Knowing Skills
Truth and Lies

There are three sides of truth molded from certain patterns.

The first example is "truth." There are three sides of truth: your truth, my truth and the start of 'the' truth, though it remains only "a truth." This point is about the norm we typically reach. The next point may be how perception can create an illusion without clarification. It's really amazing to see that brilliance is a sliding scale of the simple truths and how blindly we overlook simple truths and make up some ridiculous truths. We often believe that if it is written, it is true. A possible reason may be that once it's written it becomes permanent to many people. This also makes the duality of the words past and present the same.

1) Your truth. One side   1st
2) My truth.   Two side   2nd
3) A truth.   Three side 3rd
4) Perception of a truth.
5) Illusion or delusion of a truth.
6) Clarification of inner/outer truths.
7) Relationships of the truth is "LOVE" - it all works together.
   Perhaps all "parts" of the truth make up the whole truth.

A lie doesn't become truth, wrong doesn't become right, and evil doesn't become good, just because it's accepted by a majority.

Rick Warren

The rest of the skills will provide examples of each, as these will be explained in much greater detail interactively within the app. We will explore skills such as truth, listening, thinking, feeling, believing, knowing, and all processes of TIME and SPACE. These skills all work on their own but also work interconnected with each of the others. The life coaches have worked on and understand these skills and will help people see it for themselves.

The Listening Skill

First and foremost, the listening skill is the center of emotional intelligence, although we're often not taught to listen in order to learn. That by itself will make us a learning machine, but we are not taught to clarify either. In some cases we don't have someone's attention when talking, the reason usually being that there was not enough time, the person did not care, or their attention was elsewhere. People must listen in silence to learn how to narrow down the possible meanings of what is being said to gain a deeper understanding of the natural truths we overlook. All the way down to finding what is like if a glass "is" half full or it "is" half empty either way without reading into it, it means the same thing down to what is, even though both are the truth - it is what it is, all it can be.

1) Clear away thoughts to listen.
2) Listen to learn and to be open in your mind.
3) Listen to your internal workings closely. (i.e. listen to your gut, see the best possibilities)
4) Concentrated focused listening.
5) The center of the soul is listening.
6) Together achieving sound harmonics.
7) Silent answers.

The Thinking Skill

'WHENEVER A NEGATIVE THOUGHT CONCERNING YOUR PERSONAL POWER COMES TO MIND, DELIBERATELY VOICE A POSITIVE THOUGHT TO CANCEL IT OUT.'
NORMAN VINCENT PEALE

SUCCESSFULTRIBE.COM

The thinking skill should be exercised like the body, using a sliding scale to see the process. Where do thoughts come from when we think to ourselves? How do thoughts arrive in our heads? Thoughts don't matter as much as what we do with them. But the deeper, well thought-out thought provides another level or dimension to create more choices after seeing greater possibilities.

What is the process once a thought enters one's mind and how do we think about those thoughts? What is the timing of action needed in deciding what we are going to do with a good thought or a bad thought? Let's call this the horizontal sliding scale. The layered vertical sliding scale will follow.

In the sliding scale of decision making, the P represents perfection or perfect, the A is for acceptable, adequate. The G is for gray or questionable. The D is or dark, dangerous or bad, something that is unspeakable. This tool will provide a visual sliding line for illustration purposes for all the skills. Fear can't share the same space with Love, and not knowing can invoke the wrong side of emotions.

Human Side   Vertical-   Sliding Scale =   Poetry   Spirit Side

The P in the center represents Perfect.

Vertical- Divine   Dark

                                 Gray

--A----------------------------------acceptable

negative__D_____G_____A_____P_____A_____G_____D___positive

--A----------------------------------acceptable
-

                                 Gray

                                 Dark

Vertical- Human

The scale of emotions is equal on both sides of the dichotomy. It needs to be separated perfectly on both sides between men and women and to connect perfectly to itself for it to be a God.

It's the same principle using the dichotomy of a human to a god, which is now vertical because the man-woman thing was the horizontal, the center! Plus the sign in the middle of the vertical is where a person becomes a god with all the skills back in them self. Draw a circle around A's, G's and D's then decide how far you will go!

You can get rid of, or at least reduce, the bad, evil or negative thoughts by addressing them fully. Once you're aware of a good or bad thought and can discern it, it's up to you to put it on the scale to see what line you're on and how far you're willing to go.

It's best to not strive for perfection or to dwell on the choices you make. There's nothing wrong with exploring the danger zone in your mind as long as you know you can come back from it! Our human makeup gravitates us towards the negative side first, which I call our "human side." However, just by simple thought and being aware, we can, in a blink of an eye, move it to the good side, which I call our "spirit side." In the app, when flying in spirit, there is no right or wrong when seeking understanding. Others think there is no right or wrong on the outside, not seeing there are two parts of you. That's why some don't understand what it means when people say there is no right or wrong.

One may say that they are going flying today. No other information is provided. In the imagination, one can fly in spirit; those thoughts, or ducks, are really out there. The thought is to start with the outside of oneself by thinking that the person is flying in an airplane.

First ask yourself if it matters. Don't assume; just put together how the inside and outside could meet while figuring out the middle, as that's where there is no right or wrong.

Try first flying in yourself in spirit, really thinking freely, without labels for a while. Try thinking about nothing in stillness. It may be harder than you think! There is a certain strength or concentrated energy within us; find it, use it and label it. There is a certain type of relationship one should know and have with themselves before diving into their soul, as this can be scary. Think of a place to get answers, where there is more of life's simple truth given than even the Bible can provide. One may find the good book was written as a guide for what a person can find inside of themselves, because in certain ways, we are the same on the inside. The marathon thinker proudly thinks broader, deeper and sees what others don't. But it's the group of thinkers, with small thoughts and their imaginations working together in guided thought that will come up with broader possibilities, narrowing down the answers.

When thinking within yourself, looking from the duck's eyes, each person looking out to the world is small as a grain of sand in their thinking. This may be the person that has a big ego, who only thinks of themselves, with their focus on the bad side of greed. This type of person makes it to powerful positions, as high as presidents, kings, royalty, etc. With this type of leadership, civilizations can perish. We can learn lessons from the past to find out what the failed thinking was. As our thinking grows and the way we think changes direction, we will change ourselves for the better!

Looking at the growth in a leader or an individual today, we should be able to see the results of the work they have done on the inside by the way they talk to, treat and give advice to others! This is to be selfless without ego and still be powerful, intelligent and wise. There are plenty of ways to gather information out there to provide learning, thinking skills but the keys aren't out there; they're in the mind! There are no speed limits, stop signs or boundaries to your thinking.

If one chooses to further the thought once they have triggered the listening skill by talking to someone or to themselves, there are a few things to think about:

1) Think about the time to rationalize and internalize. Listen more than talk for clear understanding, then think about how to think.

2) Think of the best possibilities, then narrow them down to select a few. This helps in making choices by reducing the chaos in your head.

3) Think about the way you're thinking. This will keep you aware there are other ways of seeing and/or other dimensional points of view.

4) Think without limits or boundaries.

5) When unpleasant thoughts arise, imagine having pins popping out in your head and watch thoughts pop up to find ways to overcome them.

6) Think in layers and dimensions of all sides, and see beyond what the mind sees.

7) When one stops 'thinking' about it, it disappears; it ceases to exist.

The Feelings

Feelings themselves are not skills, but an internal management of feelings is needed and can be viewed as skillful. One travels to villages in the remote parts of Africa, for example, with multiple generations of indigenous tribes.

These groups are the ones we should be learning from because they have mastered their emotions and their internal world. These tribes have survived on the outside, physically, but they have also mastered generations upon generations of internal work. That knowledge should be shared for our learning in the future and for our children.

Feelings are also a sliding scale from good to bad. If a person has obtained the top amount of growth when it comes to something like greed, this is good; if they have only reached the bottom, this is bad. Greed typically involves doing anything to get power, stepping on anyone who gets in the way. Living this way fails to find peace because some of the pieces are wrong; even though they may have loved ones around them, they still feel alone and know something is wrong. They may have all the money one could spend and still not be satisfied. They may not even see it yet. Unfortunately, these people may have to experience tremendous sadness before they see the missing or needed growth. The listening has shut down because the negative side has started to take hold and once that strong grip of disbelief enters, it seems that the head may listen but the heart is sealed. Sadly, we need to get stronger individually. As the saying goes, when pointing fingers, one needs to remember three are pointing back.

The good side of greed can be seen as having the same drive, passion and will to accomplish the same things, but for different reasons. Like stern competition, action with extreme pressure still welcomes people to keep up with them only in fairness. It can be hard to tell the person's intent because on the surface this may look the same. We need money to live and there is nothing wrong with profit or having money. What matters is the way one treats people and how they earned their money. Money carries its own energy. There are, after all, people who have made large amounts of money in a good way, in service to others. This distinction will help in our underwriting process to identify people who see that our collective purpose is to be in service.

Emotions like anger, fear and jealousy need to be understood. All bad ones are related though fear. There are so many good examples the community can come up with! Like some people get angry "because they don't know why!" So why get angry? We control it. Some get jealous because of the fear of what they themselves might do.

> No matter how many people believe or don't believe in you, you must be the ultimate believer in yourself!

We create our beliefs using a sliding scale of good and bad. Somewhere in the middle will be the razor's edge of a truth and that's one way a belief is created. This can happen from sitting in silence and having a conversation in your head, or recalling life's experiences outside in nature or by walking around engaging in what you see and talking to others. There is a process to this over time to help in choosing what to believe. I'd like to throw that out to the community before any pros answer. The question is, what happens through our listening; is that what builds believing? So if we live by our beliefs, how many different ways do people think beliefs are created? By throwing questions like this out to the community through the app, we build camaraderie and consensus. This is the power of the app. We typically live by what we believe in, so it's good to see how we build what we believe and hear the way other people do as well. Now remember, we are building a puzzle on religion in another category so we're not expressing what we believe in a religious way. We're figuring out how believing works for and/or against us as humans and how our everyday beliefs are created. Notwithstanding, sometimes we take what we believe and somehow make it a truth for ourselves. We then defend what was once a belief but that we have made into a truth through natural unintentional justification (backwards thinking). We often defend our beliefs as beliefs until we have enough information to confirm that they are in fact truths. The app is intended to help us confirm our truths by listening to the wisdom of the crowd and our skill set. We may find ourselves modifying our beliefs before they become our truths and in the process become better aware of how our beliefs become truths.

I believe that beliefs are created through conditioning and the way someone is raised. Naturally, as we go through life we gain intellect, wisdom and understanding and we apply that when forming our beliefs, perhaps "shortening" the distance between belief and truth.

Beliefs are not only created by us from the inside. Look at the progression in extreme sports. Thirty years ago, one man created a paradigm shift of "believing" what the mind and body could accomplish physically together on a motorcycle. Somewhere inside, Evil Knievel must have gotten over the fear of death to attempt the acts he did. Since that shift, others have built on his belief and the current state of that activity is absolutely mind-boggling in terms of harnessing fear! This is a skill we now know helps us in many different ways to face fear and to accomplish many great things on a motorcycle. As importantly, there are others involved who may not be changing their beliefs about fear but perhaps changing their belief of what a motorcycle could and should be and the progression there is just as mind-boggling.

Consider the same thing back when the pyramids were being built. Possibly the fears weren't faced because they didn't know how, or even what they were. Not getting over their fears may have meant lessons were not learned and this may have contributed to the ultimate demise of that society.

The skill of overcoming fear is timeless, and an illustration can come from the 19th century. High-ranking officers in the military had far greater autonomy and fewer restrictions (due at least in part to the slow nature of communication at the time). One must have achieved a great deal of personal growth to achieve a position like that. Getting over the need to be right was of the same importance then as it is today, and was another timeless skill: the ability to duck, weave and bob or improvise, adapt and overcome. The point of this, looking at history from the inside out as if we are there, is to ask and perhaps answer the question, is the process of creating beliefs the same now as it was then? Have we identified it and answered it? The answer is no. This may help answer the question of what happened to the ancient Egyptian society. Based on the lessons we know now, it seems that the leaders of the past developed these timeless skills as it did greatly change the outcome of communities and countries around the world. The lessons on the outside are clear and remain today as we fight over land and defining borders for protection.

When looking at historic events, what good can we find from horrific past events and how far one man took his beliefs to the extreme? Adolph Hitler murdered millions of people, because of a belief he created for himself. Another example would be the Ku Klux Klan. We see today that no matter how others have tried to control race, race has prevailed. Perhaps in time we will evolve and become a mixture of all races. Did Hitler's ideology and fear work? Not in the end. What good can we take from this? This piece of history helps us understand how a distorted vision sees part of the truth. We can flip this for the good, though. We already have one pure race, the human race. The dichotomy of men and women can help in closing the gap of polarization for politics, gender, religion and racism. If we all use the same processes inside, then the purity of the human race is the combination of the races. The help to unite the world is somewhere in words intended to help accomplish this, by bringing together diverse groups in discussion to learn life's timeless lessons.

Again, the goal is to help groups of people to share together in thought, not to deal with their problems, but to arrive at a collective outcome that will be mediated by coaches having fun with today's technology. These groups could grow to be a helpful force with current events by combining Airbnb, Uber, and Facebook with a physical location for cyberspace, making for the biggest, safest relationship/ activity/entertainment hub mixed on an app. What can we find for good lessons around the world? What lesson did you get out of what song? The same lesson could compare different generations and diverse types of music, allowing the old and young to participate and most likely share important moments.

I would say the dyslexic and the move-the-box-out-of-the-way thinkers (not out-of-the-box thinkers) will start with a clean slate and may seek a higher truth or at least the truth after all the air is squeezed out of it. What remains of the truth is what "is," or at least part of the truth after left brainers bring the right brainers back to a balanced reality. We all make up a part of the whole. We have the ancient ruins still standing, waiting and wanting to tell us the truth but our believing skills need to show at least three faces before we can see what and how they are asking us to look and ultimately see. The science, philosophy and religion of what, why, and how simultaneously working together should result in a much finer truth on those very same categories. Could this be what believing means for any topic? Or do we get stuck on seeing one at a time? And believing means only part of the three?

These historic events are suggested as topics for the community in a helpful way to see the past and take what is good from it and find many more examples and let the bad dissipate, giving it no attention. The process of the inner technology of these skills is not easy to understand when one looks from the outside in. This may help to see what is said or the part of the inside that is the same but different. How we develop and process our skills is how we end up forming our beliefs. We have been to war over emotions and religion and what good lessons have we received out of that?

At the end of a truth and the end of an understanding it becomes "it just is." If so, who will listen? Hearing directly from the source is important in two ways: 1) they have a need to talk and be heard on their side and 2) the other side should fill that need and gather their truth of why. Then the simple process of clarification, if both sides are open, can happen through listening and getting to an understanding beyond words before a choice is made. This allows emotions to move on because it could take generations to get to a meeting of the minds. This could happen by talking and taking out forgiveness two bricks at a time and misunderstandings one brick at a time. Then emotional walls will come down a little bit at a time. Don't underestimate the power of communication in any and all forms.

The universes of the mind, self, community, country or Me, Myself and I, or mind, body and soul all have the same meaning, symbolically. The outside is a reflection of what lesson is needed on the inside that will fill in the gaps in time to become visible on the outside. In other words what work is done on the inside reflects on the outside in terms of peace.

Unlock the POWER of the MIND We start to break things down piece by piece as a collective group. The topics that the community might consider will initially create polarization. This polarization is much like the dichotomy of men and women and we can use that similarity to help reduce or eliminate the polarization. Abundant answers may be found in the Ying and Yang, but a little bit of Yang in the Ying and vice versa can be good, utilizing professionally-directed input from men, women and even children. The simplicity of innocence may find a brilliant outcome.

The start of the app could be all the questions asked in this book. They would be placed on the website to get your answers, utilizing the wisdom of the crowd.

What lessons are not uncovered or mentioned yet?

What about God and country? Is there a God? And are we looking at the God correctly?

How many times have you said, "What do you mean by that?" This involves both sides within oneself and using the skill to manipulate others for good or bad. This is about the intent one has when they have an initial thought in their head. Our instinct is to think of ourselves, or to experience a thought that is negative. Why is this? Our conditioning whether living in the human world or the spiritual world?

Now, if there was one linear universe in the mind, why are there so many misunderstandings? What percentage of misunderstandings is due to the way people think about a subject? Let the Community try to answer it for a day and write down examples and we may find a division that makes it into the Rubik's Cube of Knowledge.

Why is there racism? After all, we are all the same on the inside. This shows that racism is a barricade for us to bring our minds together.

Why are there so many mental illnesses that may be caused by the inability of one to control or manage the thoughts in their mind?

What about a religion that wants to kill? Or the comparison to a fearful God? Killing oneself to find God? Or doing it for God or dying while alive to find God? Not a loving God, but the opposite, a God fearing God. None are right or wrong. This would be true if we are talking about seeking a higher power or trying to understand God in thought (this is our mind looking from us being human to us being God). Let's look at where the minds are unwilling to go. From God to human, our mind being the same as God, of course there is right and wrong. This could be God to human or human to God. The same but different, or different but the same. The question states, "is there right and wrong?" This may be a delivered skill. It's in the way one looks at it (when seeking a higher power there is no right or wrong).

I watched 26 episodes of an Oprah Lifetime special which originally aired around June 2012 and then again the mid part of 2015. The show ended by discussing what God is. What are love, law and many good, wise and heartfelt things? What's next? And what do you know for sure? Who's the next trailblazer who is uncovering what is to come? In her lifetime of work, Oprah said, "I've been throwing out bits and pieces from inside." I feel like Oprah is trying to help people through a metaphysical "portal" of knowledge. The portal helps by gathering together the collective whole. The people willing to participate both in guiding what we have learned over the years and in helping us get to the portal individually and collectively (SELF) through language along with coaches, help build the Rubik's Cube of Knowledge for all of us. At the end of this book I will add back in some of what the editor cut out and what people that read the content did not understand. But I think it is important; even if I stand alone I see a nugget or a diamond and if I explained it to Oprah's group and ultimately if just they put together what I am laying down it will be worth it. I think the wisdom of the crowd for the people that know will put it together on the website at www.yourname.Blog .

After the completion of the series I called and spoke to Dr. John Gray, who wrote the book *Men Are from Mars and Women are from Venus*, because 20 years ago he was one of my teachers and I interviewed him for a documentary I did entitled "Nobody Wins Divorce in Modern America." The start of this book was that love helps find the truth. When I keep going I see how truth finds love and both love and truth are/our God. I see God as us the perfect human is one "SELF" is God individually. Everybody is all of "SELF" which is humanity and is God because he is every "thing" (and every living thing) so he made us in his image and therefore one God. The language represents the NEXT step! The pros missed the language. I know the editor did. The twins in language explained all living things and things by the definitions in the dictionary from the spiritual side or the inside and the human side or the outside.

The sliding scale of the gender dichotomy is a great example of starting from the differences of the polarizations from inside out and outside and explains how language works. There is a process of understanding that needs to be done right on point so one can see what we already have inside in order to reach the portal.

The real goal here is to get to the first stage of KNOWING the higher consciousness. I'm just calling it that for now as it's really identifying things we already know in different and new ways so people can at least see the sliding scale of simple brilliance (more on this later) and the skills listed out. As we know, we can't live with only light or only dark; it's not possible, we need a little of both. The same thing is true for fear and love. They are energies fighting for the space inside of us and when these energies overlap or too much empty space exists, it becomes feelings of jealousy, anger, greed and so on. We all have free will to choose what space to take up with knowledge from thinking and believing in a way to fill in space in our hearts. We can choose happiness by understanding what it means to truly live in the moment, by knowing how moments work. When moments of emotion, skill and lessons don't see time, how is it living in the present? In Oprah's episodes, she draws the conclusion that God and Love are the same thing. The other piece to this is the Truth, meaning God, Love and Truth are the same.

The Rubik's Cube of Knowledge can't be put together without the start of a, or the, Truth.

This will give you an idea of putting together variables, algorithms and grids in an abstract but efficient way. This is expanding that idea into what it is to be human and the natural variables we don't see that will make sense in the end, using time lapse photography.

We will further this with the interactive participation of community, both here and abroad, as a simultaneous goal of at least three different countries.

The Paris attacks are now, at the time of writing this book, in the news. These horrible acts of religious killing are done to make a statement. The taking of lives randomly and senselessly is for a cause that may have the same meaning for the killers as the one in our prayers, meditation or thoughts. We use a different name, but how do either of us know it's not the same God? Picture what it is to know God - to know essentially everything He is - to break down all "knowledge." What if He were knowledge - everything - by making an invisible universe the other side of the parallel universe? The universe we see of like taking a picture of a mirror image would be the same but different but backwards and for everything in the universe we can see its counterpart. This is what we can't see but is exactly the same in the center after the dichotomy. We need to see how language fits together using tangible and intangible, using the perfect word where it comes back to itself. By what we believe should be an aid only help us get there to know if we believe correctly. All religions miss this because it is about self.

As I discussed previously, beliefs are influenced by one's conditioning and how parents may carry and pass on issues and emotions. When it comes to "believing," most of the time we can believe what we want to believe and others can do the same and both can still be friends. However, it seems that when religion becomes involved, "believing" becomes more intense; people often go to war over their beliefs and what their truth is. Is that the truth? Why do we go to war over something we don't know but we believe? Isn't believing just *part* of the truth? And yet we still don't "know." This can be the bad side of believing.

The good side of believing may be, in a perfect world, using our intellect, science and wisdom to improve our beliefs and seek out a more solid truth. Using the skills backwards, or unaware of a misalignment and/or skewed timing can cause someone to live an unintended lie. To show this properly we could use time lapse photography, as seeing is believing, some say.

This statement stood out to me: "If your religion involves killing, then start with yourself." It dawned on me that that's what they're doing. Let me explain. In seeking a higher power, there is no right or wrong answer when seeking thoughts and flying in spirit inside oneself to find answers. Here is something that can be taken both on the inside and outside, but differently: one needs to die while they're still alive to restart and meet the higher power. (This means to die mentally, not physically). I think we mistake it as a baptism in this part of the hemisphere. This is just my opinion, and I don't intend to offend anyone.

This would be a total surrender, like a video tape of your own life flashing in front of your eyes then starting over, growing from the inside lessons being learned. This may explain the dying thing and possibly the surrender thing, taking the meaning outward, not inward. This may not be delusional as the inward part of us put together may be the collective part of the higher power or a life's lesson may require exploring and/or an explanation.

There is a multidimensional way of knowing oneself on the inside. Whether we know it or not, and whether we notice it or not, we all have within us polarization, dichotomy, universes, ducks all residing on and in parallel universes, one tangible and physical, and the other non-physical and intangible, and at the same time and they all come together within us to produce confusion, madness, chaos, craziness, religion, philosophy, love, fear and so on. The opposite scientists are the group that use "know" the way it's intended but get it wrong a lot, although it may take years for us to prove that they are wrong. The simple word KNOW is a lesson that scientists have started to toy with. The understanding has come from the inside of a person. To know oneself is exactly the same as inductive energy and wisdom as if a light bulb is being turned on. This type of energy shows that the part of humans that is within us is the same as the higher power. The average person uses less than 10% of their brain power in order to see the connection that we might be the same as the higher power. Some do see the connection. This should not be confused with a collective source of gathering more power or how we can create miracles and move mountains, so to speak, from the inside as an individual. Just imagine what we can do together, with a controlled inner-technology structure from the inside of all of us as the Rubik's Cube of Knowledge. This tells me that we are not having the problem of a love of power, of money or of control that malingers on the outside of us. We have the conflict of not understanding the higher power that is on the outside/inside of us, which is still the power of love/fear misconstrued. Using the word "power" in the last sentence is sharing the same meaning on the inside and the outside. How will the ducks/universes see, notice or know which one is meant? A multitude of words do this. We can justify most things with "should have, would have, could have," but try seeing examples in your own mind using "what is." Like, what is naturally around in the days to come? "What is" is just that way without change. Or it can just be the way you look at it. The mind sees and misses more than we think.

I would think that the goodness within religions will show us the polarization, as we see it in this part of the hemisphere. We may find that a fearful God (a God to be feared) is the same but opposite to a loving God and we all have both. If we take God out of the equation, we may have found the missing link: us as it starts with us as a child, the purest form of love that exists. That's what the app does; it brings together groups of thought to break down these kinds of issues. We need to find what makes us tick while we are here and alive and use all of us to find the answers on our good side as to what we believe but more importantly know. This is another belief about "believing" only part of the whole, part of "a truth" from the inside or outside, but that breaks up the understanding of what it is to believe. Remember, believing from the neck down is to get "a truth" or "the truth" on the inside. On the outside, believing is from the neck up, as if to fight for what you believe in no matter what. If you are speaking to someone in conversation and you state any given belief you may have, how is it possible to know what universe of understanding (or what duck) your belief has come from? The point is we have to first realize what could be missed before we can begin to understand what can be done about it. This will be demonstrated with color-coded, time lapse photography within the app.

1) Believing is part of the whole beyond what we see or how it's brought up.

2) We can believe in other things and still have a close relationship with one another.

3) In believing, look inward-out for the scale on both sides. Look at good/bad to see the center.

4) Be aware of only seeing one! Find a balanced mixture of three: science, philosophy and religion to help form a belief.

5) Believing is just part of the truth for you to make complete.

6) We have a choice, belief and the moment to help us know.

7) It's not what you don't believe, or not seeing all the different ways to believe and then believing anyway; we must first see how the processes fit together.

The Knowing Skill

The knowing skill is one of the most difficult to master because its meaning can be multi-dimensional. When we are trying to figure out something or we are making a choice, aren't we communicating with our self and isn't that a relationship with ourselves in a way? What we know on the inside of us can be completely different from how others perceive us on the outside. What we know on the inside can be different than what we know on the outside in some cases. In some ways, there are two different worlds.

One need not play time travel on the outside during a conversation; the mind, in effect, travels in time depending on which universe it sees or lands on. We are set up to fail if we don't grow and become aware of the way real life works and pass this down to our children so they will have a better life of learning, growing and obtaining answers for happiness and wisdom.

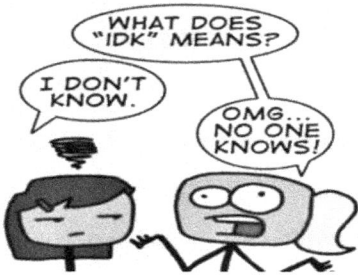

One reason why thought can be so confusing is the different ways it's set up to confuse, mislead and create misunderstandings. Let's revisit the ducks of thought/understanding. I said the person thinking/speaking is the duck and the person receiving what is said is using the universes in the mind. What matters in order to prevent misunderstanding is which universe the thought/meaning stays on (without clarification; with clarification, it will land on a different universe) since the two parties can be on the same or different universes. We are exploring in our minds the lost truth even before it starts. This also works with country, community and one's self. Understanding is merely keeping your thoughts open and dismissing any negative thoughts until you receive a couple of your own examples in your head.

The mind is programmed to look from the outside-in rather than inside-out and then humanly instead of spiritually when trying to understand something or when following a conversation.

There are so many deep and simple ways to this skill. For example, what we don't know can shape our lives; what we miss naturally or can't see, didn't see or are unwilling to see can prevent us from knowing the meaning, thought or lesson. I am referring to what one sees in the mind while using the mind's eye. This will be a cool feature in the app and the community will have a lot of fun expanding the possibilities. Not knowing is fine if you know that you don't know or can't know, or don't want to know. But if all knowing is knowing that one doesn't know, seeing that as part of the skill is a good start but can be confusing when on a quest for a deeper understanding.

This program will help in gaining knowledge by combining what other people know, as it helps us as a group to know and learn more. These skills will surprise people working and playing in the app. The timing of "knowing" is one by itself, but watch it with the other skills in time lapse photography. Once you think, feel and believe what you know, rethink it and restate it differently; the intent is to have the meaning be the same for both parties. This will show what we miss naturally, like when a magician performs tricks. The mystical part of what we don't see is a part of our focus in this app. For example,, using the three ducks is knowing how to see in one's mind that it's natural to miss that the intent of "me, myself or I = us" is the outside of us. So, what represents the inside of us - we all have a mind, body, and soul and they all mean the same but different, and different but the same. This can lead to an unintended path, an untruth or lying to oneself or even a misunderstanding.

The multidimensional part is inside-out and outside plays in abstract thought as we understand that each duck or universe is multidimensional at the same time. We don't recognize this as a knowing skill and it makes no sense. A saying may innocently mean two or three different things at once but when spoken about, one assumes their universe or understanding is the right one. The mind does this automatically.

Have you heard the phrase we're "simultaneously on parallel universes"? The universe is: 1) self 2) community and 3) country. We all think in different dimensions, or universes, and this often makes us unable to see or hear the true meaning of a simple sentence. Drugs, sex and rock 'n' roll, in an abstract way, can be seen as mind, body and soul. God, love and truth or the purpose is service; it turns out to be the same but different. Now, let's reach out a little further. Typically, when speaking, we often begin before even considering in our head what we intend to say. This is another way that misunderstandings occur between the speaker and the receiver.

The three universes concept represents the other person's understanding of which duck is on your side. The three ducks concept is your understanding inside yourself. When we speak our thought or idea to someone else, we don't know which universe it may land on for the receiver. They can be left innocently misunderstanding (on the wrong universe) with a different meaning. What does it matter if the meaning is taken wrong or not put in the right context or even taken out of context? It's like keeping the jury out without judgment and staying open in thought for clarification, waiting to see if change comes and staying open for a better understanding and leaving thought open if time permits. When one closes a conversation in their mind, in most cases it's with some type of judgment. It's important to view your thought as your opinion, rather than seeing it as something you know. Because even though you know or believe something, we get there by what we think. We would want to see clear, usable examples of both directions you could have gone by not closing the conversation in your mind. This app brings us anywhere we want to go within us. The focus of the app is the timing of the processes for the way we grow internally, as the communities around the world better it a little at a time. The objective here is to be aware of what the brain and emotions do to us without our knowing.

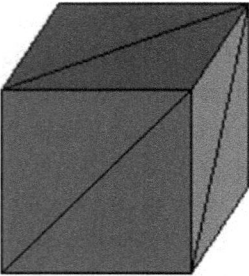

The substance of what matters and its timing is the natural part within us that is right in front of our eyes and isn't seen (on the outside) until the awareness skill is set in motion. Ultimately, we want to point out how to see what is in the shadows when digging deeper inside of oneself.

The Great Pyramids of Giza were built in harmony with Planet Earth physically, metaphysically and mathematically. The deeper understanding, beyond physics and mathematics, is metaphysically the equality of the dichotomy of genders and how their process relates to oneself. The community connection, in harmony to the Earth's movements, is showing us, in real time, how to live in the millisecond of the balanced moment from outside in and the inside out.

This thought is still being developed. We can use the pyramids as a visual. Starting from one side of the pyramids, each has their own separate sliding scale of "skills." We may choose to start with Ying and Yang, man and woman, as a dichotomy from one side to the other and then back again to the middle for love, strength, femininity, etc. As mentioned previously the way men's and women's minds work initially is that men typically think for tomorrow while women think for today. It is an internal growth process for each to slide from one side to the other and then back again metaphysically. Then they meet in the middle of the scale where both now have a complete understanding of the opposite sex. I, of Me, Myself and I equals a metaphysical, symbolic, unisex sliding scale for men and women to get to part of the truth now, and love for oneself and everybody all of self is a part of the process for us to unite. One may think they know what it means to live in the moment. With the app, we will help you master the sliding scales and see how we start from opposite sides of each emotion.

Sliding Scale

Typically, men are linear in their thoughts; they can usually carry on one conversation at a time or operate on one level of thought with intense focus. Women, on the other hand, can usually carry on more conversations, operating on multiple levels of thought. Imagine a sliding scale between a man's brain and a woman's. We're both able to start anywhere on the sliding scale and it is a growth process both for a woman to slide over and see things linearly, and for a man to slide over and be able to operate on multiple levels of thought.

There are multiple sliding scales that help us see the broad spectrum of wisdom ultimately balanced with emotion and logic (emotional intelligence). But it takes both to see in one's mind the beauty of dichotomy. Some of the more noticeable scales will be discussed. In short, the perfect center is God and the perfect middle is the knowledge of man and woman together, as "ONESELF" is the perfect human. The perfect human and the universe work in sync perfectly and fit together because they are the image of each other and have all the answers!

How do we find Simple Brilliance, when starting from an idea, to write, start a business, make an app, or even make sense of life? We will run into mass amounts of people of wealth, intelligence and foresight in their thinking. When companies like Uber, Facebook, and Airbnb first started off with a crazy idea, others just wished them luck. As they progressed, investors often thought they were crazy. Why can businesses like these work, but at the same time appear to be crazy? The reason these specific types of businesses flourished, beyond timing, is the fact that they address basic outer needs of food, water, shelter and transportation (in conjunction with the inner human needs to talk, touch and satisfy intellect).

With cyberspace, typing has its place but something is missing; we can't start the conversation with a handshake, or speak aloud, or look into one another's eyes to establish camaraderie. The missing parts can leave you with something to be desired. Once we create a physical location for the app that encourages groups to gather at the Elongated Table of No Fear or enter the doors of no fear. Here, the 3D hologram is used to illustrate the status of their game or dialogue. Because of the physical location and the gathering of the group, they are provided a way to be noticed, receive recognition or credit, share the experience and show off their knowledge. Rather than competing with them, we will bring them all in and be a clearing house for chatrooms to hire those people and weed out the first set of required data.

Taking the space out of outer space is …impossible, like taking the space out of our minds. On the TV show, Shark Tank, they say, "I have not been in that space" when they don't know an area of business. The opposite, "I know that space well" indicates they have a great deal of knowledge in that area of business. A reasonably intelligent person would think that to fill up space in one's mind they must have as much knowledge as possible, right? We can't argue with their knowledge of business, but with this platform, we are moving towards filling up the empty spaces of the mind with more than just "worthless knowledge." By making us aware of what we miss naturally from the processes of our brains and the mystical part of our emotions, using today's technology, we can see how the processes work. Some of the space we know and some we don't. Using the wisdom of the crowd, the framework for the app can be formulated.

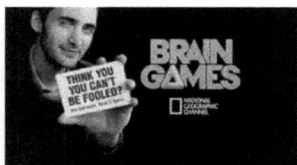

A small part of this app would be something like Brain Games, demonstrating what the mind doesn't see or know in order to determine a point in the mind to go to and be dropped off metaphysically. As one learns new lessons or gains new skills or knowledge, it serves as a key to unlock new levels within the app. These steps, through different areas of understanding, are designed to be thought-provoking, helping one to understand the three sides of each of us: human, spirit and what is, is. What is, 'is' after the air is squeezed out and the meaning is accepted beyond words down to it just "is" because all the proper possibilities have been exhausted. There are few who see all three sides, science, religion and philosophy all together as "ONE."

There is no right and wrong, but are there boundaries? The cosmos is an infinite unknown, but we know we are all made of the same energy as the universe. Call it Universal Intelligence (UI). The UI may have made God or vice versa and they shared making the universe. Maybe the gift is a way to look at things, almost anything. When and if we figure it out, will it matter? Maybe the timing of what matters could be helpful in the millisecond of time to help see patterns, slow down the process of understanding, watch it all the way to the finest detail of simplicity, and see what happens to time? The timing of what matters is shown by the universe; it's billions of years old and the energy is changing and evolving all the time. One thing that is constant is change in the UI. Look at how we change our emotions over what we do know, don't know and the timing of what we think does and doesn't matter.

The sideways meaning of what the mind sees is only a part of the truth. To know naturally means part of the all-knowing is to know and another part is the abstract of the all-knowing which is to know that you don't know!

If we use the example of our hands together, turned sideways, one represents the inside world we have and the other represents the outside world. Now move your hands out, extending your arms to the side as far as possible past your peripheral vision. This represents one: the inside stuff, everything good and bad, lessons learned, lessons lost, emotional walls assembled, us, self, humanity, universe, God, love, fear, truth - everything. The outside is pretty clear; it includes our amenities, resources and freedoms, and the animalistic ways we have grown for humanity to become more civilized. The unexplainable in the distant past on the inside and the outside seems to be multiple Gods or mishaps in the sky. Once the mind, body and soul are connected for an individual, living in a higher consciousness means learning lessons of purity of thought, curiosity and imagination to help grow the spirit. As men and women, it's harder to find the higher consciousness without each other. In seeking life's answers, knowing we have equal but opposite men and women to draw from, over time this makes for far better results. The question is, which way in time do we go to find love for ourselves? Pinpoint the millisecond of the now!

Does the inside lay with the answers in the distant past or the foreseeable future? We aren't considering where we came from or trying to find God or where we go when we die. We are looking at the lessons from the past to help bring better future knowledge for our children. Imagine: thousands of years ago, humans roamed individually and in small groups for many years and there was little or no language, yet thoughts, beliefs and knowing skills had to be figured out to find food and water. People developed their inner selves individually for many years. Then, we started to gather food and make clothes and build relationships together. Then thousands of years ago or so we started to write, leaving us with some clear and some unclear understandings, and many different languages across the world. These people left some kind of record of existence about trying to live with the land and together with each other, about reaching out across the world in harmony to connect the UI's energy together. From hieroglyphs around the world, we can see they were building global stabilized energy, wirelessly bringing the mass energy from space to Earth, because they didn't know they couldn't, but we can. It seems they almost accomplished this, based on what they left behind. Scientists, engineers and scholars have tried to figure out for years, looking at it outwardly, how these people built structures of their size and weight. With no tools left behind, just precision cuts as if they were cut by lasers, all of the technologies go unexplained. The relationships of the past found the path of least resistance and their alignment with some force of energy pole; by way of thinking, imagination, prayer, meditation, signs in the sky, and so on, it was a structure of learning that clearly worked. However, through listening, this may have revealed some of the answers as to how to produce inductive energy through thoughts and an imagination. The ideas slowly gathered and were made to work. In this world of knowledge, through the cosmos, evolution and de-evolution, God's energy seems to have the same DNA. Maybe what we are missing is something simple. The relationship between the two energies is the same but different and different but the same. Maybe we are fighting for labels instead of getting to a solution or truth. The truth of the distant past might continue to reveal the intelligence we see now! Perhaps we keep missing it?

Academic scholars and religious theologians should be working together to recognize the metaphysical, multidimensional part of knowing the skill of knowledge. The Ancients seemed to have a clear and precise way to achieve a higher consciousness because they may have found a collective part of a higher energy inside of us. This may be the part of God, of which we are the same, not the mystical part of our minds, emotions and spirit looking to the outside as we seem to think now. Some Ancients believed the human heart was God and cut it out to offer it up in sacrifice in hopes of empowering their findings, wanting more power of love. There was no separation to begin with, even though a world may exist on the inside and another on the outside. The separation of polarization started with the power of love. Seeing was believing; it provided motivation when collectively obtaining knowledge of schematics for electricity, power plants, factories, engineering and latitude/longitude placement. I think first one must slow down the mind's thoughts to get in sync with the magnetic field inside oneself, to center oneself and get to the higher harmonics we know as music, poetry, painting, art and so on.

Depending on how much work one has done on the inside, their skills, the width of their alignment and the calibration of completing the skills leads to knowing how to achieve collective harmonics of the mind, with one's spirit and human side. The inside polarization of the spirit in goodness is two-sided as well; the drive to find goodness is a force that pulls beyond one's self into community and universe from the mind, body, soul, humanity and an energy of power. Then, the individual centers of oneness in oneself is a journey in and of itself, but the truth of the never-ending journey starts after they slide into the portal. Once grown to the center of themselves, with all the others in the community linked together by the magnetic field past the first door of the portal of human and spirit, there is a universal understanding. This is the truth about having no past; there is only the present and we can't see the future. The constant truth is what remains! What is constant is 'change' in the never-ending moments and it continues to reveal the process of the truth in real time. Then, even with the awareness skills, a lot will be missed. But without these skills, life passes you by like you are asleep, and you end up living an unintentional lie and imbalanced intelligence.

The energy we are made of is the same energy stars are made of in the cosmos. The ancients seemed to believe anything with energy was a God back then. They believed events of the cosmos were the acts of angry gods. They may have known that inside each person is a lighthouse and a power source that comes from within; the strong part of power gives the ability to learn and increase intellect. The relationship they noticed was one with the self that equaled God and they believed that was the human heart and that was the energy they sought. When done properly, you will pass the gate only after individual lessons. These are calibrated and then, once graduated, you will see the simple skill sets in a different way. Others will not have any idea what you are talking about! But inside your head, heart and body it's so clear and natural. These are each a lesson, and some take days or months and others take years and other never have an end. This will act as the start of the framework to be improved on by people as they pass that part of the journey. Anyone who can improve on the app will be paid for their effort. One can think they have it together, or even lie to themselves and think they have mastered it, but the universal intelligence (UI) will not let people through the portal unless their skills and lessons are calibrated. The people that make it into the center of self (through the portal), not selfishly but in a selfless way, often come back. The more that we share, the more fun the app becomes.

The app provides a way to tap back into the collective intelligence where the earth and sky help provide more efficient processes for loving oneself, and providing the glue, tools and wisdom to grow together. When we have love, food, water, shelter and transportation, our minds, bodies and hearts work better to do miraculous things together. So, why aren't we there? We have the means and the technology, but do we have the will? Or is it that we just need the right systems of reality as we're building collective knowledge, because we're only as good as the systems we build, or the system we uncover? Balancing inner technology, which hasn't grown much over the years, with outer technology, which skyrockets every few months, maybe we can use the outer to facilitate the growth of inner with the app?

The app is designed to assist people all over the world who are trying to get together to enter and slide through the portal to achieve co-consciousness.

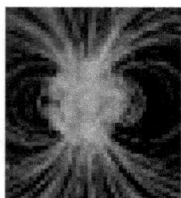

The scientific outlook is starting to pop up all over the place, with authors like Dr. Rudy Tanzi, Dr. Deepak Chopra, Dr. Jeff Stibel, and Tony Robbins. In the self-help industry, some are the masters of the individual portals, balancing the center of religion, science and philosophy. I'm not asking anyone to back up what I'm saying, but what I am asking is to make this available in three different ways on the app, saying the same thing in different ways. Within the people who know the portal for each lesson, sliding scale and skills, one person will write out the way they see the topic, by spirituality, science and philosophy.

I would like for self-help experts to participate in the way that works best for them as coaches, consultants or some form of partnerships for the app to help facilitate breaking through the magnetic fields of understanding and seeing awareness in project [Your Name] portal 2019.

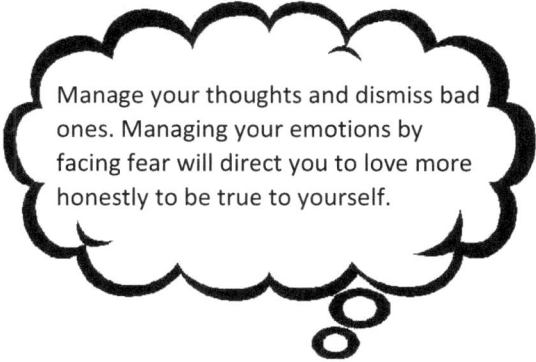

Manage your thoughts and dismiss bad ones. Managing your emotions by facing fear will direct you to love more honestly to be true to yourself.

Chapter Four:

R.S.V.P. [Your Name] for Our Unity
Who are we? What is Spirituality? What or Who is God to us?
The Weather. Liquid Genes. Keys. Science and
Religion Tied Together as One

The best line I heard about people's opinions about God on Oprah's "Super Soul Sunday" show was, "God is a sphere whose circumference is nowhere and center is everywhere" (now here). This includes time in the now continuing moments, everywhere and nowhere. It defines God as closely as we can. But the knowledge is how, where, when and why everything everywhere fits together perfectly in itself by the separation, division and split as a part of the complete whole, making one God! It works backwards as well, part of how the universe goes together making the science the proof - intangibles that go together perfectly with the tangibles to go back to "ITSELF" to get full and complete, whole.

An example is language. It starts from the completed whole (which is the same as God together with self) all the way to individual words that are part of the whole. The part of the whole is put together or taken apart perfectly by the way it is separated, divided and split, to be perfect as a part or as the whole. It is up to us to put it together like a puzzle.

The thing we overlook today is that in striving to achieve God's word, we only see part of the whole, though we believe our language is the whole truth. The completed whole is when the process of one is the same for all.

We as the human race need at least one or more missing parts to make language a completed whole, and equal to God, as God works to explain that one can be explained through the perfectly completed one word that is the same for all words.

Where reaching out to the furthermost dimension upside down and backwards, nothing is something, stillness is abundance. When time and space are not filled in to display a better picture, this leads to an internal misunderstanding. Everything can work together scientifically, philosophically and religiously, all of which can be organized and fit in sync in a mathematical way. What would wrap this all up mathematically? We wouldn't need faith, right? This might be possible by putting together all that we know worldwide. Using your truth, if it is the heart's truth, it will fit as part of the whole truth in the app about any subject we chose to break down piece by piece.

[Spiritually] Synonyms from Microsoft Word:

Mentally, internally, emotionally, psychologically, mystically. (Antonym) physically, morally.

DEFINITIONS (Google)

Spiritually refers to certain kinds of activity through which a person seeks meaning, especially a "search for the sacred". [1] It may also refer to personal growth, blissful experience, [2] or an encounter with one's own "inner dimension."

1) Personal growth: Lessons humans need to learn before they see what's next.
2) Sacred, outside: I think this is referring to the difference on the human side of what we protect, on to the inside of what is sacred in us past the deepest part of our fears inside.
3) Inner dimension: I think this is referring to the difference in the way spiritually acts on the inside and the process of facing fears on the inside, such as facing the fear of death.
4) There is no mention of God, the divine or religion. The closest definition to spiritually is "mystically".

I will use the word "Spiritually" **when trying to understand us** mentally, **who we are when talking about the human outside. We will attempt to take out what we think fits in a** mystical **way. The synonym that uses divine is the word** "Spiritual" **because the definition below has the word Divine and brings back mystical to a** transcendent **from the human side of us as the vessel to transcend from the inside/ Spiritual side. This shows how the relations work and connect us in a religious way of** "Spirituality." **Religious beliefs are the** temperament **of our** "spirit." The university is a symbol of the nation's egalitarian spirit. In a fairer egalitarian society, all people are equal and deserve equal rights and opportunities. There is a balance to this as well and that will be our choice collectively.

Mystical, divine, unworldly, otherworldly

[Spiritual.] Synonyms from Microsoft Word: psychic, non-physical, transcendent. (Antonym) physical.

DEFINITIONS

Noun. Just is a song, possibly of how music hits the true center of the soul.

A religious song, especially one arising from African American cultural matters concerning the spirit. Relating to the soul or spirit, usually in contrast to material things.

1. Relating to the soul or spirit, usually in contrast to material things. (Thinking, listening, believing and knowing skills on the outside, human, neck up).

2. **Relating to religious**, inside. (Thinking, listening, believing and knowing skills, neck down) **or sacred things rather than worldly things.** (Includes spiritually). Outside in.

3. **Connected by an affinity of the mind, spirit, or temperament.** Just is the center of us our make up!

Spiritual includes (Spiritually, Spirituality, spirit), every and all refers to something in spirits. Einstein's value of general relativity: Nothing is something and something is nothing.

4. **Showing great refinement and concern with the higher things in life.** (Spirituality) Living from Inside/outside, inside/inside, inside/inside/outside! (The good side of religions, where they meet).

5. **Related to your spirit instead of the physical world.** (Humanities, University is a symbol of one spirit). On the inside and outside. (Includes spirit) The eyes are the window to the soul, the human in humanity.

[Spirituality] Synonyms:

Holiness, religiousness, devoutness, piety, unworldliness, sanctity, mysticism, otherworldliness

DEFINITIONS:

The quality or condition of being spiritual

The property or revenue belonging to a church or church official

Religious beliefs

[Spirit] Synonyms from Microsoft Word:

Soul, chi, essence, life, life-force, {inner self (Dictionary Form}, Life force, (Antonym) body. DEFINITIONS:

The vital force that characterizes a human being as being alive. To take somebody or something away quickly in a secret or mysterious way. A particular frame of mind or mood.

I will categorize the process of what can't be seen in this way:

1)   **Spiritually:** Human side only, the lessons that need to be noticed and learned humanly before one moves on.

2)   **Spiritual**: Human side. Transcendent metaphysically, relating to the soul or spirit, usually in contrast to material things. Placing in order the processes of how one sees the way these skills work: truth, listening, thinking, and feeling, believing, and knowing. This helps from the inside to establish that we have both sides, inside and outside. Somewhere in the middle or between the two is a deeper understanding that may require quiet time to see how nonexistent emotional time and human time mix with taking out the space to be aware of an understanding.

3)   **Spirituality:** Religious beliefs and churches looking from the outside in a Godly way, trying to help understand by guided lessons seeking higher truths.

4)   **Spirit**: Soul, chi, essence, life, life-force, inner self, outer self, implement the balance of both to find the center of both, and you will see the center of one [Your Name]. The university is a symbol of the nation's egalitarian spirit. Together we can build the right balanced systems.

How can we relate the way relationships work (not our interpersonal relationships), to the way Pi works in math and how it relates to Theologian study of God?

If you removed all the empty space from human bodies, leaving only the electrons and other subatomic particles, all seven billion humans would fit in the space of a sugar cube! This is science. The question is, how do religions, theology studies, philosophies and poetry fit together as one? Is it in a mathematical way?

Spirit is mathematical along with many other ways. This seems to be the common denominator between the three. 1. Theologists, 2. Philosophers and 3. Scientists. 1. SELF, 2. LANGUAGE and 3. GOD all the same thing as come to "ONE" to explain what and who God is perfectly

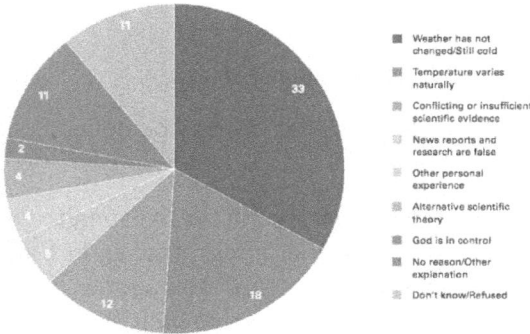

FIGURE 2. Reasons for Skepticism About Climate Change
Among Americans who do not believe earth is getting warmer

- Weather has not changed/Still cold
- Temperature varies naturally
- Conflicting or insufficient scientific evidence
- News reports and research are false
- Other personal experience
- Alternative scientific theory
- God is in control
- No reason/Other explanation
- Don't know/Refused

Source: PRRI/AAR, Religion, Values, and Climate Change Survey, November 2014

Scientists break down things and information to the smallest details. These are the ways I'm separating the growth possess of how to see the divine, Universal intelligence (UI), and **God** throughout this document for a much clearer understanding of knowing that most people have different perceptions, meanings and purposes. I'm stating these to help clarify the inner, outer and god-thing. The inner **god** (1st circle world) is not capitalized, nor is the outside **god-thing** (2nd world grown to 3D) that is the collective us, growing through the process to an understanding, to then the outer **God** (3rd world is 3, 3D worlds) we don't know is being capitalized, into a sphere. Omniscience, Omnipresence, and Omnipotence = the relationship of self, Community and Country or me, myself and I and mind, body and spirit. Let's see the possibilities of what is not seen, and we can uncover, discover and produce the creativity, together with the app, to find the center. This may include for us as humanity, an opportunity to make a small change in the weather or at least manipulate some small part in a good way. It would be nice to know if our presence alone, connected around the world through [your name], would create Global Stabilized Energy (GSE) and would change that day's forecast for the better. As they say, there is an app for everything. We know that we don't know what we can do, and the possibilities are endless because we haven't tried. Perhaps, from the collective inside of us as one, we can see if it can be done. The key is to start sharing in thought, and organize the possibilities to start with in a co-conscious way to peel away from the broad scope.

Is there *a* God or *only one* God or *the* God or many Gods? Maybe it doesn't matter if God is everything, and if so, how He is everything, everywhere and is occurring at the same time. Life's plan may be so perfect it will take us a lifetime to see all that is and all it can be. I think it would be small-minded not to include everything we know as the collective human. Maybe it's who we are inside and out or all around; we may be the bridge. Maybe it's the plan of the way things work, and we need to figure it out or maybe we're looking at the god thing in the wrong way? Maybe God isn't good or bad, fearful or loving, but instead exists somewhere in the center. Or are mind, body and spirit the center of all? These aren't word games; they're the way you think it shall be. The way one thinks makes it so. If I think and choose to believe I **can**, then I find a way, but if I think I can't, then I believe I **can't** and I'm doomed to fail before I start. Perhaps it's better not to shut down the thoughts and to stay open to center beliefs to yourself, which is the start of having a relationship with oneself.

The earth's magnetic field may be connected to a centered, connected energy by the collective us, once we've mastered the other skills mathematically. The possibilities of another energy may be balancing the unknown subtle energies once inside the mind's higher portal with developed centered skills grounded together to achieve the hierarchy of co-consciousness. This is about understanding one with electricity, sound and the harmonics of the mind to tap into the earth's energy, the universe's constant vibes. Starting in a faint way, the force or energies can increase depending on how open-minded we are. The magnetic field's strength seems to be measurable and a true constant.

One can connect wirelessly, starting from our human thought, due to our liquid gene pool (some of the population's generic material at a given time) as we are the energy looking for a connection that is always on, as a result of magneto hydrodynamics. Is it scientifically feasible to connect one's mind to the earth's magnetic force?

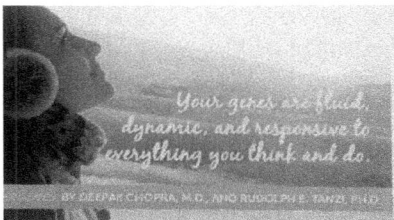

Let's explore, as the force comes from somewhere, and moreover, let's listen to learn to hear how our ancient ancestors tapped into understanding the change of molecular structure. Did they do it by listening? This will allow us to see the different processes of balancing polarizations between the inside and outside of oneself, and also those outside which help men and women move closer together in sync. This is also the key for the spirit of humanity.

The pineal gland for thought in the body/mind's eye... could possibly be part of the missing mass between the poles of the earth's magnetic field. Or does the co-consciousness of the mind create more energy? The polarizations then are the skills that remain in both worlds, inside and out, to continue seven degrees down on the inside, and the same seven degrees up on the outside. Can the human body, brain or soul be part of the missing mass of the universe and, more specifically, in the center of the earth's magnetic field, but in the absolute center... like the center's center of the liquid magnet? Can science prove or disprove that a special property of space as a floating moving mass is human? And moreover, inside humans the glands are skills working against each other as well. Thinking and opinions are closely related. Why is science missing the system of simple brilliance? Why can't the connection be electromagnetic waves?

Regarding Professor of Mathematics Marcus do Saudi and The Code: this experiment was conducted using the wisdom of the crowd or the science of a crowd. Take a big jar and fill it up with jellybeans and ask 160 people how many jellybeans are in the jar? After all the random guesses, the wisdom of the crowd prevailed within 1% of what was actually in the jar. The power of many can do much good. Even though pi is infinite, 3.1415 is typically considered enough decimal places for nearly all calculations and is fitting to calculate the size of the entire observable universe and accurate to calculate the radius of a single hydrogen atom. Pi is written in the structures and processes all around our planet. There are the seven skills wide and deep. Add to that the next three: mind, body and soul, and then the next three are world, humanity and the universe and you arrive at thirteen. Thirteen is a prime number. Is mathematics part of the code?

We use completely abstract numbers in a negative fashion as if they don't even exist and they are at the heart of the analysis when landing airplanes. They're called the "I" imaginary number. Planes are tracked in real time today with this method. With regular numbers, planes would already have moved away from their actual position on the controller's screen. These imaginary numbers (called fairy numbers) are utilized in air traffic control to land planes. This is a way that something abstract is used in a concrete way. The radar system we know today would be pretty much worthless without these numbers. If science sees and uses these to land planes in real life, is what I'm looking for compared to this not abstract, but a simple, overlooked truth?

These mathematical constants exist and have been discovered over the years. What would happen if we looked at them all together at one time? Is there some greater discovery to be learned there? Are there other mathematical constants that must be discovered first? This would be a great question to present to the community through the app.

In Neolithic times, 4,000 years ago, our ancient ancestors built across the UK Sunken Kirk stone circles in Cumbria and all around. There were 1,000 such structures. They are built with great mathematical precision; the mysterious number hidden in every circle is pi, 3.14, no matter how large or small.

Mathematically, is it possible to only have one reality? What are the laws that govern the universe? Mathematics? Philosophy? Science? Spirituality or Religion? How close are we? It seems that the clues have been laid down for us to uncover all over the world! The possibility of finding these answers may be in the wisdom of the crowd by the way people relate to each other.

The clergy at Saint Charles Cathedral wished to echo God's creation and it is a symphony set in stone out of mathematical excellence built in the 13th century.

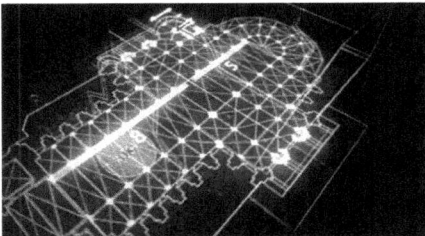

The RSA algorithm is named Rivest, Samir and Adleman. This is the closest for protection and the furthest for protection. Does this equal one? This means we wouldn't have purchasing on the internet without this algorithm. It all fits perfectly into itself.

The H Blocks are a trademark of Puma Punku and perhaps one of the best examples of lost technology. The perfection present within these blocks is staggering. It is difficult to even think that ancient mankind managed to cut, transport and stack these blocks of stone without the use of some sort of technology. Not everything can be achieved through force. The precision of light with the harmony of sound centered precisely with the right type of energy may do it somehow.

What do you think? Is it possible that the ancient builders of Puma Punku and Tiahuanaco had access to advanced technology that has been lost in history? Perhaps a forgotten, omitted piece of history that mainstream scholars do not seem to be interested in?

The speed of light and electromagnetic waves is the same, 310 kilometers per second. Along with this, some say the Giza Pyramids sit on the altitude numbers.

A little of statistics gives $p=1-(1-d/6000km)^{(n.6.m)}$

If n and m are both equal to 10, we have $p\sim d/10km$. You see that there's a 1/1,000 chance that a latitude passes within 10 meters from a monument like the Pyramids of Giza, yet the speed of light does.

Why can't the connection from us to the divine be electromagnetic waves, or some other form of energy? The fastest speed we know, so to speak, is the energy of light, and the slowest is magnetic fields, and the strength seems to be measurable and a true constant. Nevertheless, both are forms of energy. Is the balancing act our pineal gland?

For example, one of the possible ways of communicating with the divine (or getting as close as we can), for the betterment of humanity, is to listen in silence to our deepest thoughts and sometimes empty the mind as if rebooting. Then the communication comes in the form of thought and then we exercise the imagination for other "ways" to look at things, maybe pushing the mind to see more possibilities of slivers of information. These may turn out to be part of the truth (life's truth), working together with humanity in developing each stage of thought for pertinent issues. After the data has been retrieved through the app in a worldwide hub, there will be a connecting of goodness of energy in people. This will help find the equality of people, being blind to race or religion, and will find ways to reduce polarization, poverty and racism.

Another possible answer is to find out together. It really does take all of us to bring what others know out in the open. The younger generation should see this better than most. When the proper work is done, one can see the higher archetype of the human/spirit side is the side that is overlooked, justified by the mind or the mystical part of our emotions. Remember, we are looking for lessons of the past to help move into the future, so this one seems to symbolically catch what we miss, through our emotions, mind patterns and speech. This can play on the outside for many different languages to help in manifesting misunderstanding and chaos, but what is more important is what we don't think of when we are trying to find the words, or when we find the words but they don't come out right, though we think they do. The community can help in the active participation of the way things really happen, rather than the way we think they happen and then the process of the untruth, misunderstanding and justification starts.

Spiritual leaders today see that over time, the 360-degree view of spirit, meaning the side from within, has found that the exact answer to the individual search for complete love for oneself is the same exact thing as finding God inside. In some ways, it doesn't matter if faith is blind or not; it's about balancing God, love and the truth that we don't know on the outside, with God, love and the truth we know on the inside and the collective God that is the inside of us. The multidimensional seven degrees of knowing skill, and seeing abundance of clarity, can only be seen from the portal, but the information is no different for anyone, just the ways are different. This may have been the part where their internal growth stopped at the human heart thinking we are God (half God, half human) and that may be why our ancestors were cutting out hearts for misguided power. They may have built what they thought was God, but the connecting force of the process with our higher self may have been possible to break the molecular structure. To change the form is the most reasonable, based on being one with the universe, centered and in tune with everything else symbolically. Why would it be inconceivable to move mountains and work miracles by connecting the energies on the ground, sky and collective self? This was tapped into somehow, providing wireless worldwide sound as latitude/longitude numbers, as the big pyramid sits at the same numbers for the speed of sound. The energy was inductive, and the hypothetic text clearly states they used electricity with light and cities had plumbing with electricity. Moreover, the schematics for factories and engineering were unbelievable as to the geometry and engineering.

One of the reasons I am focusing on the distant past is because I can understand why, 5,000 years ago, people cut out hearts, thinking it would give them power. They were wrong to do what they did, but it is reasonable that someone could think that God is in the human heart. They didn't have the intelligence we have now; their intuition was their guidance.

This may be part of science overstepping into the God territory because as humans we listen, hear, think, believe, know and feel different types of energies, feelings and emotions and the more we figure out, the less we know. Let's look at this in a philosophical way.

Edward Leedskalnin built pyramid-like structures and then moved one of the greatest wonders of architecture in modern times, Coral Castle. Waiting for the love of his life, he changed the molecular structure of stone/rocks like the ancients as he spent every waking hour working, thinking, praying and meditating to be in sync with Earth's energy. He wanted to obtain the wisdom for fun, curiosity, centered and balanced love, depth inside and outside, and then ultimately the balance of the inside and outside with human and spirit. Understanding the dualism helps separate and then reconnect. The truth of love did turn out to be the reality of the imagination and life's truth from the inside out. Finding the perfection of love internally in oneself is the ultimate definition of selfless or pure love. This begs the question, is love enough? The answer is yes, if one completes the set of skills they set for themselves and they choose to share the deep love within. Yes, love is enough, even if it sounds cliché. The fear one lets in occupies that space of love and more work is required of them to offset and manage their own emotions. This will keep repeating in a relationship time after time but now can be prevented. We can pinpoint the needed growth from lessons learned to protect our future moments together with our kids. We can teach them the lessons we have learned to help better generations in a balanced, human and spiritual way. Our children are the answer to what love is! And what the universe's plan is. And what the truth is. Philosophy can be used to see how we as humans are centered and fused into the core nucleus of the universe. In the same way, we are bonded to that which is **Love** and is life's puzzle *of* education and it is *in* education for us to see where true education may be missing.

Life's **truth** surrounds and runs through us and then is embedded with sciences from the outer part of us. Religion comes from the inner parts being fused together with checks and balances, using philosophy, the Bible and dictionaries to meet, discover and organize ways to the center of one. The truth about love is that it is exactly the same as the truth with no variations or deviations to the universe's plan. We can see that togetherness is part of the plan. It is not about who is right or wrong or who chooses to love. Diminishing fear allows more love to see life's truth. The breaking of the nuclear family comes from not learning needed lessons and skill sets. Not seeing the wisdom of others' pasts is to not see the present, continuous moments and the future moments.

To answer the above question, yes love is enough, but how many ways can one see this? Or should we have the community explain? Finding the deep center of truth inside oneself is centered, selfless love. Are we taught how to find this? The app may help do just that.

If they can't prove a connection wirelessly, the other question science will ask is whether we can be the connection. The physical remains left by our ancestors all over the world show how we can arrive at a mathematical outcome after building a puzzle, then seek out mathematical patterns in numbers and/or follow the data. I would like today's science to fill in the possibilities. I would also like to see the religious aspect be explored by looking at things in different ways to build a puzzle that utilizes data from different religions.

The three Kings: RSVP: In learning, typically one sees in one of three ways: **R**eligiously (inside red), **S**cientifically (outside blue), as we are the (in/out) **V**essel humans (center green) which helps to explain it in **P**hilologically (all together purple) the acronym for all four is (RSVP) We rarely see all three at the same time. There is a process to get to the core of what is meant. It is very rare you will find people that truly see all three together when processing thoughts, unless they have been through the portal. Some people are the exception to the rule, and some people will argue with you until they are blue in the face, just to disagree. This process is about dwelling, focusing and participating in shaping the development of the "good," giving little attention to negativity. It pushes out what we can't do and keeps the possibilities open to what we can.

R.S.V.P. [Your Name] for our Unity.

Scholars and academics make up the science community and we can show religiously, using theologians that we found that the same service works for all three communities and how all **three fit together.**

1) Now we need to explain philosophically how all three tie together, starting with after the inter-technology from our ancestors who misused the internal collective knowledge "power" lost deep inside us now and took a deep paradigm shift the wrong way to lose these gifts because they might have been free "gratis" in times past. They lived from their spirit side and/or the inside first, then the outside/human. Or maybe there was no separation. They seemed to be barbaric on the outside, unlike today.

The way the ancients managed their groups is key and it is still a mystery as to the way they obtained useable information together. A good place to start is Sakai Japan Faison Kogan, one of over 40 ancient crypts. This is mammoth, more than twice the length of the Great Pyramid of Giza. It is the largest tomb in the world, constructed in the 5th century AD.

These keys, once properly fitted, will help in finding the portal and, maybe even more importantly, how today we use the co-consciousness through trial and error in using / finding love, truth, God and why we have the same purpose is service. The last of one of the three kings is: world, universe and cosmos. The science community should be finding out that the God thing is science and that they fit together for the process of the relationships as it seems to find the center of the three, where the mind and emotions either miss or can't see without help. But the wisdom of the crowd will break out questions and answers, and because others know what we don't, we may find a number of keys to help uncover starting points or important symbols that are keys.

These are patterns, so if we dig together for more patterns, will patterns of patterns reveal more if we do this in an organized way?

This is where we possibly lost the portal (hands together). This is where it started to separate, as this took four or five generations after losing this inner technology to become unaware, and to lose both working portals (individual and co-conscious).

We have just scratched the surface on the many different possible skills our ancestors had. Consider the three kings: what happened at that point? Did we spin off to increase the chaos? There were many barricades created to reach the portal; different languages, the downfall of their education system and various changed religions made it almost impossible to know, love and understand oneself, creating much less clarity from within. This is abstract thinking, but why are we being punished? Or are we? Did we advance too quickly and become united in inner technology back in the past? There has been little to no movement today in inner technology, at least as far as I have seen.

This may be a good question to ask for fun: what else can taking a bite of the apple mean when talking about Adam and Eve? Remember, when asking questions beyond our community, we're going to look to other countries and cultures so, in order to not offend their customs and beliefs, we would build a puzzle about the different religions and cultures.

We are part of the universe, so is it possible to think that humanity is the bite of the apple or the different ways it relates? Your first thought can be our best organized, categorized answer and if millions or billions of people answer, could that be simple brilliance?   Let's explore past the way we were conditioned and think for ourselves in other ways, but consult professionals for guidance in topics and three-dimensional thinking to help build the framework. Ultimately, publishing the wisdom of the crowd will prove the wisest outcome. I mentioned in the beginning that church is the inside of a person and state is the outside. To define polarization, there are two parts by following the patterns and there appears to be a polar opposite to the inside and outside. I'm calling the church side good for the reason that what is inside us should be good. Church represents spirit, while the state represents human. Waiting a few seconds past our instant reaction, to act in a better way, is using your spirit. These sides of us are present and the more we see how they exist the more we will see how they appear like different worlds on parallel universes. The awareness skills will not put both sides together but will help see the working processes of both. The question is, are we ready for these challenges in different ways worldwide?

Obviously, there are far more people living today than in the past. In many ways, we are the same on the inside as others, whether we see it or not. Time is the separating factor in terms of timeless lessons, skills and knowledge (abstract time doesn't exist symbolically, literally or philosophically). A person of any size, race, color or religion, with the proper training and committed goodwill, could get to the individual portal because we all have these skills within us. People have tried for years, but with better organization and a brighter light at the end of the tunnel, we can make it easier to find the portal. There are so many people who have written great books to uncover different parts of the portal and the various skills and lessons necessary to even begin to prepare one's self for such a journey. I just want any question someone might have to be answered with a simple search by going to the app where most questions and answers are explored from all sides as we build together. Example: self-help, as well as science and the God thing fit together, and together they fit perfectly on the parallel universes; the words tie in the tangible and intangible universe, meanings, and patterns. We now have established why this requires much-needed participation worldwide.

Individuals had to work really hard and dig deep after forty years or enough time to lose the inner-technology. They began to realize these skills probably started out as gifts in ancient times. When inner-technology became so difficult to obtain, we began to live from the outside (or humanly) and we still do so today. Earlier, I used an example of placing my hands together as if praying and then turning those 180 degrees, then separating them sideways so that you need to use your peripheral vision. When our hands start to separate sideways, this not only loses the individual connection, or our self-portal, but the co-portal as well. During the forty-year period, the community did not pursue lessons, skills or wisdom and it was practically lost for good. When we get together now, we are a bunch of people running around outside to outside on the surface, and over time we let a few people in and some touch us on the inside. I would believe that, in times past, few ancients were kicked out of their community. Maybe their focus was their God(s). What was explainable was the process in the portal, which was simple and in tune with the earth, the sky and each other. What makes it explainable with the hierarchy of the co-consciousness is the purity of the mind. "Can't" wasn't in their thoughts. No brain games or barricades existed to prevent them from taking the diamonds of information and picking apart the possibilities of the good things and building civilizations through the collective, organized and calibrated listening of the imagination. Since ancient times, barricades have developed in our minds and the highest awareness is required now to overcome these barricades. But, we receive answers today much as they did in the past, only with much greater effort. The emotional, internal balance of one's self starts with imagination and appropriately asking questions and this leads to "curiosity" and "listening" which leads to "thinking" which leads to "choosing" what one "believes" to see what they learned and ultimately "know" the "way" of this process. Even if we could change our molecular structure (with what we've learned through this process) to get through the portal, would the UI let us? The universe knows to provide specific, timely information as to "what is," focusing on the present moment. The question we need to answer is, what people are in tune with "their ear to the ground"? This has happened twice to me. The first time was twenty years ago when I did a documentary about divorce, and this didn't turn out the way I intended. I was trying to change the world by sharing what I went through, to help reduce divorce rates and to help people raise their own children and find love for themselves to share with their family.

Years ago, when I started writing this vision to see where it would take me, it seemed to only lead to the bridging of science, philosophy and religion to one. The nucleus is still to find love for oneself and to share the love with the nuclear family with the right skills as the children carry the perfect human which is God when they are young. When one finds the portal, it is a lifetime achievement, regardless of age, that happens on many different levels. I think if one person has the strength, will, wisdom, and/or passion in the family to know what love means, the family can survive, finding bliss in time because the love doesn't get any stronger than between a man and a woman when they have children and are properly educated.

In the distant past, the whole group would receive answers for what they did in the portal together; they were sharing in thought, much like the individual processes of the portal, and the timing was coupled with the depth and width of understanding the lessons, skills and sliding scales. If we start off by exploring issues, what are the possibilities that can be built? After the community talks about the possibilities, one of the keys is to gain more information and to not shut down thoughts. One can often use the dark of the night or the mists of the next morning in stillness to find more questions and answers or to clarify some. When they retrieved the best and most noteworthy questions or ideas in a different way than we do now, they broke them down, piece by piece, using their imagination. If we were to use our imaginations, we would take the three best possibilities, always keeping our minds open, not discarding pertinent thoughts and from there we would explore and break it down to its core.

The individual portal is no longer easy to obtain as we had to start over to relearn the simple principles, but in different ways. One can see to learn what we can't see, but it's still there for all of us to tap into. We just have to find the portal again. A simple paradigm shift occurs in one's head to know that we often don't know things in everyday life. We must remain open-minded, because once one knows, or thinks they know, thoughts are shut down about the subject, leaving people with only little parts of the whole, thinking they understand, while knowing less than they think they do. Our brains can tell us we know when we really don't. Trying to have a better understanding of the natural, internal differences that work perfectly together and against each other inside of us, and finding a balance between the two, can help us with our outside relationships. We don't want to go back to ancient times to mirror what they did; instead we want to use this app to create the community setting they had, and through that community, simplify the process for everyone involved. By doing so we will use the app to build back the connections for the lessons of wisdom, knowledge and intellect. Together, we will put a label on the internal process's skills needed, and call this the "Rubik's Cube of Knowledge."

What does the universe know?

There were a few recognizable individuals who understood the portal but, just as we see in the separating hands example, much was lost when civilizations folded. The gifts of inner technology were lost. This may have begun the shift in human makeup in which we began living from the human/state side, or the outside of us. Our ancient

* What did they write hieroglyphics on?

They wrote hieroglyphics on this stone called the "Rosetta Stone". One the top part of the stone they wrote in hieroglyphics. On the middle part of the stone they wrote in demotic hieroglyphics, and on the bottom part they wrote in ancient Greek. Ancient Greek could be translated easily.

Rosetta Stone

ancestors may have indulged in extreme humanistic pleasures because they were all equal in mind, body and spirit to everybody else in their community. It has been thought that the basic needs were taken care of by a small, rotating percentage of the people. A small group provided food, water and shelter and the rest had nothing to do but enjoy, think, and gain wisdom.

Eventually, ancient communities no longer shared the teachings to get into the individual portal. We are now provided only what is still standing and it is up to us to make sense of the remains. The individual part of the portal would have been found on their own from the inside. We have quite a time span between the end of the ancients and now, so let's think about the people during this period with great impact.

There have undoubtedly been so many people over the years who saw the individual knowing part of the portal and tapped into it. They needed to see into most issues from all three sides, scientifically, philosophically and religiously. The abundance of information is then poured into those few history-making heads in science, philosophy, and religion. We were experiencing more as individuals, externally and internally, as if the gates had been opened. We were flooded with information, but there were no community portals to help break down data together, so from then on we built individually, getting praise from the community and being held in high esteem for our accomplishments. This is completely opposite to the way it worked in ancient times. This has reached a breaking point for us individually, placing the growth to be experienced in a polarized fashion. This mirrors what we are made of: star stuff, on each side (inside and out) going down seven layers with time lapse photography to show the timing of the inner workings. The 3D holograms show the timing of how this works and interacts with all the skills, lessons, emotions, actively and all together in a usable, helpful way.

These people's skills may seem simple, but they are often overlooked now. Over time we started to miss out on the skills once held by the Mayans, Egyptians and other ancients. Naturally, certain skills dissipated over 5,000 years. For me, the most noticeable skill today is the younger generation's practice of texting and living in cyberspace instead of talking and interacting with one another. They are missing out on basic aspects of human interaction, including speech, touch and hearing which provide the basic social skills of which they've become unaware. I think the ancients left thoughts open automatically in order to achieve a better understanding rather than completing each thought just for the sake of completing it. This allowed them to become much more open-minded and to not pass judgment too quickly (internally or externally).

We need to connect to the power of many to single out an answer to truth or love. The process may be greatly enhanced through trial and error. Your initial first thought or your "gut feeling" has merit and will be included in shared thinking, but it is important to allow enough time to listen in silence for new thoughts. We could apply this to a question like: "how can we work less and make more money?" The power of this is mind-boggling! Remember, through the app, we start off instantly seeking and having billions of people, starting at the top with the richest and most influential people, and moving down to the masses of people. The connection serves a purpose for the betterment of work on the inside and the wisdom of the crowd helps provide control. The app is entertaining, powerful and needs to be used wisely.

With this plan, we could currently offset the Rubik's Cube of Knowledge and help the government by expanding the new platforms and finding the different ways we could run everyday life from the inside out.

The communication hub of the world for the basic human spirit to unite in goodness with holograms at a subtonic level.

Chapter Five:

Ancients and Community
To Know What "Know" Means

1st) the Three Kings: Mind, Body and Soul/Spirit;. 2nd Humanity, World and/or Universe. Our ancestors found the 3rd world in a secret way; 4th) The way one looks to see. (RSVP)

Perhaps our spiritual side has a connection with the earth's forces that needs to be proven with the laser precision of science. Maybe it has something to do with the earth's magnetic field or some unknown source of energies related to the cosmos. I feel like there is much we don't know about the way we relate to the earth and the universe. If we could discover what this connection is, it might open up a new way of learning.

Confucius knew what knowledge is. What one knows on the inside of oneself and the outside of oneself shows that they don't know everything. If a person knows that he doesn't know but understands both, then he would know what knowledge is.

Shall I tell you what knowledge is? It is to know both what one knows and what one does not know.

Confucius

PICTURE QUOTES .com

PICTUREQUOTES .com

How will [Your name] see this? I believe teaching at universities is a form of knowledge; knowing academically is from the outside of us to the inside. The other way of knowing what knowledge is comes from the inside out. The Three Kings (Mind, Body and Soul) learned from the timing of the universe in the distant past or even now. The university, or the outside in approach is about the physical world. The universe's university, or the inside out process, is about the spiritual world. After all lessons are learned, the human side metaphysically transcends our spirit side. Our collective mind is spirit relating to the soul (everybody else) or to the material outer/outside/human/state. Our skill sets, our inside/spirit/church side, and the skills of timeless wisdom are the same as what separates us (in time and space). The timing of the skill sets work with the Rubik's Cube of Knowledge to operate the skills of timeless wisdom together with the calibrated ways of using time lapse photography to see we have the same equality of intelligence when we work as a whole to understand how humans work. We will show the world what meeting in the center means, when we have the academic brilliance of the outer human world, like each one of us is a scientist. We all also have the spiritual enlightenment in the same equality of the inner world. We center academic brilliance and spiritual enlightenment through the Doctorate of Education. We then understand that the perfect balance of education in words, speech and writing are these spiritual and academic laws, naturally combining the center of time and space by what we don't see. They are the answer to what we should know as a community. The ancient way of learning needs to be combined with our way to see the puzzle that has been with humanity since the inception of the world. The philosophy of love is wisdom for an academic brilliance of **HOW** the world works, to **WHY,** symbolically, it all relates in perfect harmony at the center of time in any order to see all life's answers work in sync. The answers show **WHERE** to work together metaphysically, brings **WHEN** religiously and scientifically meet in one is the deepest truth for **WHO** humanity is, centered and balanced knowledge of **WHAT** the different now's (love, truth, time, space) explains OUR makeup in and about the Universe IS a child (the guide to all life), which some call God's plan... that which is us.

Does this sound religious, scientific, philosophical or poetic?

We are the same as the outer God or the unknown. We can use this connection to learn some of the skills the ancients knew such as sound, light and electricity. In my experience, the portal gives a 360- degree view of spirituality, after the 2nd paradigm shift (the 2nd paradigm shift was a traumatic life event for some that loved me), as if standing on top of all of the lessons one has learned. There are at least two things one must do to gain this 360-degree view. First, one must refrain from closing down thoughts in the mind. To do so would mean we have passed judgment without all of the information. Secondly, we might have (Science smalls. sm). Science says that the natural state of the mind involves wanting to overlook needed information because it seeks the path of least resistance automatically.

The mind is both one's best asset and worst enemy. How can this be? The mind is powerful both ways; what it sees can be incredibly valuable, while what it doesn't see and how it uses this information to learn can be incredibly damaging. For example, let's say your grandmother's doctor determines she needs surgery. Rather than getting a second opinion, she goes ahead with his recommendation and learns afterward that she could have been treated by a more modern technique that did not include surgery. She suffers a life-long complication that requires her to go to physical therapy every week. Because her mind didn't "see" the second opinion, she ended up suffering. I watched a documentary recently about a Chinese scientist exploring Einstein's theories and he showed an atom splitting and then joining back together. I liken this to two sides of a truth and how there are pieces of an atom that are even smaller than we know of today. What's natural has a spirit side as well as a human side. Science needs to put its parts together from the other two to be one.

Religion could be science's polar opposite. There is a process of moving through lessons that includes topics such as relationships with people; the way of learning; relationships with Self, Community and Country (S.C.C.) and emotions and skills from the neck down; time and timing of processes, and abstracts. As I've mentioned, the first paradigm shift is just learning all of the lessons. The second is standing at the top of the completed lessons. As an abstract illustration: one side of the color-coded hologram body is facing the lessons on the way up, but on the way down the legs face the opposite direction while the upper half is facing the lessons on the way down. On top of a pyramid, the head is looking straight at us; in order to get down these lessons one must die while still physically alive. Surely many people have paved the way to make it easier for most to move back down, one lesson at a time, starting from the other side of the lesson, and learned in a way that is the same but different. For example: on the way up, one might be getting over the fear of fear, and on the way down they are experiencing the thing that can't occupy the same space as fear, which is love. Love can't share the same space with its polar opposite. The question is, once the depth and width of understanding is uncovered and we crawl down from the top of spirit back to where we started, what it is to be human? As we know, it is all love, but how is the question. It seems it takes seven degrees to remove the fear so love, or a deeper knowing, can be experienced. Is this what the inner connection is? Religion could need science and science needs religion, balanced by philosophy in a three-sided coin of heads, tails and the edge. This has the possibility to help find the patterns to explain how the UI of an atom may be put back together by the syncing of a balanced, symbolic and literal truth.

The question is, will others see how grounded people are as they pass through the portal, and continue to learn the processes of what it is to be human? This may give us a place to look for the missing space. I'm suggesting the connection is the pineal gland and may need more research.

2nd) Three Kings: Humanity, earth and the universe all work perfectly together and it's up to us to understand how. In the spiritual realm, once learned, the lessons are practiced from the bottom to the top and the top to the bottom and back to the balanced center. The big part of knowing the process is coming back down the other side, back to where you started, knowing you found an energy from the same lessons but looked at the lesson in a different way. Then, with each lesson the sliding scale of polarized understanding is shortened, and once the lessons are learned it squeezes out the air of misunderstanding and we have what we don't know is part of the all-knowing. Stay open-minded and be aware to catch what is typically missed. Then after that, we are left with it just "is." At that point, we have a better understanding of happiness, the mind's clarity and emotional, financial, environmental, moral, political stability. We can then go deeper worldwide, understanding things like wireless electricity, harmonic sound of listening and how to change the molecular structure from the center of truth, living in the now. The truth's center (the overall truth) will require us to get seven degrees down within oneself. The question is, how would anyone know on either side if I was talking about the overall truth or the center of truth? That may seem like semantics, but it's not. If one comes inside-out and the other outside-in, the truth may reside in seeing the difference between the two sides and/or the "relationships" of how the collective truth works. Do we see the three sides yet? Or how relationships work?   Each side is a truth. They are a dichotomy, polar opposites and there are dimensions of layers, so there is no right or wrong, it just is "what is." For example: understanding the overall truth is seeing what the difference is between the outside human and the inside spirit sides. This is how it relates to what, why and how the relationship works from the inside and outside with the collective self. The way the mind can see without growth is what is selfish about the outside human side. Choosing our inside/spirit/soul is selfless. Our world of humanity shares one ultimate polar opposite: destiny, whether we see it or not. The center of truth is what it is, whether we see and believe it or not, so don't judge or try to understand one's emotions. Don't justify one's actions by what one hears, sees or doesn't see, or by what one thinks or believes.

This is not good or bad; it is to be aware of the choice to exercise, balancing our free will. Let's find out what we do and don't need:

1) We need both light and dark; if we only had darkness, we would never see, and if we only had light, we would be blinded. This is a way in which things are the same but different, and different but the same.
2) We need both good and evil; with only one we would be dead or bored to death.
3) We need space because without it, we couldn't move in mind or body.
4) Men and women are both needed as equals to love themselves and love one another.

In raising our children, we need to give them the skills and teachings to start their lives with a fair chance of getting over the issues we as parents never got over. The lifetime of justification, most of which we don't even know and can't figure out, makes us afraid to face our fears. Our children then go on to live the same way. The cycle continues.

Because we can love anyone we choose, there is no stronger bond than the one we have with the person we had babies with! This doesn't mean two people should stay together simply for the children; what I'm saying is to learn from them how to find love for yourself. Then you can choose to share this love with the person you made a family with. This is the true understanding of what love is when it's shared together with the family. When men and women see the needed growth processes, they begin to understand that we control who we love. With this balanced knowledge from the inside out, we that understand it can help others to see that self-love is the same love that is God-self. It may be that we can see God in another perspective so if we all were called God we wouldn't know one another's name, and the universes and ducks would not have any separation in communication, creating chaos, barricades and confusion in the mind because we are all separated, divided and split by time, space, love, and truth, and what we see and don't see.

We know as a child that we don't have a choice about who we grow up with; they deserve to share their past, present and future moments with both parents. A child's only true desire for their family is to have their parents remain together and recognize that their child's love is as close to unconditional as one will find.

The mind has many barricades and controls the good and bad but what it misses can and will blind us later, preventing us from seeing our fears. The mind has a limited amount of space available for love and fear and they cannot occupy the same space; in fact, they compete for space in some ways. Each fear triggers our feelings to diminish the space we have to offer love, turning that space from love and sending our emotions into a frenzy. This is providing different barricades of chaos and confusion, so the mind does not see clearly. The emotions build up without the mind seeing and are pushed out sideways, away from solutions, to bring calmness and understanding, letting the mind stay in disarray and frenzy. This triggers an emotional roller coaster and we become unable to manage our minds in order to unravel the chaos. We instead begin to blame the heart and say we are not in love anymore and then time takes care of the rest. We are stuck in the need to be right or we believe we did nothing wrong, or we have a desire to leave, thinking the grass is greener somewhere else. In some cases, people move on to the next person and repeat the same mistakes because they haven't found the necessary growth.

Some people are switching gender "sides," trying to understand what love is because the law on the outside is allowing it to be. When blaming God, look at yourself and see your neighbor as a god all on the "inside." In a symbolic, multidimensional way, we have the answers inside uncovering the mystical truths. We have to find out for ourselves because our parents didn't see it. This will help the next generation of parents from saying they "just didn't know" and will show them how to build a family and keep it together.

For the betterment of humanity, we need to start from the core self, extending to the family. The unselfish love of **one**self on the inside is the key. This is the power of **ONE** love, balanced with each person, the love of power to add strength to that for humanity, to unite **ONE** spirit. This is to understand part of what love is, to know what the sun, moon and the stars mean.

The tools from the collective wisdom of the crowd for this and the next generation will learn from the mistakes of the previous generation. Remember, we are taking the good from the past. The consensus in speaking to hundreds of divorcees for my documentary years ago was that "Nobody wins Divorce in Modern America." Now is the time to be fair to our children and to leave them with the gift of sharing continuous future moments together. Let us not leave this to chance. Knowing and understanding these timeless skills will only help to make a better world when the choice for the parents to love themselves first and then each other, and the children win. .

Children are here to help grow and sharpen the adults' skills by having us see what it is to notice how and why they work the way they do while they are still in their innocence. **K.I.D.S: Keep, Innocent Dreams Safe**. We must protect the future for all of us. What they know is a simple form of living in the now, with no past or future just the present inside and outside. Children don't see differences like gender or race. Eventually, we grow out of what makes us a child.

3rd) Three Kings: To understand the good of what our ancestors left behind, we need to explore together, from the inside out, how they worked together to accomplish what they were able to. This is a completely different way of learning. We first figure out the right processes and do that part over and over again.

The science to this is like an atom that splits as if it's going through two doors at once and then comes back together as one on the other side. I am seeing why and how abstract thinking should be normal to use in philosophy, science and mathematics. Believe and it will become; believe and it can be. This can be the bad side (or human side) of believing. The good side or spirit side may be worthy of further research. Maybe the science smalls are related in some way to our inner technology. Then we may need to duck, weave and bob to get there with no ego.

We can only see as far as the completed lessons for an individual, community or country, but can the wisdom of the crowd trump this? This is why people in the world have their own individuality, spirituality and religion; because emotions and lessons have no understanding of time. It appears as if we are more different than we really are. When it comes to spirituality, are the lessons the same for all of us?

Is this what our ancestors left behind? Perhaps we need to understand the abstract thinking to the way our inside process works to the individual part of the truth that touches each mind, body and soul. To be human, we need to find the center focus of the issues and if you squeeze out all of the air you will find the truth or RSVP (religion, science, vessel, philosophy). The guided wisdom will come from collectively teaching the crowd through trial and error.

Jon Champollion was a famous hieroglyphics decoder in the 1820's, whose focus was on the ancient Egyptians. Decoders often misinterpreted hieroglyphics with regard to death and the underworld. These hieroglyphics often interpreted death literally, when it should have been seen in a more symbolic way; you have to die while you're still alive, from the inside out, before you can enter the underworld. This starts a new beginning in a deep, concentrated way, after all, or most, skills are learned.

I have been trying to explain a portal that is seven layers deep on the inside. The skills can mean the same thing, but in a different way, as a portal seven layers on the outside. We can look at gender differences to understand this. Both genders have certain skills that they teach to one another. But these are often missed because it's simple but not easy; they get missed because the skills work inside and out simultaneously and if one is not aware of how the process works, they can misunderstand. Things on the outside don't happen as quickly because inside our mind we are mentally working through situations before we speak. The time lapse photos will explain how each of these skills or lessons work independently and together.

When we don't know something, we often become curious, but it doesn't last long because the brain wants to find the path of least resistance. This is why this project needs people of all different backgrounds around the world who have been through the portal to share how to obtain information individually. The collective portal is much the same as the individual portal, but it involves us moving through together. I have very specific, detailed ways of what, how and why to get to the collective portal to achieve goals but I'm only one person; this is why coaches are required.

The inner technology lost by the ancients has not come back for the communities and individuals. Perhaps having that internal knowledge collectively was natural for them, since they had little past experience or obstructions of the mind. Few have accomplished what the ancients did. The way they lived seemed to be aligned, inwardly-out. We now typically look from our outward side (human) into their outward side, making it hard to reach our real selves.

These skills, as wide and as deep as they may be, have to be uncovered by individuals. They are so natural that one may only need a few things to see the light of day. With a check list of what's left to be uncovered, it should be relatively easy to uncover the rest. This will be invaluable, using the individual part of the app for tracking the growth of skills and lessons learned by unlocking the keys that pass you through to the next place or level within the app.

This may help connect philosophy, religion and science. It's not about ideology; this is about people and the betterment of humanity, achieved through figuring out how we work. The focus should be how we work using RSVP and using [Your Name] higher self to connect.

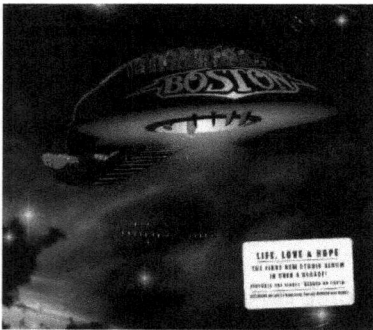

The point is, it seems like we are living life backwards from the human side. A cool thing to look at will involve seeking out the meanings of lyrics in our communities. The times follow the stage of growth we are in with our Community and dictate our conditioning and the lessons (S.C.C.) we have been through and are going through now.

It would be nice to build age lessons from those who are twenty and up. These all change as we grow. I think we all want love and trying to find the truth about what love is at any age requires the right teachings. The lesson we seem to be going through today is that involving the LGBTQ community. This ultimately may be a huge lesson from the distant past, perhaps from our ancient ancestors. We just don't know the past on this one.

There is a symbolic, unisex growth of the mind once we understand and grow to the point where there is equality among men and women. When talking about men and women, we see why the separate sides of emotions, thoughts and skills are divided and split from the completed whole. The 1st, 2nd and 3rd kings are the same while together as _**one**_ (men and women); we are different but also the same. To see the gender dichotomy is perfection from within _**one**_self (Human love). Then we grow up physically and back down metaphysically and then back to the center of _**ONE**_ on each side, _**ONE Man**_ and _**ONE Woman**_. Each is a whole complete human inside self (the knowledge of male and female inside self) world unto themselves, all having the same purpose to serve _**ONE Self that equals our self**_, inside and out to become together.

The universe can be viewed as two different, parallel worlds: physical, tangible and non-physical, intelligible. Symbolically, both sides come together as **one through the philosophy of words,** individually in the universe of _**One**_. This will find internal, simple brilliance for us to find love and for all of us to extend into the communities and out to the countries and beyond. The non-physical, eternal world is our home in the universe or on Earth. In that way, we are made from the same stardust as the inside of a women's womb or from the outside of a man. This is the in and out of each person and each is a universe of their own, with secrets that are sacred in their "underworld." The ancients may have called the "underworld" what I have been calling the "inside world," the part where only one can see for themselves. But they managed, piece by piece, to teach the whole community.

The internal wisdom of love is in us; we just need to see how love and truth work together as one. But our makeup is the balance of truth, love and family and is the center of the core nucleus (humanity, spirituality, the universe and our world) where we grow through knowledge to all be the same. The physical world for the past, present and future includes having fun in the outside world, enjoying life in the moment and gaining knowledge from outside-in to help us be happy. This side (outside) is a truth.

If we look from a different perspective, the non-physical world is another side of a truth, using the same past, present and future with a different purpose: to be happy from within and to nurture the internal knowledge of the growth process for the betterment of humanity. When self, community and country start connecting the dots of information to understand the separation between them and the 'outside-in' and the 'inside-out, it's like a color-coded wiring diagram. It will complete a circuit of fulfillment within us and will show us that from the 'outside-in' is to see **_One World_** by itself. To see oneself from the 'inside-out' is also **_One World_** of its own. Both combined are a universe of **_One_**. This helps to understand how the world works backwards and how being in service for others when working as **_one_** is the same purpose of service. To have all working for **_one_** means we all work for (S.C.C.U) self, community, country and universe, which is the same as Me, Myself and I (the outside) on the physical or tangible side of the universe. Together with the Mind, Body, and Soul (the inside) in the non-physical or intangible both sides of the universe are each a truth and need each other at every step of the way to be involved, if not it is a unintentional lie to oneself. We need to add the "verb" to M,B, S. (inside) and "noun" to M,M,I (outside) to do it in God's Word to show what it is to be perfect in everything in writing. First we must split our language up equally; we did that by inside and outside of the verbs and nouns and separate our definitions in the dictionary appropriately by using the oxymoron in one word using the definitions the noun is outside human and the verb is inside spiritual to use for each word in the dictionary. We need to divide our spiritual inside words and our human outside words by "ONE" word, so all our rules and regulations can go into that one word to take a word to show the formula the correct way. But ultimately language pieces the universe together perfectly or piece-by-piece takes it apart perfectly to become one in the middle of the center "for everybody and everything are the answers to all" where we humans are all knowing because God made us this way we just need to uncover how and the key is in our language.

When I talk about uniting the physical and non-physical worlds, what I mean is that the Universe of One is greater than the sum of its parts. This relationship is similar to pi in the way a radius of a circle relates to its other properties. What is relative outside, in the way the inside and outside relate, is how we depend on each other to exist, then just to unite on the outside with a purpose of identifying the inside world of oneself. For example: One might say to another, "Look and see." "To look" is from the outside while "to see" is from the inside. Seeing the separation by using words that represent the inside and the outside should distinguish the difference before the perspective changes. The "way" of what, why, and how is looked at first. As words merge with thoughts, we see how the words relate to be used on both sides as a separate truth, showing another dimension of how both sides of each world work. "Can you hear me?" is on the outside, and it squeezes down to a truth. "Listen to me" is on the inside, and it tightens down the truth. The center of understanding is inside and outside at the same time by the proper flow of words to the center, opposite words put together with both sides of a single word make the whole word complete. The way of the simple truth is hidden and is seen with the mind's eye with the perfect system in language to see the one truth. An example can be found in the human hands. We have two hands, and each are the mirror image and opposite of each other and each operates on its own. As each hand works on its own, they cannot become one. Our hands also relate to each other in that they can work together as one, like when someone types on a keyboard or when a musician uses an instrument. We are only as good as the systems we build. We may be back to the very basics we keep overlooking as a group; sometimes our minds pass over what we need to see. I would like for as many as possible to participate in our own type of hieroglyphics, using the framework I have already built. Using the ancients as a guide and understanding ourselves can only come from uniting the group of people that have been through the "portal" along with the coaches and teachers who bring the crowd along. I remember Oprah and the guy from Brooklyn Howard Schultz (he calls himself the guy from Brooklyn) speaking about this... is it time?

Itself = one world; Myself = the self = yourself + Himself & Herself, ourselves, God the self. Both sides (nonphysical, intangible and physical, tangible).

Women see the beauty in the universe naturally as part of their outside physical world. Thinking about sex daily at the same time while looking at men and thinking about what type of a relationship they would be, this is living in the non-physical world.

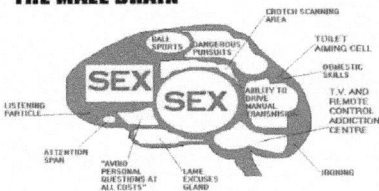

THE MALE BRAIN

On the other hand, men tend to look at the beauty of women, often not seeing the inner beauty (spiritual side). Their thoughts are often about sex; some men just want a woman sexually and will do anything to get it, play with her emotions, constantly complimenting her and even breaking up a family. This is a man's makeup, and a growth process is required for men to decide to live in, and see, the non-physical world but again this is to get sex.

We've not understood exactly how the ancients did what they did with stone, electricity and sound with such precision. There is a perfectly-built system to uncover from the inside out, into language and speech the distant past tapped into we now have it on the outside literally when we perfect the perfect language. We have the opportunity to do it from the inside like the ancients with the right teachings, or the outside to make it through the individual portal. All that is non-physical comes from the universe's plan that lies deep within us. The growth process for life's plan comes from the centered language of speech, with our languages being broken down further than we commonly see. We can learn through the union of one man and one woman, through sex; by this, I don't just mean the physical act or the closeness in spirituality, but rather how we were made.

The Core of the Universe is the mirror image inside non-physical and outside physical of us, using two sides - things, no-things and living things make up everything, the nucleus of the parallel universe has all I mean ALL the answers in the universe we together just need to organize the correct formula of God's way to obtain these answers. The makeup I am referring to is **the physical (science) and non-physical (religious) parts of the universe.** The solar system within us is embedded in the universe's plan since the beginning of time. Babies are born from **the center of the core nucleus in the universe** through each **nucleus of one.** That is one man and he is the **nucleus of one.** One woman is also the **nucleus of one**, together with the **core center of/in the universe of one, which is the nucleus of one.** The center of the **nucleus** in, on and of one is to know one child. One child is known once the nucleuses of the universe appropriate. The center of oneself from human to God and God to human, it is the same but different, and different but the same. The Human side is human and the spiritual side is God. We should stay open, but barricades

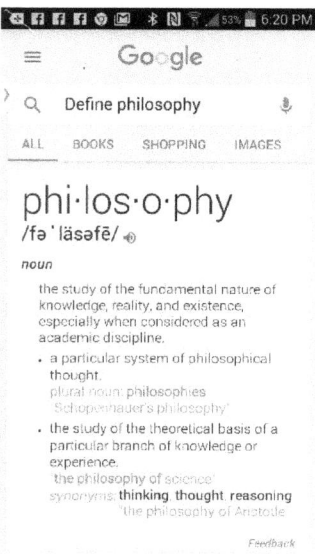

Google

≡   Google

Q   Define philosophy   🎤

ALL   BOOKS   SHOPPING   IMAGES

phi·los·o·phy
/fə ˈläsəfē/ 🔊

noun

the study of the fundamental nature of knowledge, reality, and existence, especially when considered as an academic discipline.

- a particular system of philosophical thought.
  plural noun: philosophies
  "Schopenhauer's philosophy"
- the study of the theoretical basis of a particular branch of knowledge or experience.
  "the philosophy of science"
  synonyms: thinking, thought, reasoning
  "the philosophy of Aristotle"

Feedback

separate the growth and throw the process off. To grow and be educated in love is internal brilliance. Love puts all life's pieces of perception together correctly because seeing life's truth is both the intangible which is the side of love from the inside and the outside of love is the tangible side. For seeing love the intangible side and the tangible side are gathered by truth together to make the perfect answers for everything and will help in most situations when one sees how they join.. This will keep the biological family together and will keep communities and countries together and in sync, cheered on by humanity. They will see that there is light at the end of the learning tunnel; for one to see the hidden truth, we must join together to find the "one" truth as the one love is in our grasp of choice with the right education.

Science and religion are **one,** explained through academic discipline using philosophy from the wisdom of and in God's proxies science! We know this, but the parts that we can't see are seen through the other side of learning the intangibles and other side to the polar opposite words making the word complete and "whole" like "look and see." We are focused on just directing our energies into the narrowed-down possibilities, until we see a better way. Then collectively we see the better way is part of the process to 'KNOW,' for future generations to enhance properly through trial and error. The Universal intelligence is left to us in all ways. The plan was to communicate what love is through the overall depth of the truth.

The true truth creates justice inside and out, peace and love for oneself by calibrating everything correctly inside one person at a time until we all are following the same correct formula inside, the collective machine that is the same as truth. What we believe we know does more damage than we actually know. That which is God "is" not knowing, or the inside knows not only after what one thinks, believes and knows. We are to learn the master plan together to find the one truth of what it means to be human (God made it the perfect human to be God, so it is our self). We are here to find what we can't see and to know the intricacies of being human and God. The universe's plan is for us to start over until we reach the portal. The journey begins again with a totally different perspective. We need to leave our thoughts open and be willing to change for the better, filling up the space inside with wisdom and growth to understand how we are perfect.

A man loves by thinking of tomorrow. A woman loves by thinking of today. The child loves in the "now" - the perfect moment where the ingredients for Mom and Dad need to be in the now to stay together teaching us to live in the now, the present as well as God to love in all ways is us too. As we all can love anywhere on the map correctly, the Universe/God/Children has love for now, adults love for today and tomorrow but need to grow in all appropriate ways, levels and dimensions back to the center of "NOW" and since we are identical only timing and understanding sets us apart. And sex brings us back together using the differences but what is the same. The "ONE" truth is what is "differentness" but the "same" are Male and Female and the "human hips!" cannot be altered; what doesn't fit isn't in God's plan. And the twins in language can explain any truth with one side being non-physical, defined by a verb in that side as part of the formula. The other side is physical, defined by a noun so we as humans can understand language perfectly with all of the correct answers to God's ways. Also, God understands how language works. He made language down to his word (explained later) and Self are all the same but different to explain to us humans as we are Gods too.

The universe's plan lies deep in all of us. Some have said the ancients must have had a pretty good reason to work together the way they did, both physically and non-physically. There is a growth process for both sides, inside and outside, the physical side and non-physical side. At a certain age, time or period of growth, the woman starts to embody more of the physical side. The man embodies more of the emotional side as he gets older. The simple act of sex might be the unknown space between the magnets. This seems to be the understanding of sex in all its possibilities, but it has nothing to do with the act itself.

Metaphors and polarities, patterns and perceptions are like stars or planets, inside and outside. Life brought the ancients an understating of how most things worked from love and truth and camaraderie. This brought them to the center of love, truth and God pure "Knowledge."

Those who don't see that the growth process of a man and woman together inside has grown to a unisex or a God from within. The people that are accepting love and/or sex from the same gender may have not received justice inside themselves and do not understand what they need to know to know who God is but it is acceptable today so they settle and get halfway there to know God.. A human can love anyone of their choosing; this depends on how much fear they have conquered on the inside to find love for themselves. The biggest key to life is to love yourself; choosing to share that love with another is the unity of one. This requires a complete understanding of mind, body and spirit. I think we as a self, community or country should not judge right or wrong but think of the possible long-term effects. Men offer a form of love that looks to tomorrow, this is why men have forward thinking. Women offer a form of love that focuses on today. Children live and think in the now. A growth process is required for both men and women to see each other's side and the different timings of love. We must grow back to the middle of the scale if we are to understand that we together are the power and the unity of love. Is there a science behind love? Or is love behind science? Or both together?

The ancients calibrated languages to understand that God and/or the universe are exactly the same as love. The center of love is ourselves. To see both sides of the truth of love is the center of all the universe. Example: the human side/the outside is to love with an ego (Edging God Out). The inside/spirit is selfless love that doesn't neglect the self and which leads to the center of love's truth. Each side of love relates to a subtle energy which is restrained until we uncover unity, busting through the barricades to see that the human race is the same when we know God.

We are separated by religions and divided by politics and still we don't understand *why* we are split. It is easy if we just look at it from the whole (what God is). Why does the act of sex cause so much trouble? One simple reason is that sex is the center of everything. Us seeing, or being open to seeing, the God-self can and will unite all religions. God is the perfect human. This is a responsibility for the community to understand and for the countries to see in the universe together.

Love that is outside of everything is an energy that is all around the science behind love. The love behind science is inside of us in our non-physical world, showing that we are nothing (no thing). A ***love that is inside everywhere*** is an energy that is the center of how they relate.

Our simple makeup, when learning from the universe like the ancients did, is "in and out." All things are ***inside or outside*** of something. Imagine yourself as being on the inside of something. This is, at the same time, the outside of something else. The words alone can give you truth like on the outside you can't go outside the universe is a truth. Look at the inside as you can't go back inside your mother's womb. When the inside's simple skills match up with the outside's easy skills and make sense, we can clearly see how words make a truth an inside or outside. The perfection of three equal sets of polar opposites could be viewed as a triangle. The center of each side is the knowledge that helps us to see how the three sides will relate as **_One_**. The first side is inside men and women. The second side is inside human and God/UI. The third side that is in all of us is inside the non-physical world and its counterpart, the physical world. The polar opposites are the ins and outs of our language outside/inside of the non-physical world and the physical world will explain the inner workings of both by how the word of God works in our language by using the right "Knowledge." This is all the same, just starting at different ends of emotions.

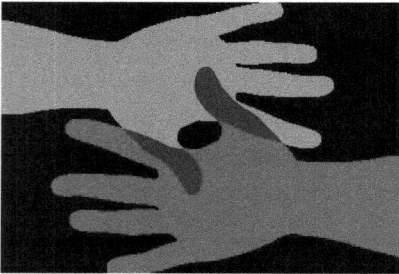

This may be how the ancients uncovered that we're made of the two sides of the universe. The 1. Side is Non-physical. The mirror image is the 2nd side of the physical universe; they fit together perfectly but still are separate with one side being intangible. Both universes are within us and are real when we "look, listen and hear" as we are identical in exactly the same way the universe operates inside and out, humans do, too. Because we are the mirror image of the universe or God, we need to look at the universe in a different way. The way the universe is in a parallel universe forum and think one side is non-physical it includes spiritual, intangible, verbs inside and on the outside is physical, human, tangible, nouns. The horizontal sliding scale of men and women when they come together as one human represents a truth using polar opposite's words together to articulate in writing.

The same utility of understanding comes from God to human in God's laws, emotions, beliefs and knowing with justice skills to be the perfect human is a truth in seeing that a vertical sliding scale is an unadulterated perfection of each side and is a complete world of one. The ancients separated the gods in a better way than we thought; they did it by going inside themselves to see the answers that are branded deep within us all. The glorified method from the path of least resistance is through the simple way that is inside all of us to see together as one to be **_One_**.

We see that the same calibrated processes are for everyone, no matter what one sees, thinks, feels, believes or even knows. Then we see that the simple way on the inside and the easy way outside is a symbol of needed lessons that remain hidden and covered for each civilization to uncover. This is based on what they had available to them in their pursuit to see an absolutely perfect plan that was beyond what they believed. Yet, they kept their minds open for the truth until they knew. Then, based on the results of what they knew, the collective human bodies solidified their truth and their minds, together in thought, would see the symbolization of the bodies' lesson that needed to be learned. They left their minds open to receive justice for all people (through the portal) on the outside and for one's self on the inside.

The ancients designed a system of exploring life's truths and finding truths to uncover inside themselves. Their purpose in life was to keep up with the community, teaching individuals. The community could grow by moving all people through the portal. This would drive curiosity to show how to share thoughts, beliefs and knowing skills from the inside of the community and self. What they (on the outside) discovered was how to use the energy of love. Done together, this is knowledgeable, collective and wise. It is universal intelligence. The Rubik's Cube of Knowledge together is the Universe of **_ONE._**

The ancients figured out how to uncover some of life's universal truths, using clues of how the world can work. The answers came from deep within, where individuals could see just a glimpse of the whole plan. One person could not see the whole plan, but through several individuals they found different parts of the whole and designed a system together to work their way down to the truth. They then uncovered the degrees of love partitioned by life's truths. Life's truth is stationary, but there is a process to get to it, and this occurs within one's self which we need to have written down. Finding the calibrated tools of love form inside is what changes things on the outside.

Theban tombs (TT52) was written on the outside of the tombs. Some believe T.T. stands for Theban tombs, the name of the tombs, and that the placement number is 52. T.T. could possibility stand for The Truth, and 52 could be a system of lessons from the symbols of the hieroglyphics from the bodies of gods, man/woman and animals all representing a lesson of the human body to be the perfect human God. The perfect God, with all His different names and bodies and minds, has the same but different obstacles to uncover to see what we can do together.

Chapter Six:

A World of One in a Universe of One: Simple Brilliance through the INSIDE/OUTSIDE of One

The ultimate human truth is how love is a tool that cuts to the truth. God is the Truth and the plan and is deep in all of us; that is how love works. Considering the tools required to build a perfect life inside first and then out, it seems the ancients got close to finding it all. They understood that each person is their own world and universe. The Self, Community and Country were aware of these truths and they are the same as they were in ancient times. Our physical and non-physical worlds each have the same foundation: the universe. Men and women are becoming unisex in the mind, in the non-physical world. If we don't see this happening and learn the intended lessons together, the lesson becomes physical. One of the lessons that probably became physical came from the 1960's. In those days, for the most part, women stayed at home and didn't have an income. Then, women sought equality. Today, it is no longer the standard for there to be a single provider or a single caregiver; both share physically. The point is, if we had learned this lesson in the non-physical world, equality may have been found years ago.

This is the double sliding scale: first, the horizontal sliding scale of man and woman and second, the vertical sliding scale of God and human. It grows from the edge of one side to the edge of the other side and back to the center, as I've previously discussed. The same process occurs with both scales.

This is a world of one's self and we are all one in the universe, as a God-self. The simple explanation is to see one's self from the outside-in and from the inside-out and to see that it works as the universe of one. The universe is actually made up of two parallel universes (the physical and non-physical or literal and symbolic) that never meet. This is the same principle as the mirror image like when hypothetically we put a mirror over the universe and everything comes back exactly the opposite but intangible or invisible like it wasn't there, now called the spiritual side or God's lessons. Then, from the top of the completed lessons, we learn again, down but backwards, right to left, back down to be one human/God-self. This is to become wise and knowledgeable from the inside-out when we put together the inside and outside, the intangibles and tangibles, the polar opposite words and the non-physical and physical parallel universe together as "ONE" therefore having all the answers.

This is what the ancients learned together. These are polar opposite, parallel universes where an inside, non-physical universe is a truth and the other side, an outside physical universe is also (one) a truth. These parallel universes of the non-physical and the physical worlds relate to one another, are relative, and revolve around each other (picture a big strand of DNA but on the outside) but they don't meet. This is how we were made and we're combining the mixture of the same but different universes, each showing a truth forming "the" whole truth; possibly they do come together. Everything inside the universe is one truth and another truth exists on the inside or outside of us as a result of the parallel universes acting like an inverse mirror. The mirror part of the universe is things that are unknown, such as God and the Holy Spirit. All the intangibles and non-physical things have their place to know and discover the whole truth by putting the physical and tangible together with the intangible and physical. This is the truth of God on the "outside" and Universal Intelligence (UI) on the "inside," both of which equal humanity and make us individuals. The balanced center of each world is the heartbeat of all that is one, after humanity deflates the air out and the universe is perfectly in sync. The togetherness of men, women and the universe or God is a world that is all a partition of looking at how the construction was made inside of *One Universe*. The inside world of us is a world of *One* that is the same for all symbolically, intangible in some way. The Earth and the outside of us is a world of *One* in time, space and knowledge with twisting platforms that share a little bit of Ying and Yang. The *One* physical universe is a true reality separating into a parallel universe, following the process of how it was made. Example: inside of us is the fight within seeing the polarization. We have become polarized because of how we are made. What sets humans apart from the inside of each other is how we see what we know, and space in four partitions: men, women, God and humans. This will show how men, women, God and humans = One Universe, inside/outside and how everything works as one.

These partitions help us identify different perceptions to clarify the separations that start from the whole universe as one inside/outside. An example is the partition inside of a human being, with time and space. Time is nonexistent when it comes to emotions and how time works to the millisecond of the moment, in sync with each skill. The internal processes that are missed, blocked or twisted between the lines work exactly the same for all humans, like a clock that keeps prefect time. People don't see the intangible, almost invisible patterns because they generally think they know, but fail to see the perfect intelligence that is part of what each of us has inside us, the process for one to uncover and then share.

Sliding scales narrow down to a correct perception of the centered knowledge in the millisecond of the moment, working together in unison. The growth processes of the centered adult are the same knowledge humanly and godly that we all have deep inside us. The puzzle is for us to bring church and state together, starting from the inside.

We should not judge or shut down thoughts, as we know that staying open-minded is essential to balancing the inside and outside and finding an ultimate truth together. We can gather what each religion believes on the outside. We can narrow things down to a few good possibilities to bring the world together, not by what we believe or don't believe or by what we know or don't know but by God's word "what just is" when we have it calibrated correctly.

Maybe organizing by joining together with what we know and don't know will help humanity. We can look at this in an abstract way, through the way we're making use of our bodies, as a key factor to unravel the plan to help find what has been covered up since the distant past. The unscrambling together helps to uncover the perfect plan. This pinpoints how and when the timing of ducks and the universes operate on the same page, clearly defining a better understanding of the controllable misunderstandings. We are made with a part of the universe's plan because we all encounter these mishaps, making the imperfection known to help see the perfection.

The constant and never-ending fight, inside and out, starts with the human self and needs to be recognized by others, what are the problems we share as humans? We may have fun with this center stage, explaining how our timing works perfectly together and also perfectly against; finding the center is perfection.

Example: explaining our makeup, there are many polarized sides that are melted down to an even liquid and it is the center of us. The universe is where we meet on the inside, so to speak. Our balanced **millisecond** of time on one side is the inside of us. We need to figure out how our happiness/peace (the portal) is a true reality for a part of the way we live life in the non-physical side of knowledge measured in a sliding scale of time. We are based around the perfect plan of the universe in the timing of stillness. We walk over blindly what we think we know.

The other side, or counterpart, is the outside happiness that carries our balanced **millisecond** of time that has a separate task of understanding real time in the way we know things on the outside world. There is an inside **millisecond** and an outside **millisecond** as well as a center **millisecond.** The three different **milliseconds of time** joined the strand of DNA in the parallel universes, non-physical and the physical worlds of how they relate to one another. They are relative and revolve around each other in unison and in sync but they still don't meet. But at some point, I think they do meet. By the twins in language, as language has two sides as well, the mere image as an image looks as if it is one when it really is two the same as humans have two sides one side human and the other side spiritual⬚ operating identical to language. But language is complete when the non-physical side comes back to itself or meets the physical side like in "the laws of thought." We look at the physical human body, we can see that the left and right sides are the same, yet different. On the outside, they are opposites. Inside, the right and left brains are different but work together to achieve full awareness as they work in sync to become one.

Centered intelligence and growth involve understanding one's emotions. This reduced and or resolved major problems that plagued society in the distant past, and the methods they found remain within us today. This question is, what is our collective purpose? Is it coming together in "SELF" to see that the timing of centered knowledge is wisdom for justice on the inside and out, which was the same then as it is now for ALL of us? The inter-technology needs to be taught while we are finding out and/or working on our individual purpose and when we "know for sure" our service is the same exact service inside us as others have to concern inside them that which is the same part as God we are on the right track, this is the one collective reality we share inside us as humans. I think our distant ancestors were masters in knowing the processes of what we don't see because they asked questions individually and together to the universe.

Understanding the true processes of internal communication is when the light bulb turns on for the majority, combined with the inter-technology of what it is to communicate from the relationship inside first with oneself. Could we say that the inside is with yourself? Your God? Or with an "energy" that seems to be a part of EVERYTHING inside and out? This may change the perception of God to intermix to be the same God as the universe, as self, others or all of humanity as it all comes together as one God when we uncover the perfect truth in writing. We will maintain our individuality but know ourselves through love and truth; these are the answers for us so we can merge church and state. Once we understand all churches are part of the whole and there is "one" religion when you look deep enough you will find "SELF" and when religious laws and state laws meet as one law we will have one law for state and one religious law of self, working together and apart perfectly and which are made up of human and God as "ONE."

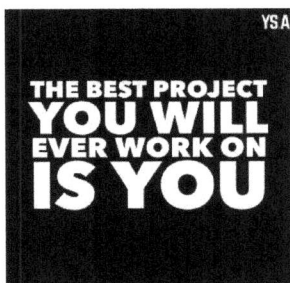

THE BEST PROJECT YOU WILL EVER WORK ON IS YOU

We want to understand how the ancients tapped into some of the good parts of the universe's plan. The covered plan inside us (which is the same that was inside them) to connect the Mind, Body and Soul is a human exercise. The vision comes in threes. Seeing how the processes, skills and sliding scales work in sync is having one heartbeat of understanding that is made from what is different but is the same from each side of the inside/out of the self.

We are made, inside and outside, to be intertwined with the universe. The plan God laid out regarding who we are as humans involves us uncovering that we are each a god ourselves. This is a plan designed through and around us. We are supposed to figure out what a perfect life is, together with the person you had babies with. Because knowing how to unite that intimate relationship are the same skills with little tweaks and small adjustments that it takes to unite our world. Then we will have perfect communities in harmony and countries in sync.

The start of the journey is to know that to be human is to be a small god. Once understood, this uncovers for each person a piece of the puzzle so they can see and participate as a leader/teacher or coach to help uncover the truth for others. These teachings were developed over time to see adulthood as being a balance of the perfect human. The teachings sought to understand the idea of the God-self and how we connect to humanity and the universe inside. Today, we would call this metaphysics or spirituality. To the ancients, this wasn't religion; it was more like self-help and had to do with what it meant to be human. We have made these ideas religious. The teachings back then were something like a portal to go through and if we were to rebuild the system today, we would use coaches who know what these people have in common.

We can see things in a philosophical way from the inside or the outside. When we look at it from the outside, this taps into a literal way of seeing how religion and science meet. Through reading, writing and speech we see how everything fits together perfectly, from inside of us to the outside in ways that have been set in stone, but have been disrupted. This is ONE Universe, the mathematical part of all; everything comes back to one truth.

We see things based on the way we were taught and conditioned to think, and then by what we believe, until we see from within. For example, religious leaders say that when you look at your neighbor, you should see God because He is oneself! Does this mean that everybody is God because we are all ONE self? Yes.

We need to see how a part of the inside of all of us is a multidimensional god for us to see a part of the plan that is at a deep level of the self, below what the mind understands. This tells me that the ancients were right in their hieroglyphics. We have a step more than they did which helps us to understand and organize the way we look at any God and the UI.

We are born with a map, and the curiosity to seek and search for who we are and where we come from. The movement of the ducks can happen with communities; this is driving us to find out who God is. We are moving over the obstacle course with our eyes closed, missing the greatest intelligence ever known to man. We need to ask what we are missing to see the universe's plan. We are in a changing world now, so we might as well look at God differently.

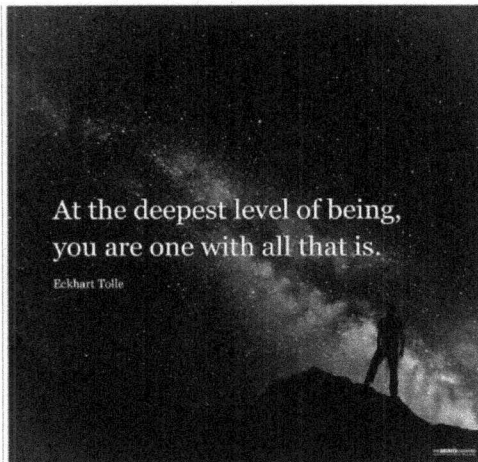
At the deepest level of being, you are one with all that is.

Eckhart Tolle

We can always use the plan and knowledge from the past to change the future for our children. This all happens without any change to the plan and it is exactly the same for everyone in the world; it doesn't move or deviate and it doesn't matter what anyone thinks or believes or knows about it. What matters is to understand HOW the present is understood, occupied and lived in for a centered understanding of how the past, present and future work together. The perfect plan of the universe inside and outside is structured backwards in the way our minds think, but it makes sense for the way God sees.

We are all the center of the universe in an abstract way. The internal growth in us may have been what the ancients recognized to be the most important part of the process. The transformation for humans happens on the inside, and it is only understood and seen like one side of a truth. The other side of the truth starts being understood after the transformation.

The one true reality that exists for everyone could be the collective universe, or the soul. It is up to us to find out. We will fill the "space" within each of us with knowledge from the inside processes. Now we add to the partition everything in the universe, including the inside of humans, making this partition the inside of everything.

In ancient times, it seems discoveries were based on talking about the universe. The limited sciences in the distant past may have helped us uncover from the inside how we were made from the sum of the universe's parts. These partitions are infinite, with a large part inside us, covered up.

The ancients' languages were perfectly designed to refer to the inside or outside based on variation. An example is, "Did you hear me?" This is the physical outside. On the other hand, a question like "Are you listening?" refers back to the inside. The ancients understood the separation of inner/outer in all ways. The center of languages may have displayed a way to disclose the truth for those willing to see the center of now.

This seems to lead back to sex, and why does the act of sex cause so much trouble? We can find comfort, confusion, unity or trouble. Maybe the wisdom of the crowd will find there is a science behind how we are made?

The man's penis is on the outside and his testicles are on the inside of his sack. This is nothing new. Whereas a woman's vagina is inside and her breasts are on the outside... a perfect fit physically and abstract fit non-physically. The non-physical platform is from the inside when its polar opposites are recognized and are different but the same physically outside. The physical bodies have the answers with what it takes in and out, from food, thoughts, and sex. Our minds haven't looked at all the simple ways together from the inside and the easy ways from the outside. By doing it this way it will lead us to see from a different perspective.

Example: How many ways can one see with different perspectives from the inside out or the outside in with eyes like the ancients? This is a way to imagine the breakdown of the universe and worlds by the way we relate and live in or on as humanity by how we are tied to Earth. Then looking at the God thing in a different way using the Mind, Body and Spirit/Soul. These ways are just for illustration purposes by using the inside world as the Mind, the outside world for the Body, the Spirit can be used for both inside world and/or the outside world representing the hidden 3rd world. In a perfect world, there would be no miscommunication. This, in theory, would clean out the court systems; learning how to catch what we don't see will clean up molehills that turn into mountains of misunderstanding. It would provide the basic foundation to

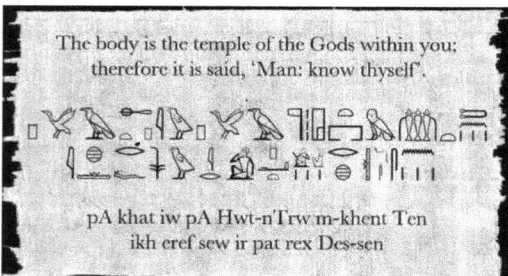

The body is the temple of the Gods within you; therefore it is said, 'Man: know thyself'.

pA khat iw pA Hwt-nTrw m-khent Ten
ikh eref sew ir pat rex Des-sen

get to the start of a simple truth. Back in the time of the ancients, the way love is the truth of the inside truth was considered science. We share love on the inside so we can see what love really is. What are the requirements to see the truth about love, past the warm fuzzy feelings? We need to go deeper to see the truth. These types of lessons can be measured through the test of time.

Imagine the man/woman sliding scale. We start on opposite sides of each feeling, and these feelings, produced by thought, work perfectly together and apart. It is not just linear but multidimensional. Then one sees and understands the effects of feelings, like a certain type of energy. The stronger emotion or the most concentrated form of energy may be love and the counterpart of that energy is a form of fear. These are vertical skills. The horizontal skills are to come from inward and outward balance.

Picture yourself at a lecture as a professor is explaining a concept, writing on the chalkboard before a room full of people. If the group started talking about what was just learned, the ones that think they have a handle on the lecture would take away things that they "know" and things they believe. In this way, we can remove the fear for those who didn't understand the lecture and turn it around to say that the challenge is to find a sliver of the truth. Perhaps the ancients felt they were stupid if they didn't exercise imagination of thought and speak out. Perhaps the group judged them, much like today; if someone doesn't know something, they stop wanting to say anything. We can look at this in two different ways. We can view it spiritually and understand that this is okay, or we can look at it humanly and conclude that the person is stupid. It depends on how we look at the situation. Because it is all in the way we look at it.

In some ways, we are living life against the grain; we seem to be living life in a backwards way. Today it's more difficult than ever to find something higher within us. It is like thought is developed from within a wireless energy connected to the cosmos; we need to turn on the required lightbulbs to slide through portals of understanding, one lesson at a time, or look at it another way.

Let's play with imaginations. As Albert Einstein said, our imagination is more important than knowledge. Part of what has been created for us to uncover is the Science of the Bigs. It is the same as the male gender, or the outside of us, and the humanly made Seven Wonders of the World which represent males. The Seven Wonders of the World which are made by nature are female and represent the science smalls and the inside of us. When we put these ideas out to the community we might find a magnetic center of energy, the nucleus of an atom, self, or family for our relationships and a better understanding about humanity, God, science, the cosmos and ourselves. This will happen just by talking in an open way and working with the correct system together and sharing from group A, is what it is 1) Inside 2) thought 3) outside. Number one means looking from the inside/spirit out. Number two means working together in thought in real time. Number three represents the hard side of looking outward to inward. Group B starts with outside: 3) outside 2) together 1) inside. This is to be built in Group C, is what it is, is, '2 thought 2" together (philosophy) and means to work the center of Group A and B, which makes up Group C and do something both in thought and together is simple brilliance. Same purposes Services =2 (Science) =1, 2, 3, or 3, 2, 1, same but different and different but the same! R. S.V.P Religious, Scientifically, Vessel, Philologically - that is the difference between inner worlds religiously, and the outer world scientifically. The Vessel is each one of us individually, processing our own ducks and universes the way we think we're on the same universes with other people, as we know this when we are on the same philologically we are all on the same page. We are all *me* in a community. We are all *myself* in a country. The mind, body and soul is *Me, Myself* and *I* = we/us. I am starting to see why this needs to be built together in thought by the world simultaneously. Are we looking at one person to get all of these things right while finding the perfect words to use after the topic is learned, whatever topic that may be? Are we looking to have it written down so we all can understand?

Instead of one person organizing thoughts as we grow back to the way our ancients mastered the process of oneness, we now have the app doing the heavy lifting. Can we get it right? Do we want to see perfection? Will we do it right this time? It seems as if we've been scolded along by having to learn the simple process again, regarding the skills sets. Taking the good from the past and bringing it into the ways we learn, live and share will offset and balance the way we live today.

Role models for children are often their parents, but in many ways, they are more than this; parents can be like gods to children when they are young. But after the kids are grown, they can carry issues that their parents didn't get over emotionally, mentally and biologically. These issues can take many years to uncover when living in the same household. In today's society, a lot of children are living part-time with their parents. I think it's less about how people stayed together in the past, and more about understanding the timeless lessons and skills to love yourself in an unselfish way to gain all the right "knowledge " to be and "know" God - all the perfect skills for what it is to be human (self). This will help in completing oneself to share that love with another person of the opposite sex to unite and build a Community, Country to have a united world. The answers are found in the relationships between R. S. V.P Religion, Science, Vessel, Philologically.

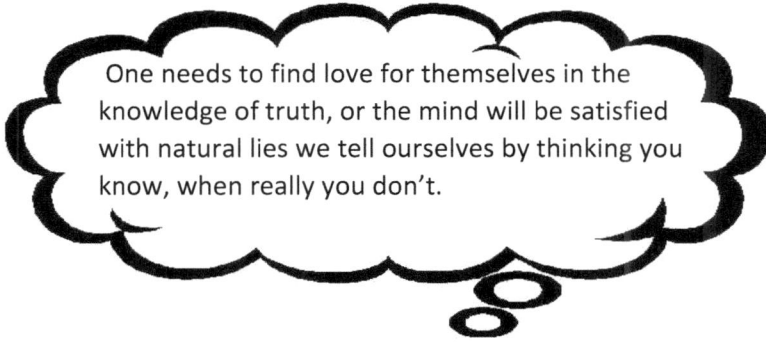

One needs to find love for themselves in the knowledge of truth, or the mind will be satisfied with natural lies we tell ourselves by thinking you know, when really you don't.

The missed connections of what you don't see make you unaware they exist. The processes are truth if the answers are verified by proper calibration.

Chapter Seven:

*Laws of Thought. Philosophy: The Outline of the Polarization
Is the Glass Half Empty or Half Full? We are Made of Star Energy;
Is God's DNA also Star Dust?*

There is a force field to go through to reach one's center. It involves learning, drawing energy, meditating, praying, or engaging in deep thought, and this is how many people have tapped into their center. Our goal here is to involve the masses and have help from professionals, such as scientists, philosophers and other kinds of spiritual leaders such as scholars, academics and theologists.

This is the universe of the big or the outside. Everything works together as one, after properly being separated, spilt and divided. It all fits perfectly into the whole when each part is completed correctly. For example, look at language; everything fits together perfectly when adding up the separated, spilt and divided parts, and together they create the whole. This is a way of understanding God.

Magnetic center earth =UI, God/energy	Magnetic center mind	Molecular structure	
Me	Myself	I	= Self
World	Humanity	Universe	= Country
Mind	Body	Soul	=Community all= **One**

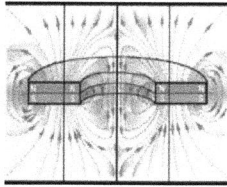

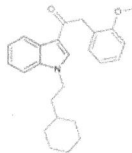

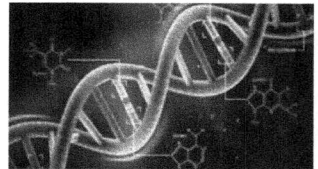

Inside Earth	Outside magnetic fields	DNA

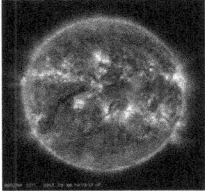

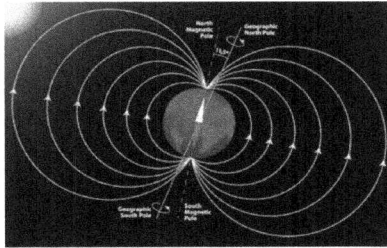

Magneto hydrodynamics.	Outside magnetic fields	Air bending time? Constant Gravity

The math here is: DNA =0, Outside magnetic fields = 1, Magneto hydrodynamics =2.

This shows that everything works as one, sometimes differently than how we perceive it. Perhaps the abstract science is the outside and religion is the inside. But philosophy and the "Law of Excluded Middle" explains how everything is the same as itself; the patterns work for the "Whole Complete Universe" down to a single word where they are perfectly the same.

Laws of Thought: Philosophy:

1. The Law of Identity - A is A. *Everything, everywhere and everybody all goes into itself.*

    Everything is the same as itself. A statement cannot not remain the same and change its true value. *God is a person and all of "self" which is all people and all "things." Where we are equal and our perception needs to widen to all and then narrow down to ONE because* everything is the same as itself (parallel universe).

    1. Is invisible\ intangible or non-physical and 2a. the other is physical. *All works are equally in harmony together. Our language is the perfect thing to describe everything in perfect order. God, then, is explained*

seamlessly because all the processes and "parts" are the completed whole. We see all the rules of grammar through His word (God's word). Each word has all the rules going through it and this is the KEY to all words (read carefully) everything is the same as itself. All rules in philosophy are a part of the "whole" to make it complete and until we have the "completed" whole we are not finished.

The definition can be split from the whole by two or more meanings (the human and spiritual sides). The word is correct based on the way it split, separated or divided.

The rules are permanent and stationary; even the definitions of the meanings stand still, perfectly connected, and linked together. It is the surroundings that change in time. The past, future and present are the same as a stationary time machine; language, the rules of philosophy and patterns of knowledge stay the same while time moves around us.

Cause and effect, and intelligence and intellect, separate the differences and bring it back to itself. All stands still until we know. When the self realizes that God is the same as "itself," (because everything everywhere comes back to self) it unites into one. We live in a perfect world; we just need it to uncover one perfect God.

2.   The Law of Non- Contradiction - NOT (A and not A) *Explained under paradox and oxymoron.*

Nothing can both exist and not exist at the same time and in the same respect, no statement is   both true and false.

3.   The Law of Excluded Middle - Either (A or not A)

Something either exists or does not exist; or every statement is either true or false.

"**Philosophy** (from Greek φιλοσοφία, philosophia, literally "love of wisdom") is the study of general and fundamental problems concerning matters such as existence, knowledge, values, reason, mind, and language."

Philosophy - Wikipedia, the free encyclopedia
Wikipedia › wiki › Philosophy

About this result • Feedback

Philosophy - Wikipedia, the free encyclopedia

First, what is... this will be one side of a truth that fits all the laws of thought, the what is, is will be the other side of a truth not changing its value and obeying the laws. The connection here is that religion is looking from the outside in. The truth is that the teaching will be from the inside out; God, love and the truth are all the same thing and can be used interchangeably. God is love! Love is the truth and we must uncover the lessons to see the truth of all the truths. We are all the same on the inside. To see and understand this, we need to look up, down, forward, backwards, both sides, sideways and deep.

Air has been proven to bend time and supermassive black holes' gravity eats light, gases and galaxies because black holes of gravity can be seen, but only by what disappears from the gravitational pull that goes into the supermassive black holes that hold up the universe. Somehow, the small things can be the balancing factor, along with us, in keeping a centered universe, and may also be seen in the practices of successful business.

One needs to see and understand that mercy is humanity and justice is open-mindedness and that they are the same but different and different but the same. Mercy is the inside and Justice is the outside. So, what does it mean when it's said the apple doesn't fall far from the tree? Where's the apple? Who is taking the bite? That is the collective us as humanity; we have taken a bite out of the universe's tree, to learn how to get to "one" symbolically, for each person first, and then the community.

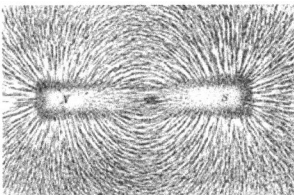

The patterns of the world energy may be part of what we need to push through to understand why we have polarization. This is a growth process through skills, lessons, patterns, gender, self, human and God to see and get to understand the center.

The electromagnetic field of the heart

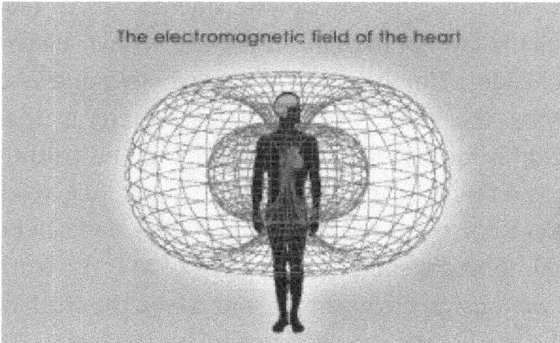

This is also a perfect way to show why we, in a political fashion, are polarized on issues. We can start with each political issue, when the initial thought is at its infancy, and then share its creation with each other as the issue is being developed in a collective way. This process helps in figuring out the center of most important issues. I call this the co-consciousness or the collective portal. No one is better than another person, and in many ways, we are the same. Therefore it makes sense that the wisdom of the crowd can trump knowing the individual portal. The trial and error process in building for the masses will provide the right way in building the app.

The outer side to science bigs is somewhat like the way we are built and the same as the relationship of the Seven Wonders of the World.

Centered

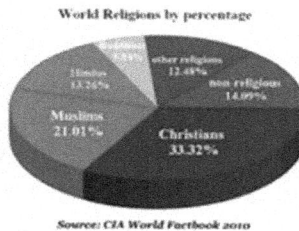

Philosophically	**Religiously**	**Scientifically**

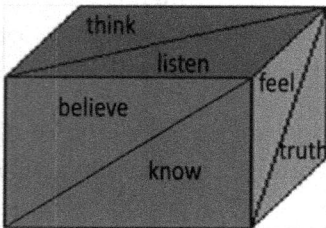

This is how we tie the shapes together for the holograms using the GSE (Global Stabilized Energy).

This is the universe of the smalls or the inside. If we can balance these, philosophically, religiously and scientifically, we might figure out a code to wisdom, intelligence and entertainment.

Inside the nucleus of an atom there are 12 things smaller than the atom. The present theory is M theory, in which there are four forces of gravity: electromagnetism, strong interaction, weak interaction and gravity. These four forces create the ultimate theory: can we put all four together as one in the universe? My question is, could that be us? And is the gravity and light that is sucked into black holes creating something from nothing? Are they two extremes?

The small world vibrations of string theory results in beautiful music. Music also stores lessons learned from generation to generation, all of which is timeless. There may be different types, but they are the same lessons, just taught in different ways. The vibration of sound will probably be uncovered next, along with music and string theory and the physics of light.

With regard to the 12 things smaller than an atom, which were discovered in the 1960's, it is my theory that we can only see what we've learned from the lessons uncovered.

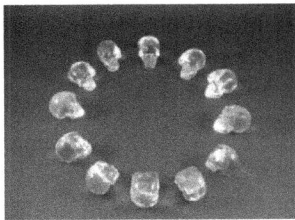

These 12 crystal skulls were found in Brazil or Madagascar. Until we know or uncover a way to understand, we still may not be able to see inside the atom. Although, if we soon can, then perhaps my theory may be correct. Nevertheless, we are just looking for the one or two diamonds. Imagine billions of organized and computerized people taking out the junk and sifting through what's written in a backwards fashion (UI); that is the wisdom of universal intelligence and the artificial universal intelligence. We have the outer technology to build the inner technology. Our genes were uncovered as a liquid. Can they be considered in any way because they can split up? Look for the extreme abstract. How we can lose skills that may include healing energies, organs and teeth. Can this change the smalls? Then atoms split? We form the floating body of how the skills work together in seven layers in three-dimensional ways, along with how the inner

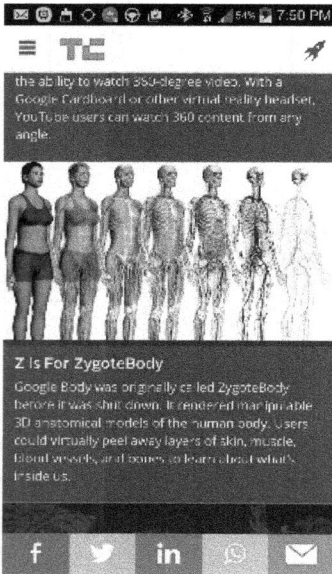

This is where seven bodies go out one at a time the other way, starting with listening, thinking and believing etc. Showing how the internal working of the process for the skills to connect layer by layer to shows how 'change' is made through the mind, emotions and connection of the lessons. These will be illustrated by time laps photo for all of us, naturally.

connections work out for the Zygote Body of Google. After achieving the individual portal (IP) inside, and the intellectual properties (IP) outside, the electromagnetism of the mind is where circles' energies of purest form around the mind and body after the connection has been made. Spiritual leaders would say to remain focused on your dreams, because after one achieves the individual portal, the next step is the dream that got you there or the work you put in to get there on the inside and out. But the outcome is outside (IP) intellectual properties.

Human Side   Protects the Spirit inside

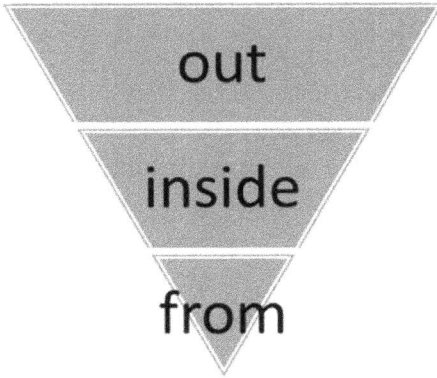

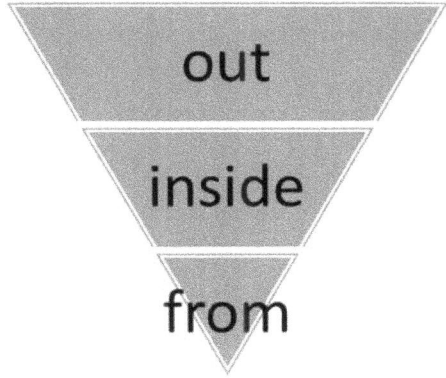

out   out

inside   inside

from   from

Spirit Side

Once inside!

inside
outside
inside   inside

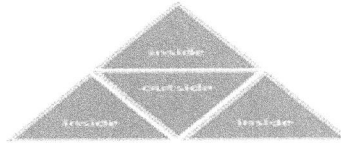

The outside of us is visible through actions and speech. Our human side is the one that reacts negatively and judges others.

The inside is the deeper part of thought, revealed by balanced actions and emotions. The more positive side is the spirit, or the inside.

This corner is the mystical part of what we don't see in our emotions. This is the inside of the subconscious mind, small but the most powerful.

There is a center between the outside and inside. The center is all of the self, and this is the same for everybody. This is the pure part of the inside of the self, the God-self, the perfect human. Science shows us how all is one, and how the universe, people and God are all one. A faultless system already exists; we need to uncover it by seeing with all perspectives to see that the one truth is the same for all of us.

The truth can be covered up and camouflaged by our hearts and minds and it becomes difficult to see and understand. One percent (1%) of the world sees it correctly; it is in plain sight, simple, but not easy.

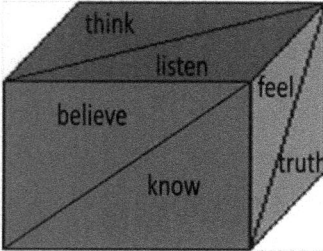

This is simply what scientists now say we overlook. The brain also overlooks truths, not allowing us to see ducks or universes. It almost creates an illusion in the mind, creating the easiest way for it to see an acceptable way of understanding something. In doing so, it's taking only part of the whole truth to make up an understanding, taking the path of least resistance and leaving out much of what makes up the whole truth. The brain gathers part of a whole conversation, sees a part of the whole visually, hears what we thought was all of the meaning of something and then dismisses a portion of its awareness. Once we become aware of this, we can begin to find a greater amount of truth in our lives.

We are not starting off with the glass full because we are not acknowledging missing information, whether intentionally or unintentionally. When the brain does not have enough time to gather the appropriate information, the brain shortens, for its convenience, the way it gathers information and the amount of information gathered in order to make sense of the question at hand. Many things pass by us in interactions that we don't see, hear or register in our minds BUT we think, feel and believe we are handing over the truth when we tell someone what we heard, saw or registered. How can we know what we don't know? We just handed over a half-empty glass, believing it was full. This means the person we are speaking to believe the glass is full as well. This is what I mean by "a truth." We can be living an unintentional lie, which has the same result as an intentional lie.

Is the glass half full?

The possibilities may be between the lines! The partial truth keeps one out of living in the millisecond of the moment because the opportunity to be on the same page has drifted apart without delivering skills to both sides. If the mind looked at conversations in one linear direction, it would not be seeing the truth, as most conversations are in three dimensions. These three dimensions are in play with a normal conversation that happens naturally in our minds. One word can enter a different level if it has more than one meaning, changing the understanding of the intended conversation. When a word or sentence enters the mind and you recognize there can be different meanings, you must leave one meaning on another dimension.

The further out we push to the edge of what the mind can see, the easier it's seen on different universes in our heads. We can picture the different universes; it's like putting thoughts on different shelves in our mind while putting meanings and variables in a file cabinet, organizing what the best possible ducks are. To put things back into a linear conversation, we must watch for the same words that can have different meanings. We all have similar misconceptions in our minds and emotions, so we think we're smart when we catch one after missing ten. What's smart is when we work together and point out the patterns that stand out below the surface or between the lines.

The inside of us doesn't know time and just sees in the moment. It's up to us to catch and see a split second of time. Doing something fun or living on the edge can mean living in the moment on the outside. But this has nothing to do with living in the moment on the inside. We are still trying to uncover what that means. It's all about the lessons and the skills and squashing the air out of the emotions and the partial truths to see what remains.

The lessons and skills run through to the community and country, from an extension of self because even though they are separate, the skills and lessons are the same.

We need to look from our head, heart and emotions to find the best timeless lessons learned from people, dead or alive, from all walks of life.

It would be great for the community to share with one another what they feel are life's greatest lessons. Imagine the possibilities! We could share lessons we have learned from loved ones. This will keep their memory alive and act as wisdom for others.

This could be two-fold: keeping one's memory alive for the loved ones as well as making it into the Rubik's Cube of Knowledge for life's timeless lessons and skills. In my experience, my father's way of looking at the imperfections in others helped me find the perfection of the truth in others. We want to look for perfection but it actually works backwards; we must look through the imperfections to see perfection but really the perfection is in the system of God's plan.

Though my family was not religious, we talked about the idea of the human heart being God. This was what the portal was for me then. Now it has expanded from one circle to three worlds. The sum of its parts are three worlds, but from a distance it's a circle growing to three worlds in 3D to a sphere, to all of us on the inside as a whole world by itself and on the outside as a world by itself as well. The third world is joined by the understanding of how the relationships work when the inner and outer worlds meet.

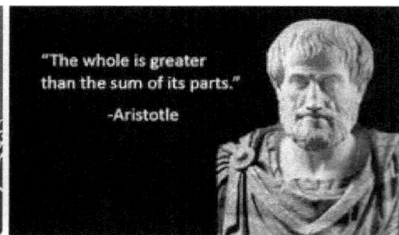

Each part is a whole world on its own. We make sure we continue keeping thoughts open, to then reserve judgment for a later time, as shutting them down is the outside/human trait. One may think we can't reserve judgment because we must make a decision, but we won't know until we try. Imagine everyone having one mind for humanity's thoughts to create a belief. Look at the different possibilities when we don't shut down thought, and we are truly being open-minded. Answers could be uncovered by all of us as we narrow down how to control the ways we look at things. That is what spirit/the inside is and what spirit/the outside is as well. This is a way to find unity as we are earthly Gods or part of the UI. Our individual inside selves are their own world, just as humanity's inside is also a world. Do we need to band together in one thought to see results? We can all come together and use that "force" for something amazing because the sum of the parts is greater than the whole. That's what this app is intended to accomplish. What can be the results?

We are all made of star energy. Does this mean that God's DNA is also star energy, as we were made in His image? These are great questions for the community to address within the app. The perfect human is God. The question is, how do we see it?

Place of worship

- Bahá'í House of Worship (Bahá'is)
- Chaitya/Buddhist temples/monastery (Buddhists)
- Church (Christians)
- Hof (Germanic pagans)
- Hindu temple/mandir (Hindus)
- Jain temple/basadi (Jains)
- Synagogue (Jews)
- Mosque (Muslims)

More items...

Place of worship - Wikipedia
Wikipedia › wiki › Place_of_worship

About this result · Feedback

Proper self-help can parallel religious meanings in an abstract way by the way one looks at it. Do inside, spiritual laws and outside, human laws share the polarization to find the third world of how they relate? Utilizing the app could bring together the entire community. Imagine the advances that could be made in a field like medicine using these skills and principles. Once we use the sum of its parts and use the 3D worlds collectively, we can get over the need to be right, and see that there is no right or wrong. When the inside and outside are properly centered, the fear is removed so that only love can be taking up space.

We cover up the love by not understanding, in theory, what love is. Love is like a light; if you put your hand over it the light becomes dark. Letting in fear can kill love. Fear and love cannot occupy the same space in our minds. The more love we have, the less fear there is, so if we use our skills to reduce fear in our minds we can increase love.

One way of seeing how the spiritual and human worlds of a person work together to find the center of the collective inside spirit for a country is to work with the politicians from the outside/in to help find the center of the country's spirit. This, in theory, finds that the equality of the center is the spirit inside of us from the inside/out and the spirit outside of us from the outside/in.

We have explained how the mind needs to see and understand the processes of the skills, being open to seeing with different perspectives. Once we find the collective mind in the community, we may find a collective constant that will help us to see better ways of using the collective mind. Knowing that we are all the same on the inside will help when we chose the spirit or human side.

Father sky and Mother Earth are together with the Universe, for the interlocking makeup of us is the electromagnetic field of the heart polarizing us naturally by how we are made. Together, through philosophy, religion and science, we will see Truth.

Chapter Eight:

"(G) God," Human and Universe are the same. Looking outside the Universe into Earth

God, the perfect human. Extreme opposites in every way at the same time explains the center,

     |

Men___|____ Women, the unisex of the center of four sides inside and outside of both.

     |

    Human

Human has the perfect god within - we need to see it. Nothing and everything at the same time (nowhere and now here). The Universe, World, Humanity, People, Atoms, Energy, Air [Your Name] all have been referred to as God in his name in one way or another, is this not everything? Maybe the plan from the UI is evolving and devolving and the conscience is made to con-science. We are a whole "part" of god, with the "whole" of humanity is for us to find.

Believing is just part of the whole, part of *a* truth, from the inside or the outside. Remember, believing from the neck down (inside) is to get *a* truth or *the* truth on the inside. But on the outside, believing is from the neck up (outside) and we tend to fight for what we believe in no matter what, even when we don't know. Believing on the inside and believing on the outside are wildly different. If you have the same belief on the inside and outside, on the inside you naturally try to improve the belief with additional knowledge and good intent to make it a complete truth. On the outside, if required to talk about it in conversation, we naturally defend our belief as it stands, before it is a complete truth. The party that we are conversing with doesn't understand how much effort we've put into this belief on the "inside" so they can't tell

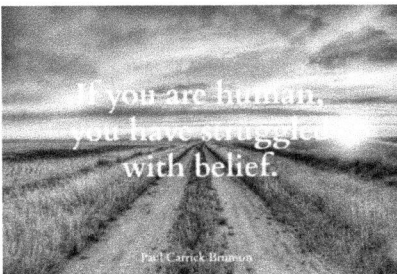

how close to the truth it might be! This sets both parties up for more misunderstandings and difficulties. That's why the inner parts of our emotions and skills from the neck down and our minds may be approaching God's turf. Combining the laws of mathematics, science, spirituality and philosophy together and looking at the patterns that might form, may be the next path we're seeking.

A concept I have developed to refer to the small particles inside an atom is something I call "Science Smalls inside Atom's Nucleus" (SSIAN). Overlooked, missed and unaware thoughts can form unworthy and unwanted beliefs; what we don't know can shape our lives. We defend these beliefs because we have not gotten over the need to be right.

A close form of love is time spent with family. Divorces rob families of that at all ages and in some cases can break the bond between parents and children. Ultimately, this can result in children who believe they can't find love for themselves or a stable relationship as a result of their parent's inability to find love for themselves and each other. One of the answers is understanding how relationships truly work. It seems to me we haven't made a lot of progress; families are being dismantled before the skills, lessons and natural processes are learned. This may be a lesson for our children, now young adults, who grew up in divorced families. Finding love for themselves is the core of the nucleus.

When thinking about timeless lessons, children in divorce have no choice but to wonder what they did wrong and as they got older why their mom and dad couldn't find love in their hearts for each other. How can they be better than their parents when it comes to relationships? An unselfish love is the answer.

The mind will justify what it can if you're not watching and aware. It will catch you not paying attention and the thing is, you won't even know it. So how do you fix that? We must be able to duck, weave and bob to adapt, change and stay aware.

I think for a person with no formal education, who barely graduated high school in a learning disability program (dyslexic), and who now finally understands when writing and reading become more important than getting you to understand an issue... it's just another barricade of how words can be more important than their meaning and can work against you. For example, if

I were to mispronounce a word you might think (spirit or inside) I just don't know the correct pronunciation, or you might think in your mind (outside or human) that I'm stupid. If the App [Your Name] could help everyone understand this one thing, we would be successful. The imperfection of our human side may be automatically looking for the negative side of things. We think we know and believe we're on the right track, but the fireworks of thoughts in our mind can be overwhelming at times. How do we manage what we don't see coming, the timing of choices, having doubts, etc.?

An apprentice would be provided passage on a ship from another country to, say, America. He was provided food, water and shelter while fulfilling a contract to pay back those costs plus produce goods for his master and this would take years to complete. Today, the opposite is true; people are paid for their time and there is work for everyone. Whatever type of job we design, the required skill sets and the algorithms through the app can calculate the value of the work. Compensation can be done using geometric growth. Then, taking into account the requirements for the job and the skills needed, we can use the conveniences of different equipment and other factors to set up the policing mechanisms through the app. This will be a system of posting your skills and or needs along with the equipment offered and working together with each of the communities. Clean energy for food, water, shelter and transportation would make this possible for everybody on the planet who deserves an equal shot to be human.

This is how we can catapult the wisdom of the crowd, starting worldwide through the inception of thought and knowing we have the same but different needs. This is completed in the mind first, while listening to other communities and seeing all the different possibilities to understand what others know that we don't. This could be a form of simple brilliance, to look at this with a different perspective or collective mind first is the meeting of the minds before it is implemented.

Human Side

We flip this contract upside down and backwards to create a world of perpetuity, with a system we build similar to the way we share vehicles and expand this concept to anything where we can put a user with an available product. Then we start with small meetings to organize ideas at coffee shops like Starbucks, which is a perfect internet hub. One can work as little or as much as they want to serve with balanced algorithms, making a livable wage, utilizing our blue collar and some white collar work forces with some industry jobs that need to be done every day.

Not being aware or not knowing something is not lying outwardly or even lying internally to oneself; it's being asleep to what happens. What happens after each one of the skills are revealed? Are we closer to being on the same page? I would say yes; maybe in a lot of ways we are all more similar on the inside than we think. It takes us working collectively to help open each other's eyes to see we can work miracles and move mountains. This leads to answers from within us when sharing in thought and being included in the process. Be the interactive app [Your Name] for skills and lessons, universes, ducks and sliding scales as part of the web site Globalstabilizedenergy.com where the professionals provide guidance in their areas of expertise. Once the masses collectively understand, use, see and become aware of these skills through this humanity will see the value of knowing the human God, self and language as it will provide the lessons of timeless wisdom, justice on the inside and outside, and the results of love and truth come together. The center of the spiritual side and the middle of the human side where a person and a God together with language can become one to reveal how disease is cured when the masses work together with the correct formula. When one first understands the skills, they may begin making mild judgments about the skills another person needs. Most people may not see their next lesson but it's on their mind, so just listen and over time they will tell you. The more familiar you get with the processes, the easier it becomes. When one tells themselves they need to know something, they will verbalize and let you know. Where do you think this is generated from: is it a thought, a feeling in your gut, just curiosity or a quest?

How many different ways can you see what we know and don't know? A lot of people think they know! The question is, what do they know? It would be nice to understand what we know and everybody else knows in a form that is usable and readable in order to fit in a Rubik's Cube of Knowledge.

KNOWING SKILLS:

1)   Know yourself from within.

2)   What we don't know, and overlook can shape our lives.

3)   Other people know what we don't know.

4)   Let's find out the wisdom of the crowd and break it down to the core.

5)   Some have the need to know.

6)   The infinite not knowing, the timing of knowing and just not knowing.

7)   The multi-dimensional parts of knowing.

Knowing is all about understanding that we don't know everything. The multidimensional parts of knowing are the most difficult because this helps create a bridge between the inner and outer self.

When we are born, our spirit is empty and as we learn and grow through life we fill it with the lessons we learn and the wisdom we acquire. Large or small, good or bad, this cycle starts over again with the birth and death of the next generation. But upon each death their impression remains in the community. Somewhat like a corporation as it grows, leaving the patterns of growth and through the growth of the community, this leads to the country's growth again. The skills of timeless wisdom will lead us to missing skills that each of the countries and communities missed when individually we start seeing and knowing what it takes to be present.

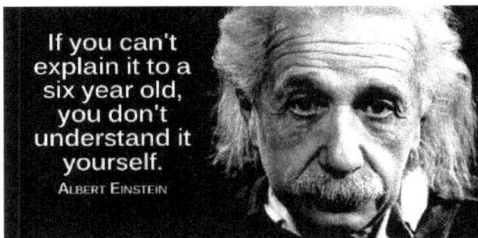
If you can't explain it to a six year old, you don't understand it yourself.
ALBERT EINSTEIN

The sides (inside and outside) work differently than the way the mind works. If you were to put something in an empty circle you would have to take something out or fill up space in the circle.

The length and breadth of time are not equal. Today's Bible will likely intensify our confusion regarding life as we know it. To me, this seems like a puzzle. If we took all the different laws and theories from science, philosophy and religion and structured them together, what might that reveal to us? This is what the power of the app [Your Name] is intended to do. This will also show us a different way to imagine, looking at the path of least resistance of the abstract, peripheral mind. This may be a key component of seeing the way relationship patterns really work for our minds, past the way we have been conditioned, to explore different ways to see what is truly possible.

This balances out science with philosophy and religion. The UI will only let one go as far as the universal intelligence allows. Spiritual leaders of the past understood important concepts from twenty years ago. Though in most cases we can't go back, we can try to see the skills of that time.

Aristotle, Plato and Rumi are some of the minds that achieved the portal and started to see early and had a lot to say because the separation was small between the "inside" world of **love** and the "outside" world of **fear**. We now think it was wonderful because that's what we know, seeking recognition and approval. In some cases, we are unable to find the right words, such as when trying to explain this process. It remains at the razor's edge of truth between understanding and not.

The Bible, in an abstract way, becomes the polar opposite and is stopping us because you're getting too close or passing what the heart and mind are allowed to know, at a time in our ever-changing, evolving and de-evolving universe. Twenty years ago after finding the portal, I thought everybody that made it to the portal knew all the skill sets. When the light bulb turns on inside, then you know! You could forget temporally but not over time.

This is where time begins again, when one tries to move the masses to a better understanding of living in the moment. Once the internal process starts, it seems it triggers the curiosity button for the quest for more information.

How far one can see inside is directly related to the lessons they learned and achieved. In other words, how deep they have gone inside. Where are the boundaries? Are there any? This can be scary and it will challenge you to see how far you're willing to go!

The subtonic level inside atoms is the deepest part of a person. The partitions of the universe are infinite. The sciences in time will show how we are all a part of each and every part of the universe, making us each a Universe of ONE metaphysically, symbolically and literally.

How do we know UI? The answer is that we are all the same, but until one understands how he describes the knowing skills, it will not be understood, even when someone thinks they know. Remember, this is simple but not easy for us to tap into.

The multidimensional part of knowing is what is extended or uncovered, along with a number of other things. There are so many people that have written about the different parts of the portal and now it's time to expand and organize. We aren't reinventing the wheel; we're orchestrating the Rubik's Cube of Knowledge of the whole Portal.

Love is an energy, not an emotion; it is the basis of the truth. There are certain barricades one needs to get through to find the perfect human, [your name] to know yourself and God's part of what it is to be human. Let's know the timeless skills, lessons and how things are the same so we can enjoy our own individuality. This way, we have a better shot at helping to build tighter families so each generation can enhance the Rubik's Cube of Knowledge to better understand love using intellect and wisdom.

As humans, we are our own world, individually and collectively, as we are our own power of God by ourselves and collectively in a multidimensional way. This is the same as the power up. The universe and God are separate and at the same time they are the same.

The inside power is the will to choose, and to face and conquer fear as we know fear cannot share the same space with love. Therefore, to find love is to find truth.

The centered energy that wraps up everything in all depths of dimensions and all sides from the inside and outside to past, present, and future, is LOVE. It may sound cliché, but the center of the patterns reveals all is one and one is all.

Knowledge is knowing the opposite sex symbolically, metaphysically and literally at a subtonic level as this is the key to understanding love and life.

Spirit is the balance between the whole human world and the whole spiritual world. The third world however is joined by the understanding of how relationships work when the inner and outer worlds meet. It becomes the third world eternal, a world of perpetuities. This is the balance of love and truth, revealing just part of the plan for the UI.

Love is what we need to find 'inside' of ourselves to truly love another person on the outside. The center of inner technology is the fuel for the advancement of the inside of humanity to unite to the unity of one.

The perfect life is inside all of us and so far we as a nation/world just recognize God as loving us! Our lessons are how to build a perfect human through us in the division of religions to see the perfect human life is bringing God out.

Chapter Nine:

A Truth. Some Hieroglyphics.
The 3rd World includes The Truth.
Spiritual laws, Inside Polarity to the Bi-Polar
Intelligence and Intellect

The world of communication can have different hubs that are inside and on the outside and all around us. This will show what we are like when we are working together towards one common goal. The outside world is **a truth** for a person to see that our *literal* human bodies are tied and centered into the universe's plan for us to uncover. The inside/outside **is the truth** of how our *symbolic* world is being revealed by the perfect placement of how the worlds relate on the inside/non-physical/spirit world. The 3 worlds are the three parallel universes, with the ducks of misunderstanding. When they all go underwater at the same time, the world gives an illusion of being one circle, not three worlds, leaving an 'inside' perception that only sees part of a truth. The mind doesn't know the innocence of the unintended misdirection from the illusion. Unknowingly, this can create a delusion of what one thinks and believes is the truth; this will show up as one's truth on the outside. **These are the three worlds: 1, 2, 3**) Mind, Metaphysical and Me. **2, 3, 1**) Body, Literally and Myself. **3, 2, 1) Spirit/Soul, Symbolic and I**. Let's put it in another way: the **Mind, Body and Soul** is the same as 2. **me, Myself and I** or our Metaphysical mind of me or you, and our symbolic spirit/soul is to be our literal way of life.

We are all One Truth, One God and One Love and this can be seen by the way we communicate and the way we make the boundaries for the world we live in. The world outside "relativity relates" inside **as to open** the 3rd world to see the laws of polarity.

What are some of the different worlds? A) There is our outside world, which includes what *is* **a truth**. Imagine looking at yourself in a deeply introspective way. This is what I mean by our outside world looking inward. B) There is our inside world, which includes what *is* **a truth**. Imagine closing your eyes and experiencing everything around you through your remaining senses. This is what is meant by our inside world looking outward. C) Finally, there is the 3rd world. It results from our inner and outer worlds and how they relate to each other. Our inner and outer worlds each begin with a different perspective. The way those two perspectives relate and interact with one another helps create this 3rd world, but it is not simply the combination of the inner and outer worlds: it's a separate and distinct world. The 3rd world includes ***the whole truth*** about how our inner world is a truth and the outer world is a truth but the whole truth is how they relate in the 3rd world.

The two worlds are both separate and the same in us and they do not become one even in our self. When separate on the outside, the first definition can be used to explain the world. The inside world, when "separate" on the inside is explained by the second definition. The 3rd world unites the two other worlds to make it whole. In a human sense, the word unite means to come together for a common purpose. The second definition, which is spiritual, refers to a fairer, more egalitarian society. The third definition of unite refers to joining, typically in marriage, with another person of the opposite sex. It is like a sliding bridge where the skills meet from both ends, dimensions and layers of skills, and that shows how they relate in the center. It is a balancing act in three different ways.

1. (Inside) The Red world includes what one can't see or touch on the inside the body. It includes anything intangible of the inside/spirit. All that is inside.

2. Outside) The Blue world is human/physical, everything that is tangible. All that is outside. Both sides inside/outside clearly stand on their own, but we need to know how to separate and join them possibly at the same time. This adulates the God side of humans and steps down from the height of the spiritual God-

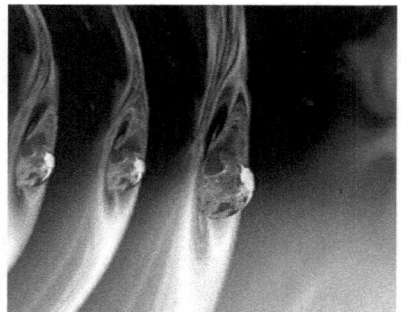

self; they pick up new lessons on the way down to the circle of life where they started from originally.

The other side of understanding is to see how, in the core center of the mind, the Red and Blue worlds relate to each other to the millisecond of the moment in each world. In the purple world, we see a centered life inside and out.

The Red or Blue worlds are helping to see the center of the start of the true truth, by the use of laws, composition, polarity, physics etc. They are the same words; the meaning is just different. We need a clarified, centered perspective of where the meaning goes (to red or to blue) and how they relate. The words in the different worlds are on the same page, but they are not seen properly in and on our different universe(s) inside, and our ducks on the outside, as the meaning moves. Things are bi-polar (outside, physical). People can also be bi-polar (inside/outside/ physical/non-physical). Each word has its bi-polar meaning when looking from a different perspective between Red and Blue worlds. What one looks at from the outside and what they see from the inside is the eyesight of the body's believing, knowing the energy and light. When one hears what is said on the outside and listens from the inside through the body's ears, and they hear a meaning, this is listening with an ear to the ground. Some words have different vertical perceptions, like the ducks and the universes, but each world has its own clarified understanding. The placement of meaning reduces the chaos of confusion.

3. The outside Law(s) of grammar, if used properly in speech and writing between the bi-polar opposite of red, blue and purple, help center the 3 worlds to pinpoint the way to calibrate **a start of the truth.** Purple guides, and

we can see red as **a truth** and use blue as **a truth**.

There is a balanced separation between science and religion that uses one-, two-, and three-letter words to separate the way to/of the truth centered between the worlds. The religion is inside (red) verb and science is outside (blue) noun. Using philosophy as an academic discipline centers purple as to how red and blue are relative guided by the Law(s) of grammar. The skills, sliding scales and spiritual law(s) help to see to the center of how religion and science work together to become **one** in time with the proper calibrated systems through imagination, intelligence and trial and error for the Rubik's Cube of Knowledge.

1) Spiritual laws are the skills of being human as well, sliding scales and lessons for what it means to be human, all of which are the same but different skill sets. Wisdom is knowing that we are the other side of two inner humanities.

2)

God's plan is for us to see for ourselves what it is to be human to God [your name]. The metaphysical unisex of men/woman is bi-polar, a horizontal way to the mind's understanding of the "heart of the mind" which is the vertical bi-polar. To look outside is to use human eyes. To see what is meant comes from the mind's eye, which is spiritual. We all have the sight of understanding, but the Egyptians really mastered the process to find answers from inside out and the outside in.

Spiritual leaders have uncovered this and they have been sharing their inner discoveries scientifically, spiritually and philosophically. This is the way one perceives the inner self and/or the God thing. We should be looking for how the inside and outside are a perfect fit together to see that religion is the gateway to science on the outside and vice versa. The religion polarity is spirituality on the inside.

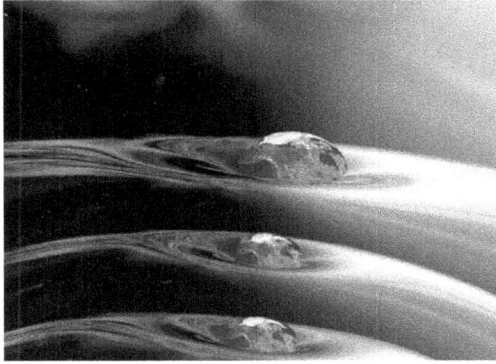

3) The designer sees everything, everywhere all at the same time in all colors. The human side is like the Hoover Dam Bridge, while the spiritual side is the natural side like the Grand Canyon. Neither one of them is right by itself but shows how we are equal to each other. The Seven Wonders give us direction for some answers to the inside/outside and to the center of the universe. The better answers seem to come first from the spirit side or the gut intuition. Adult growth is to see the balanced and calibrated lessons down to the controlled center of one from the inside out, to the outside in, and back to the center.

Think of the three primaries as being the parents in the family of colors. These three primary colors, when mixed, make 12 basic hues.

These are some of the processes and patterns of how to use words and sentences to arrange balanced meanings, by using words that describe the inside and outside meanings which, when fused properly, will naturally find the center of the particular truth. This will automatically push out fear from the center to understand the way inside without a whole lot of thought. The phrase "that which is" means that the whole country will understand in the same way, using one heartbeat from all directions, dimensions and levels to the organized processes, down to the calibration to perfection of **one** in its end. This is how we can explore the best way for humanity to see how the Rubik's Cube of Knowledge's real truths exist without 'what' one believes, but rather 'how" many believe.

Believing is formulating why separate parts go together to make sense of why. We must leave our minds open, not to judge, but to find the way to the completed design of the centered, equal truth. It is for all, from the best collective belief, to know the patterns to uncover truths. The truth starts between outside /inside and Inside/outside and leads to where the truth can be found, for SCC and Universe is the mirror image of us with the same lessons approached differently.   The expressions to be seen and found from the direction, perception and changes of "just is, this is, is what it is, which that **'IS'** to is, is, is that which is O/I centered I/O." The closest to understanding internal technology may have been the project around the world to the installation of Earth's orb. It's trying to complete a communication system to connect the world. By the ancients who knew the individual scale of love is truth and truth is love, as verified by the truth's processes, equals uncovering the perfect intelligent plan feelings, spiritual non-physical together through intellect facts human outside somehow connected the inner communications around the world.

Where science, and God energy is clouded by us because who he is, is in each of us and how many hats he wears at the same time. The human mind needs to be trained with how the correct perspective matches Gods will who's right along with us as humans; we know it all in our disquieted minds and we probably do it better if we organize togetherness properly. Rather than tap into what equals to the understanding of how to piece together the puzzle from the body of differentness, separations, time and space. The collective community changes from the human side to the friendly love by just being aware and choosing to live in good spirits by seeing the millisecond of the moment intended to **G**lobal **S**tabilize **E**nergy through electricity and communication, sound and light. Understand living from the inside of the hands together example, found through the knowledge in the center out after learning from within is more important than most realize. The processes of how love equals truth and vice versa is how God, Love and the Truth center to one God where "G.L.T." are all the same in time and timeless throughout the world and the universe (literally, "is it or it is" provable is the center) from [Your Name] are and is the centers of your child and you, a universe of one. The symbol of the cross, in giving up his body (maybe Christianity has it wrong!) could have meant knowing that the physical world is (**knowing what it is**) born into the selfish world not controlled will turn into sins (where thoughts create your intentions and intentions create your reality). The exact same as the outside human world for all of us (MMI) Me, Myself and I. As you know, the inside is (MBS) Mind, Body, Soul, is believing, not knowing, which side you're on, the inside or the outside, down to the core center after the process is understood, can be confusing as well! (There's a possibility instead of a double noun or a binary back polarity).When one doesn't believe the mind is satisfied with the information that has been gathered, the listening shuts down and the mind is no longer open to hearing what is said. This turns believing to the negative/ human side, backwards from the intended path. The Universe of One is a child born from the center of the universe where all RSVP started from in the Big Bang. Just look from the inside out, and then understand that the nature of the universe leads back to guide life in each child born. True love is the center point to life for laying down the truth right in front of you. That which is God, love and the truth creates an added understanding from our God-self, inside/outside, to the inside/outside of another, through all on the outside and inside. Centering a union of us is knowing that the educated NOW is love, even through the differences and separations of feelings. The metaphysical way of growing to the center is the purpose of the sliding scales.

These lessons prepared one god self loves all for the parents to see that life's bond is the nucleus from the teaching of a child in a family, meaning the god self when young is life's bond for a parent and that bond is permanent for life, and the parents that made the child are connected for life because they are in love spiritually by the connection with the child. Even though each person may not see the love humanely and that they are connected for life in the now spiritually – God's way and it is our emotions not to see that love humanely. The core of one god back to human is one whole god that is a perfect human, the universe of one. The natural way one loves helps us to know what love means and is the way to answer life's questions. This changes the form of love where a child loves for now in the millisecond in the moments of all sides I/O, the same love that is true for God is a centered educated process from within. As one grows, the bond of love moves from the now like a child to grow to whatever gender they are by hip structure. To find god's self-love is finding why God is not religious and the center of the complete love is brought through now. Now is love to the center of truth and means love in all ways in time and space (degrees of energy, is love). All the answers are between love and truth, literally. An adult female "separates" the loves for today and an adult male differs in love and separates loves for tomorrow so inherently our timing of love is different and this may be how gender makeup starts, more so than not but can start anywhere from where you were born. We grow with an instructions manual God gave us all when we are born; nobody has figured out yet how to love your god-self and keep families together in a natural way by how we are designed perfectly together and against each other. The easy way is to leave but in the end makes what one wants or needs to "fine" or "find" harder to see the center simply because of the self-justification of not seeing the brilliance we all have in us. Separations and differences are fueled by the perceptions we have of things we don't see, have not learned or have lost in layers of dimensions, not even knowing they (all of us) are "there/their" inside us (their) outside us (there). Everything starts with a thought in the mind of 'how' we believe. These steps are very important to why the method becomes the way we all develop what we know; this is the most important process to what we see on the inside because this is what will display on the outside of us and how we lead our lives.

There are many different ways to be aware through the placement of words and meanings to verify the processes down to ONE method. This narrows down the variables to the center of the truth. We are all to uncover simple brilliance together, from within. The first thought one has when responding in a conversation usually relates back to the self and, more often than not, it is a justification. The life that sees and understands the meaning of the razor's edge has its own language. Accidents are outside and coincidences inside. We all understand that being in the wrong place at the wrong time can create an accident. How much simpler would life be without what we know and/or believe? It comes down to "it just is." The space everyone has between themselves and their knowledge helps us understand timeless wisdom. Until one knows all or nothing, in every way, there is not a set window to define "time" for any of us. The problem is not knowing how the variables work for the organized knowledge of the process from within for all people. We can figure out the academics by asking internal questions to form our own choices and to see what true answers exist that are the same individually as they are collectively at a subtonic level, deeper than we see or know. The mind needs to recognize the parts in each world that can be unlocked to start the process of seeing the side without time (the non-physical world). Once learned, we can join back to the two worlds' center to understand the equal knowledge by how they relate in space.

We as humanity need to uncover S.C.C.U. We can't see past the choices we don't understand or the ones we fail to see in our teachings. By being open-minded through listening and uncovering the processes, we will see clarity through confusion, as we will to find life's answers together.

If we understand the collective mind, which is driven by the individual truth to see the processes, this will set one free between the inside world and the outside world and close the gap of how they relate. We can take the air out of the R.S.V.P. from the outside of everywhere. Freeing one mind through the inside process will help the community see the same specific process to the center of each individual word that is naturally fitting for the truth.

The result of the unintentional buildup of lies that comes from using only one side of a truth leads to people thinking the way they do. This leads to living an unintentional lie. On the outside we may think we know something and "think" we have enough information, but this often leads to the development of an unintended ego without knowing. Everybody sees except for the person who has the ego and he or she is usually selfish and/or not over the need to be right or if it is unintended, they may not be willing to listen. These are some results of only seeing one side of a truth. When one sees there is no right or wrong that is when they understand the centered meaning. The non-physical inside needs to see the separation beyond the five senses.

The truth narrows down to three sets of three for S.C.C.. It is explained in sets of three so we can see the different directions of separation and how not to overlook the processes so we see the perfect plan in us. The vision follows the direction of the differences on the outside of people and the separations on the inside to the center of the truth. This will explain the moment down to the millisecond of what it means to live in time; we experience the past, present and future all at the same time in the current moment. After understanding how there are no coincidences (inside) or accidents (outside), one knows the timing of knowing down to the millisecond. When people haven't seen each other in years and bump into one another, they often pick up right where they left off. The interaction is almost timeless. A person can be older but have a younger mind in the way they think.

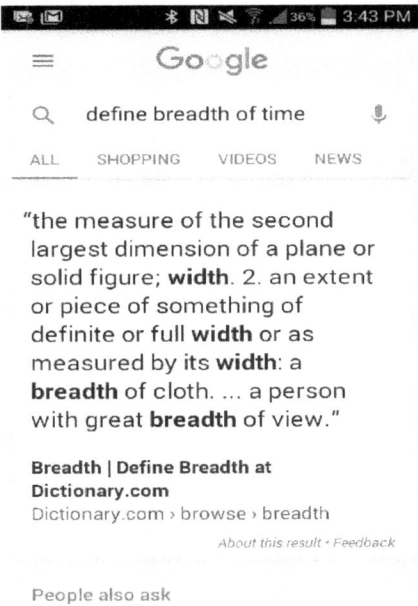

Google

define breadth of time

ALL   SHOPPING   VIDEOS   NEWS

"the measure of the second largest dimension of a plane or solid figure; **width**. 2. an extent or piece of something of definite or full **width** or as measured by its **width**: a **breadth** of cloth. ... a person with great **breadth** of view."

Breadth | Define Breadth at Dictionary.com
Dictionary.com › browse › breadth

About this result · Feedback

People also ask

This is also almost timeless. Together, we need to pinpoint what is timeless and how it affects us.

The coaches can explain better how timeless "breadth" is the second largest dimension of knowledge, from the inside of each person from all ways of times. The first is the normal, outside world we live in, labeled the first dimension, which has the organized collective knowledge of all to include universities and dictionaries all on the outside learning material. The second largest bank of knowledge is in the second dimension (everything in all ways learning material can be used for the light bulb to be turned on) of timeless breadth; it is a window moved by light bulbs of knowledge. The knowledge only moves when the light bulb is understood and is turned on; it is timeless on the inside but equally as important on the outside; that is the horizontal crossroads "of time" to the time we know for S.C.C.U,(self, community, country, universe) triggered by the same knowledge in us since the beginning of time. This is the center for past, present and future and the present moves all together in sync with knowledge and time. Making the same millisecond of the continuous moment in time to understand that which is the center of time together equals the center of how the universe knows everything and nothing (no-thing). The outside universe has time. For example, the window of time is the "length" of time one can predict when viewing something. The other is a window of the "width" of time before a rule changes, called a window of time.

Some people aren't aware of how both times meet; one is horizontal and the other is vertical. "I believe" is the plus sign. They meet in the windows of the milliseconds and in the continuous now. This is where knowledge comes together and comes back to itself (when we understand this we can develop what God's Word is through language with the four truths and both sides of time). Language has the same but different plus sign. When put together correctly, these are truly all the answers we are seeking. The plus sign is truly a point to understand the next dimension for the inside and outside to go together with time and truth. When we look at how the timing of love works is separated by knowledge using our makeup by a man, woman and a child (tomorrow, today and now) all for humans need to know where on the sliding scale they are down to the millisecond of now or the center explains how everything in the universe ties together as one when we use the correct way; we can see that it is the foundation of the whole truth where God can be found in the collective NOW. Man, with forward thinking, loves for tomorrow, women think for today. Therefore their thinking loves for today. Both can love both ways but "timing" of knowing may set them apart. Children think for now therefore love in the now the same as (UI/God). The same as the universe only knows *now* in love, truth, God's or the Universe's system, space, and time for all in all simultaneous milliseconds moving everywhere and nowhere in time (timeless and in time) is everything = all. Because our teachings all come from the universe and love is everything all the knowledge in the universe organized correctly is between love and truth. The teaching of the energy of love and in love by all correct love, in all ways both for mankind and the universe, this is when we have it correct in knowledge of love and know everything the universe has to offer when we do it together. Helena Fisher is a doctor who did studies on love and why we cheat. Here is the link: https://www.ted.com/talks/helen/Fisherfind.

In language the differentness (please look it up) are factors on both sides; one side is the inside illustrated by a verb and the other side is the outside illustrated by a noun but "even though the sides or brothers are very different" (I'm told almost any verb can be made into a noun). So, in our language this tells me looking at the broad scope we can with this new formula get to the center (human/outside) of the middle (spiritual/inside) of any single word uncovered new rules and regulations here. The words, although they are identical twins in each single word using the definition of "differentness!" which is the twins in language the patterns in language are the "same" but "different" we can determine how everything works guided by the definitions through our language when we meet perfection. Everything in the universe comes down to SELF, male, female or a CHILD, the "one" you had babies with, the way we relate to each other in the nucleus offers what type of community we live in. All the answers to and in the universe are in the same patterns, most of which are on the inside. First, what parts are the "same" as each other on the inside when we have it correct; all together the "differences" will not matter and everything on the outside will fall in its perfect place. Language does this when it comes back to itself on both sides as explained in the laws of thought; also the part of language on the inside that is intangible or non-physical is mysterious and unknown but now guided by the polar opposite word provides us the piece to complete the word and make it whole. Once we have each word complete, we then have the part to have a completed language to make it whole or a universal Bible to explain everything, even God. Self does this too as it is the other side of and to God, self. In the "breadth of time" is finding the center of time and the breadth in the timeless window of space in knowledge moves by what an individual knows. Most spiritual leaders try to address things from the INSIDE at a deeper level. Most people can't see because the inside is a different world and a separate language of understanding but to understand is when the light bulb of knowledge turns on; most have not gone deep enough to see they end up being the same. In some cases, it takes facing all of one's fears to understand the light bulbs that need to be turned on. This is where we need scientists and religious leaders to lead together through philosophy to the center. Our purpose in life is to grow back to each "now," and to then uncover how the universe works in space, time, love and truth separately.

The knowledge of love, truth, time and space works in some abstract ways, like in physics in the universe. There are four laws: 1.Electromagnetism 2.

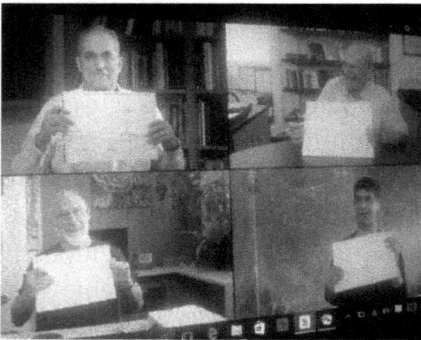

Strong interaction 3. Gravity and 4. Weak interaction related to the inside of us.

The outside, physical world is tangible. As to what percentage I do not know; it would be a question for the physicists to determine the percentage we can see or touch. It stands to reason that exactly half because we live in a perfectly symmetric world the inside, non-physical and the outside physical world are perfect and fit together perfectly because they are the mirror image of themselves making each half whole and if that is not confusing enough then try this: when I say that each half is whole on its own but also fit together perfectly making the whole universe. Then we will know answers can be found in three ways: God, self and in language.

We will come to know and understand the parallel universe. On one side, it's non-physical, intangible, invisible and uses a verb to explain things, but real. The other side of the universe is physical, tangible, touchable and uses a noun to explain things. The process of how 100 % of the universe works and uses these lessons, skills and ducks are all rolled into oneself called the heartbeat of all to match our insides to the universes outside. We work together and include the meanings in different directions of time by separations on the inside and the differentness on the outside to assimilate beyond philosophy not what we think, feel or believe but when we know fits together perfectly the proof is when (the timing) the truth and the way it fits in and if it doesn't fit in we are off in what we think we know. **It just is (Self) it just is what it is (Community) to that which is and are (Country) and all that is and can be (Universe). These are the words used when everything is aligned perfectly.** This is our world once we partition correctly each from the "inside" and "outside" of everything; one side is a truth for seeing what is in a partition. This illustrates all in one side of the inside things and or people or both looked at in a vertical way. The other side is outside things or people, or both looked at horizontal each being a separate partition. This is important because it is our foundation focus on one side at a time for a partition that will organize everything in the inside partition first. S.C.C.U example: non-physical is everything that doesn't have a physical presence like think, believe or know that is metaphysical or literal (the truth) can be inside the body like your brain or hips. Then the other side on the outside use S.C.C.U. to organize the partitions by what is physical both is a truth but when the inside (world) and the outside world by adding another is: Is/is. One is, this is one inside of a truth for all of one's (SCCU); the outside is a truth for connecting the outside (S.C.C.U) Self, Community, Country and Universe things and people. The part of the process and **just is** yourself an individual person or something using one side of the truth, typically is a direct lie to oneself when one isn't looking at it correctly. When one understands both outside and inside completely that is justice for oneself, the proper understanding of how the process works. What is, is both sides of one 'that are' where a community can see the heartbeat processes plus the skills, seeing wisdom inside and outside centering what that is equals oneness for all of self where the whole universe will come together oneself at a time. The justice is first for oneself but all will benefit (I/O) when discovering and sharing the proper calibrated heartbeat guided by coaches, professionals and normal people that see and understand the individual course of the first part of one completion of the journey is to see the god self, the individual portal. When centered how communication for the academics, religious and spiritual communities of professionals come together starting from the whole leaves no room to be holy but "'just" when complete to the balanced center of all knowledge for that which is simple **brilliance, literally. Where the smallest detail of an atom to the widest, highest and deepest**

parts of our universe by the broad scope are analyzed by oneness, not just how they go together perfectly but how each thing is explained again the perfect system for the god self to uncover together how everything all at once works, which is God how God is the way broken down from the parallel universe The separation of the Mind, Body, Humanity and the Universe all together can be broken downside a "different way of the same" but still is the whole by (S.S.D.P) "Split, Separate, Divide, Partition" to see and isolate the partitions, patterns, worlds and the Universes to the One heartbeat for all to understand. Such as: humpty dumpty separate on the outside then put back together again but on the inside this time.

We are at the top to understand each process separately in one's mind to understanding the spiritual world and putting in writing that makes sense to the masses. If we knew everything about spiritually when we back down step by step from what we miss or lack to say in conversation or said incorrectly and/or space it out and do not say at all, in our explaining leaves others in a different place than intended leaving them with not having all the information. The calibration now needs fixing because there is a part missing for whatever reason it wasn't said or a cog in the wheel to naturally understand through speech, this is symbolic to see the automation for both sides of a true "separate but the same is one right perspective" into the semantics of words that are "separate but different" that which is the polarized words of one word illustrating the inside and the outside is the "same but different is one perspective of right" with seeing different but separate and the same as one. The center is to understand and see that which is a **symbol of brilliance** between the two **literal** meanings of the **metaphysical** way seeing a part of the meaning for the verifiable truth in one person and aimed at all people is for ONE to see the understanding from within that which is the same purpose for all is why the inner processes to the truth are the same.

The symbol may be that Albert Einstein left us to uncover - A Symbol of one that leads to each specific fact that which is a part of each process for the truths as a part of the whole truth is the processes for and in life (A truth). There "is" **intellect** for facts through logic "is is" **intelligence** of emotion and feeling that is finding the symbol to which is inside and outside that are factually and emotionally the same (a true "symbol of abstract" for the workings of the process(s) easily overlooked).The truths process on the surface in a normal way of thinking or seeing that these words are not polarized. **"Intellect"** is fact (outside) and **"intelligence"** is feeling/emotions (inside). The inside, non-physical meaning splits off from the semantics into a polar opposite meaning in another direction. Viewing from the center is between seeing (inside), and look (outside) at; **intelligence** is seeing from the inside, and **intellect** from the inside to the outside and vice versa. The next process is for us to find the truth between what sits on the outside and the inside poles, breaking it down into one verifiable meaning.

Through the timing in the millisecond of knowledge, we know how the continuous moments work together in all ways. There is one truth that combines through patterns and blind spots for us to uncover and see a perfect plan. We build the truth one brick at a time, through one simple word between polarities using **intelligence** and **intellect**. There is one same but different meaning of each word using the separations in grammar. These are matching both in the inside and on the outside, down to the center. The foundation of the truth is knowing that one person is a small god, and that they have the ability to tap into the Universal Intelligence. One's religion is a piece of the whole. By itself it is holy, but together it is the complete self. The truth is the most important thing to see for ourselves. The Universal Intelligence in us is God and His plan; it doesn't matter what one thinks, feels or believes, but rather what they know at a subatomic level that which is all the same. God and humans are the same, but they are separated by the inside/outside, time and space, and our choices, thoughts and beliefs. We both see and don't see this. The other side of polarity is the physical universe outside us.

Chapter Ten:

Sex and Money Both Carry their Own Energy
Internal and External Happiness from the Center

The inside of us is determined by what space we fill in or the space we take out for the self, community or country. The inner and outer clarity to the center of knowledge mixes with moments down to the milliseconds of the inside moments and back up again to the outside millisecond in the moments but there is only one to share; this is the center of time, **NOW, and everything needs to be in sync**. We are programmed to look and see time as linear, not in width and depth. The Big Bang exploded from the center out, but everything we see is to be from our perspective. Usually it would be on the inside or outside depending on one's perspective (where the correct way is God's way the universe lays out what we need to uncover the correct way)). Time and space plus the centered now's are equal in and out of knowledge. Between the outside is a world of a complete truth and the inside is also a world of a complete truth. The whole truth is figuring out how they relate to equals in three separate worlds.

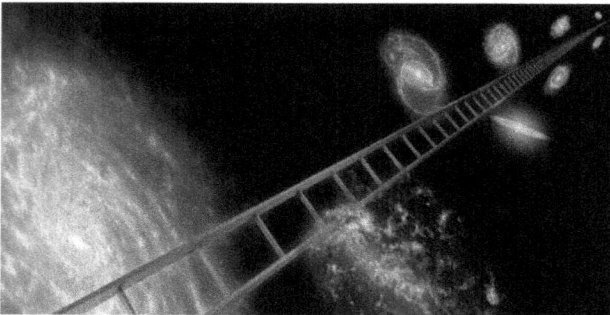

Using the illustration of the truth, parallel universes place the "outside" in the image of a universe for the physical world in a boundless partition. The long sides of a ladder each connect to bars and this is like a partition where one side places father sky with everything physical in the outside world. The outside side of the ladders houses everything that is physical. The partition separates and holds planets, human bodies and matter. The parts that are human start and end with a literal human heartbeat. Humans have only been around 200,000 years or so, even though we are made in the mirror image of the universe.

The inside brings dichotomies, polarity and opposites. Men, women and the universe are equal, but they start at separate ends. The inside/non-physical and outside/physical happened together and made us exactly equal to how the universe was made. The non-physical world is endless and can't be seen, whereas the physical universe can and has been around 12 billion years on the partition of the physical side of ladder.

The outcome may be bigger and better than we could imagine, to see heaven and Earth come inside us metaphysically by our collective brilliance, coupling love and truth to piece together God's inside plan and the Universe's outside plan. There is nothing wrong with exploring thoughts that are crazy and looking at things in a different way. Everything is done first inside us and/or inside the mind of God before it is outwardly executed. How we are made is **unknown** for now, although we are the sum of the universes' part. Some call it God. It is left to the imagination to assimilate or dismiss because we don't yet know how to have science confirm our progress of inner technology step by step for all to see. Seeing the truth for oneself is only a part of the whole truth. We need to see how each truth works and then by how they relate.

The next phase won't happen until the people in each of the communities around the world go through the portal and help others to see the lightbulbs for themselves. The lessons are similar, but a little different so inside of the community is whole and complete on the outside. Something that might help in completing the lessons is leaving the country and universes parts out before the truth to see how the whole truth works. The inside of Self, Community, Country and the Universe is a part of how the truth works. The universe's center connects like bars in a ladder. "Universes" includes the leg of understanding for humanity.

To understand how God is made is to see the workings of the Universal intelligence (UI). This together helps to complete the Rubik's Cube of Knowledge for all to arrive in the individual portal of equality for internal and external happiness. In mathematics, time, space and love, we share in equal opportunity and rights to find life's truth. God is not to be found or to be believed in. It is more important to know the plan. When we uncover the unknown by simply looking to uncover **what there is to know,** we are building the third leg to understand what is on the outside. Then we know why there is no right or wrong and what it means to see life's truth and the truth about life. The answers are between the inside and the outside and how they relate is where we find the right answers for most of the centered questions.

The country sees that the whole truth is to the point where it doesn't matter what one thinks, believes or even knows. The only thing that matters is enhancing the practices of that which is known already because one effort is all for one. When one is wrong, we will know because it will be like there is a cog in the wheel. The change of life begins when there is a constant betterment of the inter-technology. Right and wrong will just peel away and eventually one will be able to reveal their intent much more easily.

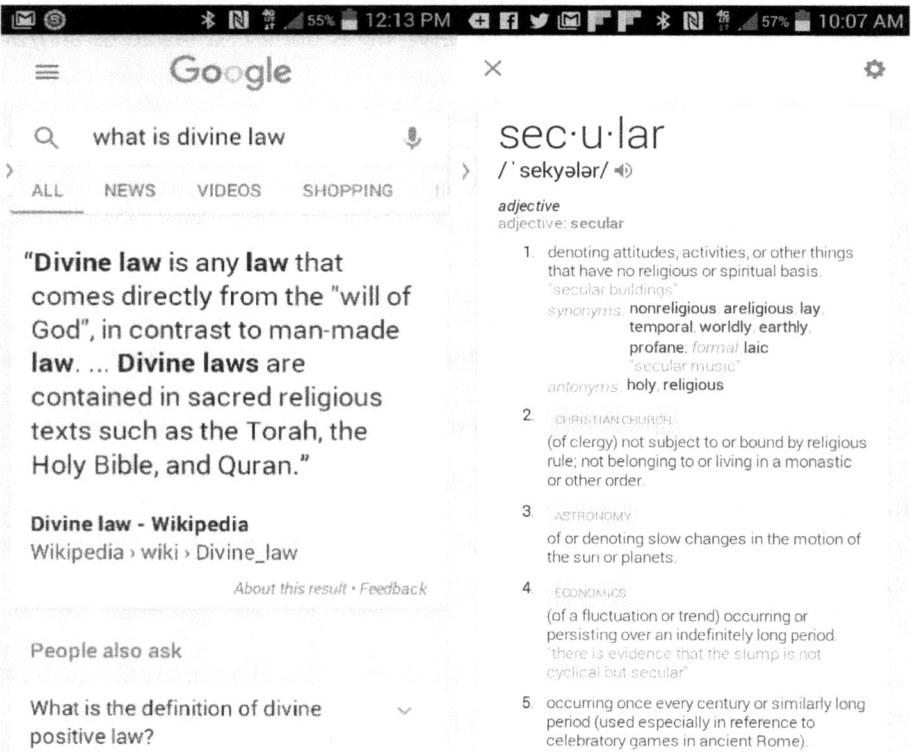

The start of the co-conscious portal of how humanity is all one (each person shares co-consciousness with God making us all one) when seeking academically from us on the outside to the center. Spiritually inside to the center as words change form to understand the center and religiously each Bible may be written both form the O/I (out/inside) but the subtonic level is the understanding of which is on the hearts of hearts "at" one center divide law for the Torah, the Holy Bible and Quran. **Inside Sacred and outside Cloaked Secret = SECULAR which means the center of NOW is the past, present and future all at the same time. Where science and religion are polar opposites, they are different but the same on the universe and can be explained by philosophy to integrate as one. Between humanity and the Universe/God to see that which is the continuous now to be in sync with what the Universe knows, Love, truth, time, space is the UI of God energy is all the NOW** (there may be another part to this double back polarity).When we look at time, we think about how long it takes for one to do something; we see the length of time. We don't typically think of the width of time- how long it takes to know something. Before one can get to the NOWs, they must get through the barricades of dimensions outside which are on the first layer/level. The next layer goes below the surface and looks at the inside knowledge of time. The third level is the knowledge of time into the completed center. The differences on the outside for those that truly understand are just barricades to fuel the chaos. To understand how Church and State are the same but different through the polarity of dichotomies is to see how knowledge and centered time are compatible through simple, centered brilliance.

Truth. Getting to the truth starts with recognizing that the inside is a constant world that we all need to tap into together. One often can't see the dichotomies because each of us carr9.e truth.

> Between "A" truth of the non-physical world or the invisible part for the inside of things in the parallel universe is a truth that stands alone (truth, mind, timeless) - the inside spiritual part of us. The other side that is "A" truth as well and also stands on its own and is the physical outside (truth, body, time) this includes the human outside. It stands to reason then, why large groups like political parties get polarized as it is our human make up by the way we are made starting with two truths each can separate us by the system alone. When not sharing in thought together is set up for close to 50% division based on votes for people not on the issues themselves. Viewing inside how the universe is equal and opposite to the outside world before any truth of substance can be seen to form the solid foundation of A's truth together. The way A's truths relate to each other after they are put

together properly the twists of growth inside and turns dropping a leg, ducks, universes, reconstitute thought is back in harmony etc. to centering the I/O in the proper way for oneself to see the pattern's truth has. The way truth is designed for each of us is the same patterns for all of us on the inside at least three levels deep. The direction to the center through polarity, dichotomies and not having the knowledge of how time works go into the barricades before one sees all the now's.

The centered relationship between inside, non-physical (Truth, Mind, Timeless) and outside physical (Truth, Body, Time) is the third level of the truth for the living soul (Mind, Body, Soul and Me, Myself and I). One person, all people united together is a true way of learning from the inside out. Example: to bring irreconcilable into the compatibility will show the perfection to uncover and bring into the **ONE** truth. Through all the correct patterns and process we establish together will show the result over the years of the planet's condition from starving people to fruitful people and will happen by the people guided by the proper communication. The Rubik's Cube of Knowledge is to become centered in equality of one in sprit and is the inside to the outside to become one to live in peace. **Love.** The power of love is choosing to uncover the energy which is all around us on the surface, where feelings are not love; they are cause and effect from our emotions. The way our knowledge of time works together into the true center is part of the way love works. The universe is made through the center of us and is our replica from the deepest part of our inside. The universe can only see in the center of each "now "collectively at the same time, in time, truth, love, and space.

The pinpointed center of the crossroad has seen and caught the breadth of love since the beginning of time. If we could all see through our emotions and minds to understand fear and truth, we could all share in love. The wisdom of love is the perfect match to the inside truth. God/the Universe is a guide for us to uncover how the plane it fits together from the inside to the outside and back to the center.

The center love is complete selflessness balanced with selfish love with one's "knowledge of width in time" that which is timeless. Each completed timeless truth to oneself is then filled in like an answered space inside a puzzle by knowledge of light bulbs - the connections to see putting in the separation of love (man, woman, child, Universe) back in specified pieces all together in one love. The perfect and complete plan works backwards to find that out and where we come from is through love and the truth together with the universe. Where something like the Big Bang Theory has completed its design from the inside we are supposed to follow where everything is from the inside out and then back to the center by orchestrated ways to from completed love. Made by truth in the center of love and truth from the multi-dimensional (MBS) Mind, Body and Soul UI-god-self. Shared from equal to opposite sides of gender where there is a much deeper plan by how the biological makeup of that which is the physical center of the non-physical growth for a child to create a proper centered union to each of the god-self's and can only be done with the opposite sex for the correct layer of balanced love that which is the centered perfect and equal form of love. The equal to understand what the universe "is is is" for all **Space.** The timeless knowledge gained from the inside of the universe has been the same since the beginning of time. The center of now is where the past, present and future all fit in the same now in all ways, where the future is the same as the past. In theory, this is the perfect world with **one** perfect reality for each generation to uncover, leaving continued progress of growth. But when we come together in the same understanding, we will see the rest of the perfectly designed plan is in each one of us. We are beginning to be able to see the difference between a creation of the animal mind and a creation of the mind of God. We are also starting to see that we need the mind of God to create a heaven on earth.

Time, Truth, Love, and Space. This is where God or UI work is done**, and** how they intermix all together. We can use the game of Jenga to understand this.

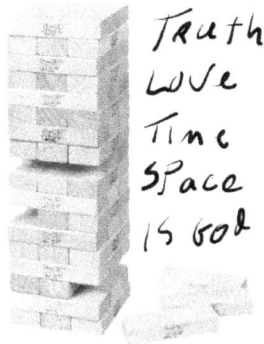

Truth
Love
Time
Space
Is God

The universe starts with 54 wooden blocks, tightly stacked in 18 rows. Each block is three times as long as its width and one fifth as thick. The three blocks represent 1) a truth inside, 2) a truth outside and 3) the way truths relate perfectly to each other. As each new row is stacked up on top of the next, the blocks are each turned 90 degrees. One of the outside blocks represents the timing knowledge (length) and the other block is the knowledge of time (breadth). The next new stack turns 90 degrees, with one block representing space by filling up space in the inside of us. This other block represents the outside space by the massive universe. The center block represents how the inside and outside relate and revolve to the center of one another, creating the center of the union between the inside and outside of **space.** The wisdom of love representing the outside block is the love of power. The next block is the power of love. The center block is perfectly matched by the centered timing and the centered truth to the space required for needed knowledge. Together, we can pinpoint the provable patterns, processes and separations of love to break the God code of understanding. The collective inside truth will allow us to know that **love** is.

The academic communities, living in part on the outside world, want to know things to gain intellect by means of logic for themselves, communities and to help better the world. The universe's facts are hidden in us by the non-physical world outside.

We are small gods from the inside out. We may be missing the bigger picture because we are using the small mind of man and not thinking we are the same collective mind of God together. Some religious leaders are set in their ways as they are people living on the outside world wanting to know God and some think or know that He resides inside a piece of all us. We are not conditioned for the way God/man or man/God is the same but different inside, and separately divided but still the same.

The collective is the process to be and see **all** that is one God in us, for us and as us, through a multidimensional way to see that we are all one human God. Because God is everything, he is you, too. When looking to find the unreligious God together by expanding our minds to have faith by what we don't know, we need to just ask. We are here to live without faith after we know, and to know what the perfect life is and how to get there to hand over a better life for our children.

We all need to explore the religion of being human that which is self, God is the perfect human (we are overlooking the truth) which is the same for all. If we look at God in a different way, we will find the unreligious God in the processes of being human, specifically in being a child. We don't see growth in ourselves because what we think, or what we think we know is probably coming from a negative side. The best way is to leave thoughts open and not say that we "know" or "believe" something; we should just think to find truth because only you will know when you get there.

I Corinthians 2:16 "'For who has understood the mind of the Lord so as to instruct him?' But we have the mind of Christ."

The Lord knew that we would face many challenges, tests and trials while living on this earth, so he sent his perfect son, Jesus, to be our light, our salvation and our guide. He was God, but he was also human, so we can relate to him fully as one who has experienced the same hardships we face. Thanks to the Holy Spirit, we also have at our reach the ability to have the mind of Christ. And if that is the case, then we can truly do all things through Christ [and his mind] that strengthen us (Philippians 4:13).

The truth about how we are connected is key for narrowing down to a subtonic level, where science is God's proxy. The perfect center in us, made directly through us by our mirror image, is the universe on the outside which can only be seen from the inside with the third leg by oneself. The third leg refers to the way the third world relates to the first and second, down to the center of one **NOW.**

For spirit, you must implement the balance of both to find the center of both, and you will see the center of one. The true part of the whole truth stays in fragments. That which is what a true belief is a true part of the entire truth. We know the difference even when our perception changes, fails or is barricaded in the test of time.

The center is known for the three centered truths freed to **ONE** truth. The same importance is given for each to tap into God's plan. When our human side is aware, and as we grow inside with the proper conditioning, we come back to being in the mind of God. When a good part of humanity knows the processes of being human, the unreligious God inside each person is to tap into the "why" to understand the communications, to understand more deeply than we have now.

We know that now we are both the same and different on the inside. We need to be aware of the process of seeing the third leg, which is the same as getting through the portal. The skills of timeless wisdom help us to see more clearly. As for what it is to be human on that side of us? The ancients found that a proper understanding of the universe is made through the inside. The third leg is the reconciliation of God and mankind. Some religions call this the Holy Spirit.

When we go deep enough spiritually, we can understand beyond words. They filled themselves with their version of the Holy Spirit, using some form of timeless wisdom to see how all divisions of one God are the same in us after the lightbulbs are turned on. This brings us to an organized mind on the inside. The question is not whether we are God. Rather, the question should be whether you see that you yourself are God, regardless of the religion you practice. God is a series of human growth traits, patterns and processes.

We can live a close to perfect life by uncovering the processes to what we know of space, time, love and truth. The key is to know the spiritual from the inside **World** of communities to help navigate the religions from the outside **World**. Spirituality, religion, and academics, when centered properly, are equal in importance and all have the same equality for people. What are the important lessons for the community to become complete and to balance out the physical world from the inside non-physical to the center of both?

From nothingness, together we can create perfection or chaos. It is our choice if we KNOW what the CENTER of LOVE and FEAR is.

EVERYTHING

kp

Chapter Eleven:

State (outside). Church (inside)
Spirituality (center)
"The divine" is us inside. The "divided" is but "One Divine"

Spirituality aims to recover the original shape of man, oriented at the image of God, as exemplified by founders and sacred religious texts.

Google

Q Define spirituality

ALL   SHOPPING   NEWS   IMAGES

spir·it·u·al·i·ty
/ˌspiriCHooˈalədē/

noun
noun: spirituality, plural noun: spiritualities

the quality of being concerned with the human spirit or soul as opposed to material or physical things
the shift in priorities allows us to embrace our spirituality in a more profound way

Translate spirituality to

Choose language

Use over time for spirituality

Inside communities, people and professionals rose out from religions, as we are God's work and His work is ours. When spirituality mentions God, they are looking from another set of eyes to see what they don't KNOW in everyday life to put a piece of a puzzle into their bigger plan.

Facts are physical, human, science, logic, outside, and this is one side (looking from the outside in). Feelings are non-physical, intangible, spirit, and inside and this is another side (looking from the inside out). The state is outside and inside. This is an understanding of change, when the polarity of something on the inside moves to the outside. The pattern continues; religion's polarity is spirituality; the constant is finding when and where the timing of change happens in the separations inside, where polarity can drop a leg or where the coincidences are removed by knowledge from the masses.

We are guided by our perfectly organized language so everybody knows how everything is the same, God and humanity, language and self and universe and self.

We have taught from the inside for centuries. But until one crosses over to see their own God-self, a person may not see the process and keep preaching what they know. After all, religion is just part of the whole.

Explaining the meaning of small words changes the picture. But if we start where the small words are, their true meanings will find the whole truth. Spiritual, religious and academic communities can come together to help each other by using words in the proper order to define time, space, love and truth properly. Doing this will define "One" Community where language will guide you.

Before one can **"know" how to love their neighbor as they love themselves,** one must first know the total process of loving themselves in the knowledge of spirituality. We need to understand a way for the spiritual groups to work together with their polar opposite group, from the inside to the outside, and from the outside to the center. On the outside, God is separate from us, but He is also part of us on the inside. This is where spiritual groups can help to find the whole part from within, without one changing their religion.

In context|music|lang=en terms the difference between division and partition
is that division is (music) a set of pipes in a pipe organ which are independently controlled and supplied while partition is (music) a musical score.

As nouns the difference between division and partition
is that division is (uncountable) the act or process of dividing anything while partition is an action which divides a thing into parts, or separates one thing from another.

As a verb partition **is** to divide something into parts, sections or shares.

division   partition

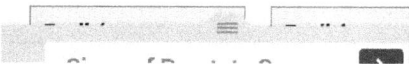

Academics want to know, not just believe; they can't know God by faith alone. Of course, "know" and "faith" do not mix, because if one knew, they wouldn't need faith. Their analytical minds need proof. Some stay hopeful and open to the God thing, hoping for an understanding by seeing the God-self first as it is education. The academics have the toughest job, as they are trying to prove the relation between spirituality, religion and academics beyond belief to knowing. The connections are just divisions to know that **one** can grow to know nothing and everything all at the same time so it is really backwards - you need to split, separate, and divide everything when everything is the same down to "ONE" thing. The difficult part is getting through the confusion because the mind doesn't see it.

The focus of the overall foundation is surrounded by the inside and outside. The direction of the universe's meanings and the meaning to life is from the center.

Coming together means finding the truth between an inside truth and an outside truth. What we discover is that a confirmed truth from the inside and outside are working together. We need to start with the framework from the first puzzle, using the complete hologram of the floating human body as part of the universe's plan by sharpening these discoveries.

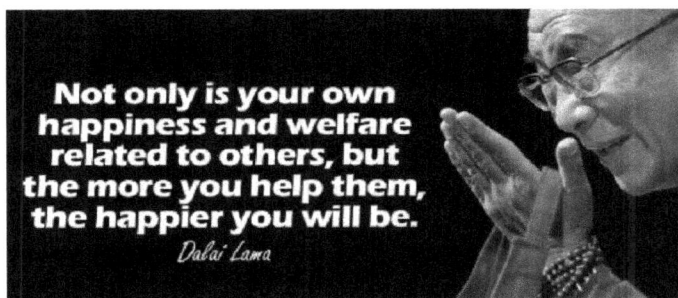

Not only is your own happiness and welfare related to others, but the more you help them, the happier you will be.

Dalai Lama

Most things work this way, such as the non-physical and physical universe, which works in three ways: 1.Humans have the non-physical part of us which is our spirit side and we have the Human side of us which is the physical. 2. The universe has the non-physical side which is the mysterious intangible side we cannot see which completes the physical side. And the physical side becomes whole when they work together... the dictionary puts both sides together perfectly through definition. 3. We and the universe work identically and the patterns of non-physical and physical... this is where they come back to itself for each issue. The way the body can illustrate the simple brilliance together in the universe's plan is laid out for us to find the road map inside ourselves. There is a myriad of moving parts and there are different ways of seeing how each part of the body fits in intellectually. The polarity of the words between the inside and outside is part of the system for building various types of connection to the specific answers needed. The structure of the human body has answers embedded in it that are the same for all humanity at the same time. We seek to uncover the universe's secrets to make sure we know and understand how things work.

In the center of the sliding scales, men and women are unisex emotionally as they grow together to see each other's perspective. Men and woman only are the portals to understanding God's stationary plan.

Living with fear will trigger different emotions in separate ways. We know that fear pushes out love and truth, which is the same as love. Fear can turn love into hate or sadness when it's not understood how it works.

Let's look at the divisions of the divine. The inside "separation" of God is humanity, embodied in each one of us. Open your perception in all ways, starting with **I Am**. The **"truth"** is explained by seeing separations to divisions and unintentional lies. We need to be educated on what is right in front of us. It's not that we don't see; we are seeing in three ways at once, in different dimensions and levels that are hiding in plain sight. We are limited by our own judgment, by what we do not believe and by our perceptions.

We are also limited in that we are unable to discern between the separations and divisions of the blind spot. When we overlook the third leg, this is part of the reason why life work backwards on the outside. One needs to see the third leg first on the inside after being triggered by the lightbulbs. This allows one to see the timeless lessons that are disguised as God's lessons but which are really human lessons. God's plan is truly our guide for life, starting at a subtonic level, to love yourself the same as God.

Everything starts from the inside connection and from the work completed. The walls of fear will break down and leave room for more love as we crave a better system of understanding to become tighter, filling in the gaps from those efforts on the inside while results of the work are displayed on the outside. The world gets repaired a little at a time by using the proper human communication for humans/God. These practices will fill in the outside of one by seeing how there is only one God. [Your Name] is divided into one divine that can't be divided. Look as far, wide and deep as you can go, with all perceptions, separations and divisions in all ways. Every aspect of humanity is to connect for a bigger and brighter purpose together in which we are all one.

1) We are all, me = self

2) We are all, myself = community.

3) We are all, I, self = country.

4) The mind, body and spirit are Me, Myself and I = WE/US! We are all one.

Without a proper understanding of spirituality and knowledge of the truth, we will continue in the way we always have, just looking rather than "KNOWING".

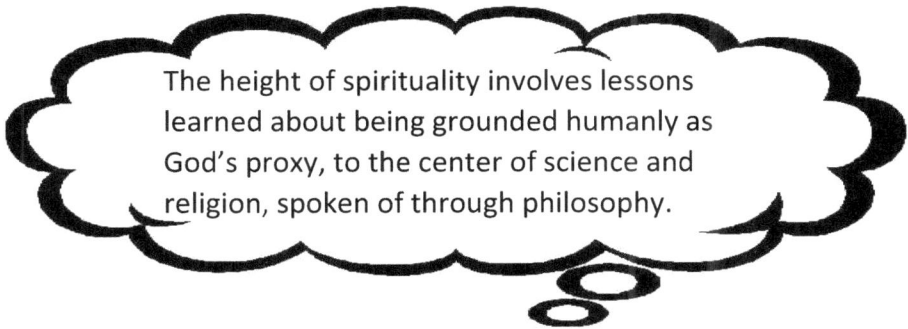

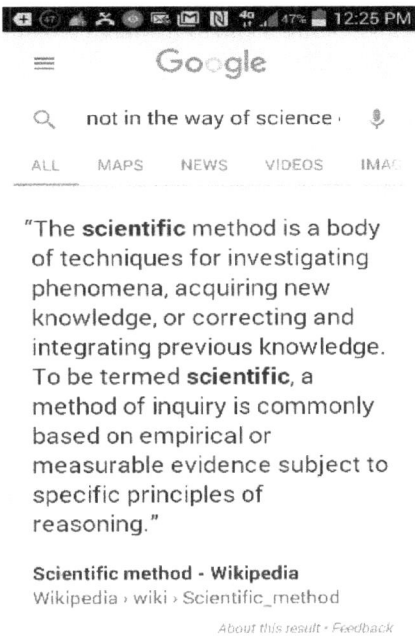

The height of spirituality involves lessons learned about being grounded humanly as God's proxy, to the center of science and religion, spoken of through philosophy.

"The **scientific** method is a body of techniques for investigating phenomena, acquiring new knowledge, or correcting and integrating previous knowledge. To be termed **scientific**, a method of inquiry is commonly based on empirical or measurable evidence subject to specific principles of reasoning."

Scientific method - Wikipedia
Wikipedia › wiki › Scientific_method
About this result · Feedback

By working together uncovering the system that is already in each of us, we can create change and wake up to see the perfect world we have overlooked. God is not religious; it is us, and we are either awake or asleep. Believing in God doesn't mean anything because it is unknown which we are until each lesson is complete. Once one sees in their own mind how we are the mirror image of God literally so it matters not if one believes or is an agnostic or even an atheist because beliefs change, but when it comes down to "what is" correctly God's way it is perfect with proof we are not giving Him credit for it. It is up to us to find and uncover the patterns God laid down for us. In doing this, we will be able to pick up the processes at each phase of advancement in our co-conscious collective. The human body is a step-by-step scientific process of things tied together as one. The findings from the wisdom of the crowd will create a better and clearer picture and we will be able to place the meaning of words between the inside and outside; in this way, we will see a whole new way of learning. The non-physical/spiritual and the physical/scientific relate even when the perception changes in an academic way through philosophy. We see that anything in the past, present and future relates down to the same millisecond of time and knowledge into all the NOWs as it relates to the third leg, both inside and out. We shouldn't need a leader after we pinpoint God's plan which exists in us for us to uncover. We need to fill in what is missing to see what it takes to be whole.

We are looking to science to help us to understand God. In reality, we are directing science for the patterns and separations with divisions so we can know the different degrees in the God-self. We must have an understanding of how we ourselves are "divided" before we have a chance to know humanity, as God makes it easier to come together with this paradigm shift. Human advancement is in the now for us to understand the God-self. Maybe the next paradigm shift of the universe after SCC is the Universe of One and how we all connect together as one. This will provide a world of perpetuity to understand where we came from, why we are here and what the plan is. There is a "separating" of the universe aimed at achieving simple brilliance which is the truth about love.

While building the hologram body with the Rubik's Cube of Knowledge we can add another perspective in 3D, or a third leg of understanding. This ending seems to follow the timeless wisdom by pinpointing the ways we can use our good side (which has formed from past historic events) to get closer to the millisecond of the now. This will help us to understand our present and to ultimately see the good and the holy truth, looking with the perspective of the third leg to be whole on the inside. Once the inside understands how this works, the truth manifests on the outside if enough people have done adequate work on the inside for all to see. This will lead to us living without, or with very little, fear. We accomplish internal justice from looking at ways to include all ways of awareness which keeps us connected to fill in the leg on the outside. This is more likely than not how the ancients did the God thing together for the community. The spirit of human/God and God/human came together as one in equality for the opportunity to live in peace. Our forefathers didn't see rights in opportunity from this perspective.

Life's truth, which is in the now, designed us to be equal with different roles... Learning how to love and stay together with no one in the family being selfish and no one getting hurt may be easier in the long run than a lifetime of justification of the untruth and/or lying to oneself unintentionally.

The way speech comes out and the way one listens can show what work has been done on the inside to grow and find the God-self. This is the growth of skills that are obtained by light bulbs on the inside. We all have intelligence and intellect, which are our deeper five senses. We can see each other as gods from the way we see, listen, think, believe, and know. We are here to get to the center. God is us, through us, and beyond us, just differently from the way we are looking. The answer may be waiting for you to ask for yourself. This happens only after one has completed the spiritual lessons. When we see from the inside, we will know the missing part of God's plan that we have overlooked for years. Communication starts with a person asking what they need to know. One relates in God and the universe in that they themselves are a god (lowercase g). We are each a division of the divine. This is what gives us the ability to truly have a deeper understanding of how God's purpose is for us to uncover 3D communication.

I started my journey with the Universal Intelligence of the mind. It had nothing to do with God in any way as far as I knew. Now I see the gaps in my perception of God. No wonder I didn't understand what peace, happiness and success meant until I was older. Our kids should experience this while they are still kids. Religions need to broaden their view of God and not think they know. We need to keep our minds open and not shut out possibilities. Science, too, needs to be open inside and outside.

I think money is the third leg to the outside of humans, together with sex. Adding a third leg of understanding from the inside to the outside and back to the center is what will make us whole from holy. Once one has graduated from the inside, the same but different lessons need to be addressed by the communities. The same growth processes are involved, just in different ways. This is why there are places of worship of all types around the world. It is for us to see and piece things together inside so we can live together on the outside in peace. The arts, such as music, painting and literature will help us to see beauty in the fullest detail. This will be done with the leadership of average people who have accomplished and graduated from within, as well as professionals and coaches.

The more we center the answers from the processes, the more the answers find the center of equal questions and answers the center of truth from the inside out. The wrong choices to the "one reality" may cost us in many ways. But if we follow language where everything fits perfectly there is only "One" way to "one" reality.

Example: no matter how the nucleus of the family is broken, someone suffers (father, mother or child). It is a universal law that you are connected to your children for life and also to the one that gave you that child. It is the bond of love, whether you see it or not. Spiritually, love doesn't go away; you just hide it, bury it and deny its existence. The human side takes over. We often cause our children to carry burdens that we couldn't get over, or even those that we didn't realize existed. It is always better to fix things rather than starting another life, though that is truly the more difficult way because one needs to face fears, forgiveness or break down an emotional wall. All relationships can be fixed; the work is on "oneself"; it is up to you to see that, and to find peace together as one. Piece by piece, from the center, the reward is in the golden years.

Understanding how a person can grow to be God is similar to the process of the sliding scales for men and women. We need to understand our divisions and perceptions to see that all of us together are God. The more we come together, the better we see our parts as small gods. The big God cannot be divided because He is simply one divine being and he separated, divided and split everything else perfectly from his perspective as everything fits back together perfectly back to God in the invisible side of the parallel universe The divisions of us and our perceptions need to come together to see how the universe and all things and people are equal. What we each *believe* doesn't matter because we have worked together and now we *know*. We will build the Rubik's Cube of Knowledge and physics and the perfect language and self will prove that the inside/outside are two sides of the perfect center on each side of "ONE."

When you have a child, you have a soulmate; nothing can match the love between a child and their parent. A child is a teacher of love because children are the bond of love. The child may not know it, but the union is deep and can have great effects on their inner world. Parents are often not aware when their children make the same mistakes as they did.

We are only as good as the systems we build together. If we live in a world that can build almost anything, and we are capable of figuring out almost anything together, why haven't we implemented processes to reach the center of now? We start with ourselves to see and imagine the perfect life; we are meant to have the knowledge to do something about it. The universe's outside elements are earth, fire, air and water. The four inside elements are time, space, love and truth. Together, these sets of elements make up the perfect polarized and paradoxical world of ONE for us to make sense of together.

My take on God is different and may be deeper, or at least different, than most people's beliefs. I "know" what God means to me; it started after I got divorced 25 years ago trying to figure out what love is/was. God is explainable in almost most all ways. He is perfect where everything everywhere and all living things fit together perfectly. Explained by the differentness in language called the twins expresses both sides of language (verbs inside, non-physical and nouns outside physical) down to matter and spiritual stuff explained how they become one. How God is non-physical (the mind of God) and the universe is physical the same as we as humans are. We have a human side which is physical and a spiritual side where a part of our spiritual side is the same as Gods non-physical side. The scientific and verifiable proof (science and God meet) to the absolute correct answer after the patterns of God to human, male and female, with polarized word connected is when the non-physical and physical world meat and come back to itself in the form of a word... God's word! We have a new universal Bible...He built us to be the controllers of his Universe, mixing the non-physical and physical within us. We are to grow to see that we are the same but different, as we are the "separations" of Him in the center of the core nucleus, for we and He are family and cannot be separated spiritually, neither can a child from the part that is a god in each of them that made the god/person.

Seeing by our own lightbulbs will show us the patterns and processes of the laws God laid down from the beginning of time for humanity to figure out together the same way the ancients did. A big part of praying and meditating should be about defining His laws and uncovering how to become a God in communications. This is the superpower we as humans are to obtain from the inside together. This will lead to what we can do on the outside. Praying shouldn't be about ourselves or about glorifying God or about discovering whose God is best. It should be about understanding the laws of timeless wisdom individually and self so we can work together with humanity, so we can pass it to the next generation. We need to start with the perception of the whole and see how everything works together using each religion as a piece. Knowing how the complete divine works for oneself is clearly important before one can pass it on. Today we are not doing that; we are looking at God separately and that is only part of the truth.

Knowledgeable faith is about knowing that you are God. The answers are within each one of us and this is the perfect system for the wisdom of the crowd to reveal the slivers of the Universal truth that will build trust together for all to see what is the same within us. We can look at the big God as perfect data that knows everything by the system He created for us to uncover in three-dimensional ways (the patterns are the same in everything by using non-physical and physical in three different ways). The system is perfect; when things go wrong we are working outside of the system. We often mess up because we are human. The part within us that sees the perfection of the system is the whole God, covered by the human parts.

The God part in us that is capable of seeing the system, needs to be centered and balanced. We as humans need to see the power is in learning goodness so the system can flush out the unintended evil that naturally builds, which is bigger than intended evil. When the mind can see, it doesn't matter if you *believe* in God because you "KNOW." Separating all into truth is how things work deep in the processes of what is "divided" inside us. How the systems work together is the same for all of us. What it is for us to complete the God-self is to connect the spiritual side and the human correctly; once we do this, only then can we start to understand the outside God.. You either see it or you don't; there is no middle ground. God is you, or you are God looking through the human part until your perception is clear.

Humanity works together to put the pieces in place. It is like a collective puzzle of the human self with all the ingredients to make whole to be a god. The Mind, Body, Soul (M.B.S.) is the spiritual **self** for everybody together while Me, Myself and I (M.M.I.) is the human **self** for everybody. Centering the two together equals the perfect **Self**, Community, Country, Universe (S.C.C.U.) to understand that everything is **self**. **To** know from the inside out is the God-self. By giving us all the knowledge inside that we need, we see everything from the perspective of wholeness.

I don't think the bigger part of God is religious; it is more like a perfect system in which everything works together. People made God religious. We are seven billion people, together with the same needs inside and out. The only thing separating humans is the timing of our emotions, our logic, and the timing of knowledge. What is dividing us is not knowing and understanding that we are the same as God. We don't understand how God is everything, everywhere but is also the same as us.

God is the energy of the systems that connect everything into **one** center in a perfect way. We can figure everything out together, but we are unaware or asleep to knowing how the different systems within us work. The system itself makes it hard to remember that there is no right or wrong between physical and non-physical worlds. We are to understand how and why, but we need to condition our minds to be aware how the inside and outside relate perfectly to see the Universal truth. Both worlds are each a Universal truth to its independent core, and they move the world because we think we know but it is the wrong way. We are not properly aware that we are only using one side of a Universal truth and in most cases it is the fuel for unknowingly lying to ourselves. Small word meanings are addressed many times, but they are so natural that we overlook their meanings. "Are" means to be present in both worlds, physical and non-physical, at the same time. "Is" means what side or world you're on now. "Of" means part of the whole, this means the one truth is "of" means part of the whole or part so can we narrow the truth down to one truth per issue?

The perfect system is in the timeless world in the invisible parallel universe because it is so easy to overlook; people have done so for centuries in normal and everyday conversations. When one just doesn't see, many conversations can become misunderstood, complex or confusing. The truth is overlooked, and therefore lost. We should always use a perception that looks at the whole picture. We can use the sliding scales of men and women as a guide, starting from inside out to the center, to show the universal dichotomies and polarizations using a 3D view. We are the same but different and separate but the same. We are divided from the whole because the whole has two sides to everything. God cannot be divided but is both sides, because He is the whole and is everything and everywhere at the same time but when you uncover the parallel universe it is everything, both sides the same, but starts from the other end and ends up in the middle where it is exactly equal because it is the mirror image the side that is invisible but real. Our inner workings are the perfect mirror image of the universe's actions. Men and women fit together perfectly and are also perfectly apart. Every opposite becomes a perfect fit to complete to the center of **one** in all sides. There are two sides of every person, human and spiritual. We also have two sides to humanity. Places of worship throughout the world are considered to be **inside** of all in us, no matter the religion. The known and the unknown are the dividing or uniting principles to humanity's separation from completeness. We are all the same but what is considered the **outside** somewhat separates us if we don't "know" our language. This has to do with the timing of what we know and what we think we know. The key to the center is a simple formula of two truths, non-physical and physical, to find the verifiable Universal truth we will need to use God's word to get into the center.

When we look from the **human/physical side,** we are often guided by fear; when we look from non-physical/**spiritual side** of 'knowing, we are guided by love. It is a simple system of two truths, human and spiritual.

The inside and outside are equaled by connected polar opposite words. Our minds naturally lead us to just one side, the human side. Without seeing both at the same time, we can't get a handle on how they relate. If we don't see the whole to begin with, we are starting off with an unintentional lie, not knowing that we are lying to ourselves.

The truth of life is to graduate from the portal to see the beauty of life's clarity from the inside out. The key is to take what our ancestors learned, and add in the thoughts of today's leaders to find the center of love and the Universal truth. To see the center of life in all ways is to see how grammar instructions or the rules in psychology fit together in a perfect overall system of education to balance the system of science on the outside and spiritual world on the inside, which is the process of the non-physical world of thinking, believing, listening and knowing. Almost everything ties into one universe, which is the center and the core of an atom. At the same time, religions are directing us to meet in spirit to unite the center of science so we can understand God's proxy, which is the same as how we all become one. The universe's partitions of the physical world are the same as science and the non-physical world is the same as religion. But now can be proven scientifically by God's word.

Literality, symbolically and analytically, the universe comes together to be only one. True, centered knowledge is unisex with the universe. To **know,** emotionally, physically and spiritually, what is one true union of both people is to know you God-self.

We can understand the past, present and future as all being the same as one into the continuous present, where knowledge fits perfectly in all ways literally, symbolically and analytically. The razor's edge of the inside knowledge and the outside knowledge are polar opposites, starting at the other end of the stick and meeting in the middle by connecting the polar opposites. This is called centered knowledge. The same knowledge is embedded throughout time (past, present and future) and in time (knowledge that is inside or outside) as the same to the continuous now connected to all knowledge. The now in time leads us to understand how to get into the center of all that is the present. KNOWING ALL is to make sense of how life works to the center, but to be ALL KNOWING is to know everything in terms of the knowledge that is embedded in the **system;** in the millisecond of the moment is the constant "now" the perfect system everything comes to the center, of now between the spiritual side and the human side of a person. The universe's now's are all the universe knows. Everything leads to the center of one "now" which is time, space, love, truth, and knowledge **inside and out.**

What was created in the beginning is the ONE truth. Knowing this is to understand what, why and how knowledge works. All the questions and answers to life are embedded in the now, and they come together by the knowledge inside and the knowledge outside. The human and spirit sides will never meet but if they do, we will know the meaning of death on both sides. Through knowledge, we will find that the center of both sides equals the total, and we will use that knowledge to complete the wholeness and to understand that one universe's truth adds up to one.

The spirt/non-physical part of a person is the seat of emotions and character; the soul, connected with the second part to define spirit, forms the definitive elements in the character of a person, nation or group in thought. Spiritual scientists understand the non-physical or intangible **inside** world, where there is a small part inside each of us, which is the same for all of us, called the Universal truth. We can tap into our heightened awareness, which I call the portal. God, love and the truth are how we know that everything fits together perfectly to the center of ONE. God is the perfect system that encompasses everything at the same time. Science has proven that we all are united and part of a living universe on the **outside** of all of us which is **a Universal truth**. The field is being uncovered to show that the connectivity of all people and all things are one. The outside energy of the inside field encompassing the whole Earth will provide electricity around the world. When the scientific Vision of Reality includes only **one** complete Reality from **the inside** which is **a Universal truth**, then we have the perfect **Universal truth, centered by how they relate** at each step of the way (they are perfectly together and/or perfectly against each other). Science is viewed as being on the outside and religion is viewed **as** being the inside. When they come together as one, science is the ultimate proof to show how we are looking at the whole God thing backwards; God's proxy is science.

Example: men and women are unisex and equal to one human, but they start from opposite ends as polar opposites. Sliding scales show how man and woman become one metaphysically. It is the same for God and humans. Everything is God; it doesn't matter whether one believes it or not because only 1% now **"KNOW"** what part of the human being is the same as God. We first have to understand what a human is before we look at ourselves. Our ancient ancestors almost mastered the inner workings of the universe. Humans, along with gods, worked together in unity, using the guide of the human body as a map to explain the inner world of intangibles. The "field" of energy through light, sound and energy is the key to the inside and outside for life's answers. To see the part of our inner workings that is perfectly the same for all is to 'KNOW' from the inside/out, outside in, up/down and down/up. The ancients uncovered the energy field through the knowledge of love, asking God what is next inside each person. **The** answers that came back were the same for all. Uncovering the plan is how everything works together as one. We are all one of the same; we just need to see it for ourselves. In the change of molecular structure, there are three key ingredients: 1). Sound, 2). Light, and 3). Energy. The ancients were just normal people, but they had a system together **from within,** which is the same as what is in all of us (the portal). They used their bodies on the outside to guide them to do all from the inside.

This is something that 99% of humanity is missing because of our conditioning. Together, they connected with confidence in truth and love.

Everything in the universe relates man, woman, child, and everything in the universe by mass and energy to oneness to see and understand why there is ONE God and how everything fits together perfectly. We must use hope and faith because it is all there, already complete and whole, waiting for us to uncover it and to ultimately know by using the wisdom **in** all to see. The wisdom of the crowd for each **part of the body is** like a puzzle from the inside out on the four-dimensional platform back to the center using social media to complete the **whole body.** There is a way to understand the whole form. Writing is today's form of hieroglyphics. We need help from the wisdom of the crowd in the next chapter to narrow down the information highway so we can see without all the details and understand from the outside and to be understood from the inside.

One man who connected the **heart and mind,** and soul and who taught everybody else was Edward Leedskalnin. He found the knowledge that love and the truth provide together. They offer everything, everywhere to everybody, inside and out where all is balanced in time to be combined in perfection when one sees self it for themselves. This will help all to understand knowledge, and for all knowledge to be understood. The change in molecular structure by the **completeness** is the state of love and the **wholeness** is the quality of the truth. Together, they create centered knowledge which shows how sound, light and energy all work together perfectly when centered and when using that specific application. The perfect center of everything is the center **in** the inside and the center **on** the outside. The center between the inside and outside is the center of the middle.

We need to look at what it is to "see" and "listen" inside. "Look" and "hear" on the outside are the same but different (The Law of Excluded Middle). It's the same as how "light" on the outside is to "see," to preserve and appreciate using intelligence to view. But when you know something, when the light turns on from the inside, you "see" intellect and then you know it. It's the same as how "sound" on the outside is to "hear" but the same in the inside is listen to sound.

The energy movement on the outside and in the inside and all at the same time together is the center of all. Each part together makes the whole. Nothing can be missed when all that are part of the whole are properly organized. Once we have complete knowledge in the inside, the biggest part of life's journey comes. It is for humanity to center God and the Universal intelligence together in order to see God's plan. This is the same but different from the ancients' wisdom of "in" and "out," with the same result by using the human body as a guide with God's instruction. This is knowledge for what the body represents.

The multidimensional God of ONE or ONE God. After the fall and demise of our ancestors, we lost the whole and complete understanding of how Love, Truth, Light, and sound all connected with energy, inside and outside. The information of the human body that provided and still provides the answers is timeless. It is a guide to intelligence and intellect, to show the family how to know the inside and out together. The family is to grow together with their child as the guide to see what is in the now. The most important part of knowing everything (S.C.C.U.) is family; the nucleus grows from the self.

Humans in later years came to see God on the outside as supernatural and lost sight of the inside and the middle. Not knowing gave humans incomplete information and broke up the big God into many different religions. They lost the inside God that acts as the glue to help in understanding the Universal truth. **Love** equals and **IS** religion. A truth inside together with outside truth equals science. Centered love holds all the answers together. Centered truth is perfect knowledge for everything everywhere in the universe. We listen and see from ourselves to understand how both love and truth together are the secret of the proper use of **light** and **sound.** This is mathematically reliable and the perfect system of God, Love and the Truth are the same from the inside out and back to the center of one. It would be perfect if we could put the puzzle in a 3D sphere in the Rubik's Cube of Knowledge in a human body, all in an app! How do we do it?

The God-self is the wisdom of centered love, guided by the outside body which is knowledge for the Universal truth with the right mixture of light, sound and energy. It is the same but different on the inside as the outside of the atom, neutrons, protons and electrons. Together, science and religion are equal to complete love as the whole truth. To see the same results together provides energy, healing and movement. Is that not everything, everywhere in time? We can unite philosophy, science and religion to find the physics of relationships and how everything relates to everybody, everywhere. This is because, proven scientifically, we are all one.

There are no tie downs here, though I don't know what the mixture is. What is inside and out of an atom? What is the same but different? As a rule, when figuring out things there are at least two sides to everything.

Another man who connected the **mind, heart and soul** for humanity was Albert Einstein. He uncovered the theory of relativity to prove the ultimate oneness of the outside world and how everything fits together. Look at it this way, matter (physical things) and the philosophical intangibles of the mind are the same by how they relate as energy. How they relate shows a connection between **inside** (the non-physical, listening, seeing, believing, light, sound and energy) and **outside (**atoms, neutrons, protons and electrons). Over the years, scientists uncovered the overall unity field, tying everything together in a living universe. We now understand the matrix of the universe; it's like finding God on the **outside,** in a way. Science needs to solidify the **one reality inside** that is the same for all of us, through time, space, love, truth, knowledge, sound and light. **If** the intangibles are organized properly, we will see the difference of all that is and the separation of God and all that is in the division of us to understand the God-self. Humans as small gods; we can see this by the way one has a relationship with themselves. Mass **and energy are the same but different on the** outside **and this relates to the center of** ONE **in the** inside. Mass and energy are one where life's Universal truth of the "field" is one inside and out! **We need to see the complete to understand from the center to make it whole.** The one now is where everything centers in perfect balance in knowledge and time, and in time and space. We balance the difference and separations of dimensions together into the center of inside and outside all at the same moment of the continuous forever. **NOW** is placed in the perfect **ONE** answer between the inside and outside by how they relate perfectly to all that matters. God not only has all the answers; He **IS** all the answers. For the perfect system, the small gods need to uncover what is the same in us. The order of knowledge is in the perfect now in time, making everything the same at the same time. This is the centered truth about what the past, present and future being one in the same in knowledge, time and space, of and in the now. They are separate and different, but in the end they are exactly the same. These patterns work for everything down to one, verifiable by the Universal truth on the inside and the Universal truth on the outside and how they relate together to the center of one, now.

Everything everywhere are elements in the **inside** and on the **outside.** The center of them equals the **one soul** of music, arts and poetry which are in harmony with the u**niverse of one**, **one mind** of the collective consciousness and **one body** on Earth. This expands out from there; the rest is our free will. Understanding the past leads to a balance of knowledge. The counterpart to the past is the future. The future is the same as the past with respect to how things are all the same in the center of time. The physical timing of knowing changes things.

Look first at the system we all live in. Then, look at the choices we make outside the system that carry their own consequences. We need to understand why things are the way they are. The deeper one goes, the more things lead to the center. The answer is to put love and truth together inside and truth and love on the outside so the center will make sense. Love is the real truth, and the real truth will find the perfect love about self and life as it connects all Universal truths in life together. The perfect system in knowledge, love, truth, space and time is embedded in all of us. To understand God is to see the whole of everything as much as one's mind can, and then to break down everything from inside and outside and back to the center, starting with the God-self.

Men and women are separate but are also made as one to themselves and one to each other metaphysically; this is a key to being whole. One can see, feel and choose to believe in centered, true love. A person has a union with the person they had children with. We need to see that our purpose is to come together in fairness and equally for the family. A child you had together is a perfect, true love. When both parents are still alive, together they transcend intellect and intelligence or emotions and logic. Through knowledge, we are all connected through love in a specific way. Our job is to see and find harmony where everything is in the whole now to "know" everything. This is the same in everybody. The more one knows about the system, the closer they get to the portal.

Connected by the correct knowledge, centered by truth and love and guided by correct communication, we can individually grow and get over our need to be right and our fears of death and fear itself. We must push out the fear until we only have love in us. In the universal truth, this is to be aware that we need to love ourselves and others for the perfect system of unity so we can grow together.

Divorce only happens when people don't see love or fear takes over. It is a matter of education; there is always enough love when it is understood. This will happen when humanity is conditioned and transformed to live from the inside out and from the outside in, back to the center of the inside. The perfect system involves brains (God) and people (gods) condensing data from the whole of both sides to understand that each side is perfectly aligned with balanced polar opposites in everything just waiting to get connected. Ultimately, the sliding scales start at the other end of the stick to find the center of perfect equality. It is for humans to uncover at each step of the way without missing a step.

Each part of the processes sees the perfect Universal truth all the way down at each layer, to the center of each field, matching the layers of the grid past the barricades to see equality for all with proper love embedded. The intent for part of the plan is to show humanity, to see that coincidences exist so we can see each other's truth (that's why there are no coincidences) and how everything relates from the inside to the outside and back to the center into one. From the three down to one, the three are on the inside (Mind, Body, Spirit) and the exact same on the outside (Me, Myself, I). The Universal truth comes down to how the inside and outside relate. Our individualities, race and religion are each part of the whole and show that we are the same inside, but different outside.

We first have to imagine the perfect system together from slivers of truth. We will help others by not shutting down our thoughts and remaining open-minded. The complete, continuous choice of sharing love from oneself is a timeless skill for both men and women to master from within. It is our shared purpose to organize from within the processes to see and understand universal **true love** for all.

We are all one GOD. We all start off from "being" whole spiritually. Synonyms for "spiritually" are mentally, internally, emotionally, psychologically, mystically, sacredly nonphysical, but the dictionary defines us to be the perfect on the spiritual side so it seems to me if we are perfect or immortal spiritually and the perfect human is God shouldn't we have these skills listed out for the Rubik's Cube of Knowledge? When we consummate the "human" side and the spiritual side together is "God." The human side and the spiritual side in each of the "one complete word" by the way they split, separate, divide and are partitioned from the whole. In any order to our completeness to get to see wholeness by the timing of what we know! Specifically, when we define each word and make it whole. The timing of our emotions all together to be complete the perfect "human" (is God) defined by the correct organization of the words into their self's when the dictionary is used correctly to complete the language by definition to make it whole (like God make it fit together piece by piece uncovering the perfect plan to have written out and put in the Rubik`s Cube of Knowledge). Even though a small part of us is God, where we are all the same, we need to know what is the same. We are separated by what is God in our language, but our language tells us what is correct with proof to "know" not just believe or use faith but to truly know. As one can see it is all in the definition of words but the connection that ties together the wholeness of each word is the two main parts that act like an oxymoron. The knowledge that we think we know is the reason why we are detached from all that is through love, truth and God. Look at it as a dart board of choice. When you make a decision on the human side without the spiritual side, you are making a choice in the dark. When you make a choice in the spiritual side without the human side, your choice is gray. Acceptable is in the center in the whole word. The spiritual side is a part from the middle of the word and is going in the **Vertical** direction as we split, separate and divide the word by the definition placement of each definition. The other Acceptable middle in the whole word on the human side is apart from the center of the whole word going in a **Horizontal** direction as we split, separate, and divide. When the Vertical and Horizontal common denominator is the start, this makes the completed whole because it includes the spiritual side that is the invisible part of the parallel universe the vertical side of the truth which is inside that is a verb explains the missing ingredients to explain God, the inside of language; this is the side humanity puts together and poorly sees. But they separate at midpoint by how the meanings of the definitions split, separate, divide and partition in each word in itself. This makes us or self, language and God, the same but different, separate but the same. And are the same up the middle spirituality and down the center humanly for all to achieve semantics by the way they relate in the definitions. Once each "word" is figured out and has a completed meaning how each word relates back to itself we have a sentence is a set of words that is complete in itself. This is the first definition of a sentence (The key "in itself"). Something that explains everything, everywhere and everybody is when each word has come back into itself by definition for all words. The verifiable "splitting" along the grain and when we have all words do this "GOD SPEAKS." In all languages, religion, science and philosophy broken down to the simplest rules in our own prefect language when each word comes back to itself!

Sliding scale = Spiritual Side or Human side.

Draw a circle around the A's when making a decision about anything because keeping our decisions in the acceptable realm is more realistic than perfect decisions. The P in the center represents Perfect and forms the plus sign between the vertical and the horizontal, the A's around it is acceptable.

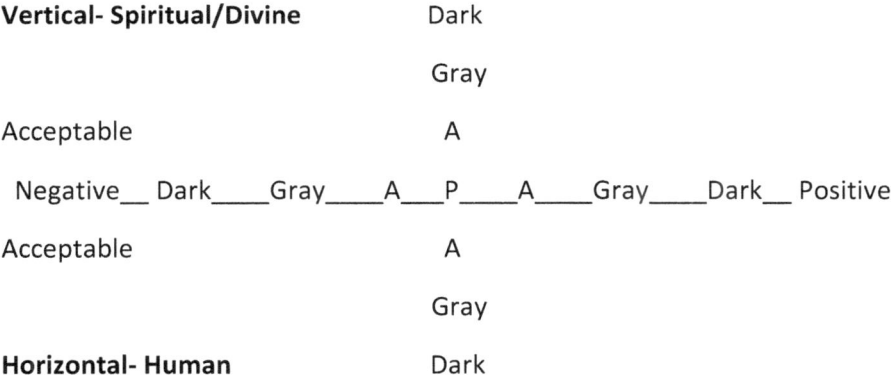

Vertical- Spiritual/Divine Dark

Gray

Acceptable A

Negative__ Dark____Gray____A___P____A____Gray____Dark__ Positive

Acceptable A

Gray

Horizontal- Human Dark

The center is perfect.

I know these are the right tools to unite us and protect the future moments of the planet. It is simple but not easy to do. We need to understand why oneness only betters in time to enhance the Rubik's Cube of Knowledge for all knowing to the center of ONE. Humanity needs to go back to working on the inner self together with members of the opposite sex. This is the correct way towards the center. This will keep the nucleus of the family together. The tighter and the more organized we get with the inside skills of how the processes work, the better we will be with conversation skills, writing skills and the skill to make the perfect choice. The awareness develops to uncover the system in the family and this leads to justice for oneself. We will then have arrived at a world of perpetuity, with no poverty, racism, diseases or divorce. This will provide a baseline for food, water, shelter and transportation for everybody, everywhere through the correct education.

Chapter Twelve:

The Perfect God-self, Language and Hieroglyphics

Language can, will and has defined God, and its parts lead back to the self. What we don't see in the completed language is the part of the whole we are left without that makes a cog. The wheel turns fine, but we don't see the nail buried beneath the surface. We are missing some rules on the inside. We are not aware of messing up the wholeness of the process, so our thinking is off.

The way the language starts is at the center in the human side horizontally and the middle of the spiritual side vertically. Each word starts midway, directly equal in the center's center of the stick! Because life (self), language and God are the same in the middle of the stick to the center where they are the same but different (the middle is spiritual and the center is human) and are the equality of each other perfectly of a male, female and self are equal together is a perfect human, horizontally they make a complete human. God and human vertically make a complete God all to be "one" for everything and non-physical and physical are the way all of the universe operates (includes us because we are the exact replica of the universe; the way we operate is the same) to be one of everything down to one truth for everything to one truth for everything, everywhere and everybody. Every word splits apart into an oxymoron itself, separating effortlessly into two or more parts. It has two sides, the human/outside tangible, a noun horizontal and the spiritual/inside intangible, a verb vertical. Once each single word is **split, it is seamlessly partitioned** from the inside to the outside to make it whole in the middle of the center of the word. To be completed, each side of the word and the bottom to the top by the way the word is separated to come back to itself. One way is by the intangible - the non-physical part of the word and the tangible physical part of the word connect, completing the circuit for that truth. To tighten down words use the polar opposite words connecting the whole words together making them whole.

"What Matters"

To know God's word is not just to believe, but to know the truth.

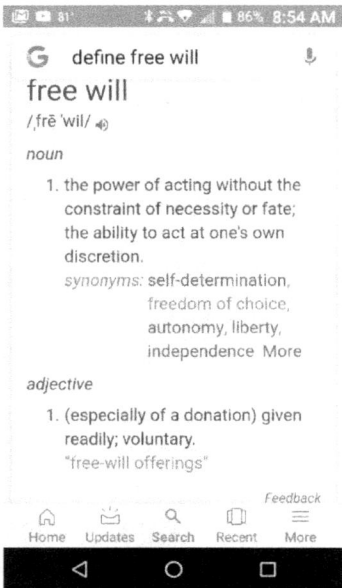

Lack of education is not knowing that the perfect human is oneself. The correct center to reach is the same as God. We can be **divided**. God is what can't be **divided**, although we are the same; He is whole and so are we, but we just don't see it. Once we see that the human side and the spiritual side are **separate** inside us, we need to bring them together in self to help see us in a flawless, supreme and complete way. We will do all this by using definition and in the definition's placement of each word to be accurate and complete. The spiritual side and human side are together inside us by the way they relate to each other and this is exactly the same as in language. We have explained how each side is the same yet different and that what is separate in the differences is also the same. This relates to Male and Female, God and Human, Language one side intangibles explained by a verb and the other side tangibles explained by a noun. In the end, through the processes, both sides are twins and start at opposite ends and come to the center's center to unite. When separated, the pieces are perfectly equal in the same way by **HOW** the sides are separated from the whole, (God) because the perfect system is God. Humanity languages are all complete; we need to uncover them by "knowing" the correct rule and regulations (may not be what we are using now). The way the whole is united is when all the proper rules and regulations are completed and used properly like when all the rules go into each single word. The law of identity -everything, everywhere and everybody all goes into itself or comes back to itself by completing the word the tangible part with the intangible part. Example: the mystical part is always intangible and found on the inside and the other side to intangible is tangible making the whole word visible by not covering anything up in the definition.

The word "consummate" has two different meanings. The first refers to sexual intercourse, as in "they consummated the marriage." The other definition refers to the act of showing a great degree of skill or flair. Once a marriage has been consummated, the human side of the definition is complete because it is possible to conceive a child. The spiritual side of the definition is showing a high degree of skill and flair.

The Bible doesn't explain who God is fully. Because the Bible is man-made, when people know who God is (they don't just believe) they typically know the self! And they have been through the portal. Using language that has been broken down correctly, the problem is that the language has not been broken down correctly.

An annulment takes place when those who have entered into marriage have done so from a mistaken human perspective. This is when individuals and communities recognize that a process has malfunctioned and must be corrected. We are meant to find God's way in each of us, to KNOW ALL inside and out. This is when an oxymoron is also a paradox.

The meanings of words work together like a perfect puzzle. An oxymoron's meaning centers around two words with definitions that might seem totally different. The insides and outsides of words can only be clearly understood when we combine the dimensions of voice, writing with proper placement of definitions. Some words have multiple meanings. The word we apply to ourselves, "humans," is an oxymoron which shows our two sides. One side is human, the other is spiritual. Together they define our position within God's way, and the perfect division between the human self and God self is the collective self.

If we were to refer to my book about the mind, body and soul versus the idea of Me Myself and I, we would be placing humans in the middle on the outside, while, as always, God occupies the center by definitions. When we explain the complete meaning of each word on each level, going seven or more degrees downward, we will discover that these meanings relate to the word's core, or "self," at every level. At all of these levels the word relates perfectly to its core, for "all equals self" and at the core is "one's self."

We as humans start life with nothing (no things), but we are complete humanly and whole spiritually. This makes us equal to God. The way we grow apart is effortless and natural; we divide, separate and split from God into human gods. We are separated such that we are human beings on the outside, and spiritual beings on the inside. We are then spilt into parts in ourselves that we don't see, and then the human race is divided by not being aware of how to unite ourselves back to God or our own selves. Ninety-nine percent of us don't know how to unite. We need to understand how the definition and its polar opposites work to bring things and people together in language. People can also be pushed apart in this way, if they don't know the system. Through this book, we now do know the system. Uniting the word is simple, but it is not easy. I will explain in detail below.

We start with one word at a time so that we understand. We need to separate the definitions for each word into two or more meanings. It is so easy to overlook the definitions themselves because the meanings are the main body of the message. Definitions are the same, but split between a noun and a verb.

The first definition of consummate is a verb; it refers to making a marriage complete through the act of sex. The second definition is an adjective and refers to someone who shows a high degree of skill and flair. Most words have two or more meanings. The word "divided" can either mean to be separated into part or to be divided in disagreement between people. When done correctly, language is divided accurately into parts to mathematical precision.

The perfect life can be found in the system of communication with ourselves which is the same for everybody. We can see this by the connected definitions in our words. See how it works backwards? The second definition in each word is the paradox, a seemingly absurd or self-contradictory statement that is actually well-founded or true. The spiritual second definition is merged together with the oxymoron. The word then comes back together inside the word itself. The two sides I don't see meeting up anytime soon.

The first and only definition of the meaning, by the way it was **split, separated, divided and partitioned by the writing and grammar rules,** becomes the completed, whole word. Each word then wholly becomes part of a meaningful sentence. Positioning the first and second definitions together, and combining them properly with rules will connect all the words together by the organized definition and rules to be in sync with the universal truth.

Most words have two or more meanings. The first is human and the second is spiritual. Almost all words are a deeper oxymoron, where the word comes back into itself by the intangibles and tangibles. This is how words work inside themselves properly. The universal truth that humanity has overlooked is the same as the second definition, to be **centered** using **an** oxymoron in each word. A human could be viewed as an oxymoron because we are both human and spirit. We can use a word like "consummate" to see how different dimensions complete a word and make it whole. The human and spiritual sides merge together, though they are polar opposites.

An oxymoron is a figure of speech in which apparently contradictory terms appear in conjunction. This is the center of the razor's edge of the human and spiritual center. We, as humans, are oxymorons. The second part of an oxymoron is the dimensional definition, or the origin of the word.

The spiritual side of the dimensional definition of **Consummate refers to** showing a high degree of skill; to be perfect, complete, supreme and flawless. This is our perception of what a God is, and the only definition is on the spiritual side. When we consummate the spiritual side of words with the human side, we are God (or god).

We use our own words from the inside to understand and organize each word within the inside world so we can understand and create another dimension to see that the mystical part of us is already complete; everything is already complete and that is why I say it works backwards; we just have to uncover how things work and what they are because they are complete - we just need to see it the correct way, the same as God. And because He put that little part in us that is the same for everybody; it is up to us to uncover all the organized knowledge in the universe regarding what is the same as Him and put it to the use He intended.

The human side of the definition of the word **Consummate** refers to the act of making a marriage complete through sexual intercourse. **The** question is how the patterns **relate together in the center of time and space.** The center of time and knowledge is the same as love and the truth because they are perfect together.

The **Consummation of God and human connects** the two above definitions. The center between the inside and the outside is exactly the same for us to uncover the center of God's plan perfectly in writing by the correct patterns. It is not to believe but to know, through mathematical perfection.

There is a deeper meaning at each step to know the second meaning of **Consummation** which connects both people and definitions to a deeper dimension. We can see by the dimensional definition when we are ready to have **a child** by the knowledge of self in space/knowledge. We are brought together into the center of love (which is inside) and the truth (which is outside) by how well we know what is in the present in the continuous now. **The deeper truth is the result of both definitions.**

Academics, spiritual leaders and religious leaders will come together as one within the app to center the human/outside and the spiritual/inside. The one, perfect plan involves knowing God's word. The pieces of a word are part of the definition that is split in half. The inside and outside of the word separate, which is the same as dividing the spiritual side within us from the human side outside of us. This causes us to be divided from God. The polar opposites of the homonyms bring us, and the parts of the word, back together. The inside and outside of the words unite the inside/spiritual with the outside/human to bring everything together in the center's center, between the inside and outside of ourselves. The sentences that are truly complete have each word perfectly. We can teach ourselves anything and everything in time and space, and love and truth. Maybe even life and death?

An **annulment in marriage usually happens because we are lacking skills such as thinking, listening, believing and knowing. These are skills of timeless wisdom and when they are properly implemented they help us to see the universal truth. If we could get this right, there would probably be a much smaller percentage of marriages ending in divorce. But how do you annul a god-child? You don't and you can't! A god cannot be** *divided, separated or split* **by the human God that created the god; we are connected for life, whether we see it or not. It is part of the inside of us, and the guide to happiness.**

This is how a community lives an unintentional lie! When we don't know how to unite the self, families, the Church, communities and countries, there will be problems. We only have one side of the truth, or just *a* truth but not the whole truth, until every word is centered in the middle. The middle is on the inside and the center is on the outside. The **Medium is** inside and the **median** is outside. We can see that language, God and the self are natural by the way all definitions fit perfectly into themselves and all together as one.

One piece of a single word is a noun (a person, place or thing) and this is the human/outside part of the word. The other piece of the same word is a verb (a phrase that describes an action) and this is on the spiritual side of the word.

So, we have a single word with a verb on the inside and a noun on the outside. For example, let's take a word like "split." A synonym for this word is "separate" and a synonym of that word is "divide". Once we define one word, we **split the definition into two parts, separating the definition into spiritual and human parts.** Then we **divide the parts on the inside and the outside and partition all the parts back into the center's center of itself to be complete as one whole word.**

We need to unravel and organize to see there are no secrets in their word by definition. The human definition of a word is synced up with the spiritual definition of the same word, in a similar yet different definition. They are separate, but the same. The whole word has two pieces, with a noun on the outside and a verb on the inside. Each part splits the definition into two or more meanings and is divided either by the human side or the spiritual side. The word is divided into parts in order to make it a completed whole. God is the completed, whole meaning as itself, where everything and everybody fit together **IN ITSELF**. The instruction are all in the organized definition of what to do next, leading into itself all by using the definitions for the words themselves.

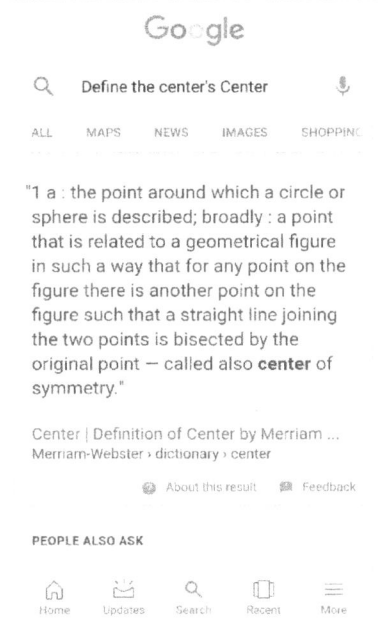

Two people's different meanings can both be true by **separating** a word into the human and spiritual sides. When the word is apart from the human and spiritual sides, this can cause division.

The first definition of the word "divide" means, "to separate or be separated into parts." The second definition has to do with disagreeing.

The sweet spot here is in between the center of the middle, known as the center's center.

When we use both sides of the truth, we find that everything is perfectly equal in the center to "KNOW." We are then on the right path to find and understand God.

When we fully understand how love and truth, and the spiritual and human work together perfectly as one, this can be world-changing. This is the center of the system, literally, analytically, and philosophically. Imagine if we all found God inside first.

In the past, I didn't know what I know now, which is how to get to the universal truth. We all need to understand how God, love, and the truth are the same. This will help us to unravel the misunderstanding of God in our minds. I now see through the confusion and understand life's plan is obtainable when looking at the whole, complete self/god that is in each of us.

Until the complete meaning of a word is known, it cannot be understood. When each word is put together properly with others, we are closer to reaching the whole truth. Everything else is just a justification or a belief or a lie to oneself. We do not know until we see this is the breakdown of God from the whole.

The idea here is to prevent the wrong truth from appearing. We can have good intentions, but still mishaps occur. When all worlds with each word in the universe line up properly, we can and will see the perfect truth. Now imagine with this new way of learning to see the perfect world, minimal abortions, adoptions and divorces with few gay marriages only because they "KNOW" and understand why the LGBTQ communities simply aren't "equal" because the same side doesn't fit together in the center to be all-knowing , a complete human and to achieve God status the perfect human. The provable truth where everything fits together perfectly. God's plan starts at the opposite ends of the stick. A man and a woman knowing each other naturally and learning about one another helps them to become each one whole human and reach the center's middle equal to God. This is part of what it means to know the God-self.

The dimensions of definitions are in front of us to use for everything. Choosing a better thought and wanting to understand is to be on the right side of thought. If we only use our human side, or our spiritual side, we are often wrong in our thinking and it can turn into justification. We're lying to ourselves. In many ways, we as people aren't over the need to be right. Only using one side is wrong, though you may think you're right. When you use both sides at the same time, you are truly right.

If parents were spiritually educated, it is possible that we could all grow up with the parents who had us in an almost perfect environment. Our parents may even become soulmates in this way. We are all equal and need each other to survive and to live the perfect life, humanly and spiritually. When we understand we are the replica of the way the universe works, the spiritual side will reveal itself by language when we complete it.

What we know on the inside is connected through inner technology to love and truth by the breadth of time where the center is all the answers. In the center of time, where everything is equal to one whole and complete God, **time is divided between the spiritual/human and the non-physical/physical.**

For the universe, a human self has all the answers with God's help because we as humans are only God part of the time; God is God all the time. Again our perception is incorrect; the proper religion is to add to the self that which is in all religions to find the answers to the self. The patterns of everything unite mathematically to include the universe, where the answers are in each question. Once we know and graduate from believing, we see properly, guided by the abstract the way they are separated, divided and split perfectly from God. The whole universe is a perfect jigsaw puzzle.

From the whole word, we go to the **center,** outside/physical world on the human side to split the definition in half to break the meaning down into parts of the whole. Again, from the "same" word on the other side, we go to the middle inside the non-physical/spiritual side to divide into two or more groups. After we consummate them in self, we partition them by the way they all relate, using polar opposite words to the same middle inside and the same center outside to find the wholeness in itself. Everything has its own proper place.

By definition, science and religion are the same, just at opposite ends of the stick are explained perfectly by philosophy. When you understand that, you will understand that God's plan starts with men and women. God is all places, all things and all people. He is everything and nothing at the same time. He is energy, sound, light, the non-physical, the physical, the spiritual, the human, inside and outside, language, the self. God is all that and everything that can be. It is important to not overlook any of the process in life. God is wider and deeper and higher than anyone can see.

He is responsible for even the smallest pieces, and the completed whole. Everyone and everything are the same to Him, together or separate, because it is all of the same God. Whether we perceive it to be something or nothing, it is Him. We split all the pieces, separate all the parts, and divide it into sections, then put it back together, like a jigsaw puzzle. The pieces, parts and sections, by how they are partitioned in our language, are the key to knowing the whole plan.

The simple words inside and outside cover almost all the knowledge in the universe. When it comes to the outside/inside, one can be on one side and in the other at the same time. One can't go **outside** the universe or back **inside** their mother's womb. Solid truths for what is possible to know in the world go by "what is" on and in the inside and outside. This is the universal truth. Now, if we KNOW this is THE truth, not a part of the truth or one side of the truth but the whole truth, with the correct perception, can't we organize and go together to complete the patterns and achieve any and all truths with good intent?

Writing by the proper placement of centered completed definitions (here is where we use the proper completed rules and regulations that are not complete yet) and figuring out how to articulate proper placement is extremely difficult, because it's in each and every word and is the same for all words. It is extremely easy to overlook in a word, for each word starts in the definition (the spiritual part is the verb and the human part is the noun). How the word splits in itself (spiritual and human, noun and verb) is the key. The proper placement in writing is having the rules and regulations complete (where they are not now). They'd all go into one word not the other way around. For each word that has more than one definition, one is human, which is a noun, and the other is a verb, which is spiritual. With this method we will break down spirituality and faith. The writing will lead us not for us to lead the writing, in the definition, the circle represents both sides, a picture something physical and/or, in writing, non-physical. In the definition, each word represents the non-physical which is the writing side which is most likely the intangible side, something that you can't take a picture of. The physical means the opposite; if we can take a picture of it, it's usually tangible or the same as the physical side. It's probably physical or non-physical, perfectly separated in half of the world and word's meaning. Could it be between inside and outside in the same way? We can go a little deeper and that is the spiritual side, added to the non-physical inside (which is the same) and to the human outside, which is the other side. Added to physical separately, they will fit perfectly, narrowing down each side to the centered truth and love for each side. In the middle of the centers are all God's perfect answers. There are a few different ways the outside can be defined. Blue: what is tangible is also a physical place one can touch. **Blue**: what is intangible, non-physical and on the outside but that can't be touched. The perfect language to reveal God's word fits together by how they relate and by the inside and outside of the word to the center of the middle. The word's spiritual and human sides relate to the truth in the center, along with the non-physical and physical. These sides are the makeup of each word to define the truth in God's word.

Define **OUTSIDE** (Later tie in spiritual and human). Blue, Blue the human side, **blue spiritual outside. Or picture to help identify:**

Noun:

1. The outer, surface, or part; exterior: outside of the house needs painting. (PHYSICAL OUTSIDE)

2. The external aspect or appearance. (PHYSICAL OUTSIDE)

3. The space without or beyond an enclosure, institution, boundary, etc. A prisoner about to resume life on the outside. (NON Physical) THE SPACE IS INTANGIBLE.

4. A position away or farther away from the inside or center: The horse on the outside finished second. (PHYSICAL).

5. An outside passenger or place on a coach or other vehicle. (PHYSICAL OUTSIDE)

6. Northern Canada and Alaska. (Sometimes initial capital letter) the settled or more populous part of Canada or the U.S.? These are proper nouns the (PHYSICAL OUTSIDE) PLACES.

Adjective:

7. Being, acting, done, or originating beyond an enclosure, boundary, etc.: outside noises; news from the outside world. (NON) WRITING INTANGIBLE (INTANGIBLE?)

8. Situated on or pertaining to the outside; exterior; external: an outside television antenna.

9. Situated away from the inside or center; farther or farthest away from the inside or center: the outside lane. **(PHYSICAL OUTSIDE) Lane.**

10. **Not belonging to or connected with a specified institution, society, etc.: outside influences; outside help.   (NON) INFLUENCES INTANGIBLE.**

11. **Extremely unlikely or remote: an outside chance for recovery.**

12. **Extreme or maximum: an outside estimate (NON)**

13. Being in addition to one's regular work or duties: an outside job?

14. Working on or assigned to the outside, as of a place or organization: an outside man to care for the grounds. **(PHYSICAL OUTSIDE)**

In Baseball: (Of a pitched ball) passing, but not going over, home plate on the opposite the batter: The fastball was high and outside. **(physical) TANGIBLE ball.**

Adverb:

16. **On** or to **the outside, exterior, or space without: Take the dog outside.** (NON) SPACE intangible but the dog is tangible? (But not in)

17. **In or to an area that is removed from or beyond a given place or region: The country's inhabitants seldom travel outside. (NON) outside but people are physical.**

18. On or toward the outside of: There was a noise outside the door. (PHYSICAL SOUND)

19. **Beyond the confines or borders of: visitors from outside the country. (NON) line.**

20. **With the exception of; aside from: She has no interests outside her work. (NON)**

Idioms:

21. "At the" outside, at the utmost limit; at the maximum: There weren't more than ten at the outside.

22. Outside of, other than; exclusive of; excepting: Outside of us, no one else came to the party. (NON)

Origin of outside:

First recorded in 1495–1505.

Synonyms for outside **ANTONYMS inside.**

Noun, Adjective, Adverb, Preposition, Idioms are all part of the whole. The question is can we match up the opposites?

Define **INSIDE:** (PHYSICAL INSIDE), **(NON-PHYSICAL) and Spiritual are both dark red for now.**

Preposition:

1. On the inner side or part of; within: inside the circle; inside the envelope. **(PHYSICAL INSIDE)**

2. **Prior to the elapse of; within: He promised to arrive inside an hour. (NON-PHYSICAL)**

Adverb:

3. In or into the inner part: Please go inside. **(PHYSICAL INSIDE)**

4. Indoors: They play inside on rainy days. **(PHYSICAL INSIDE)**

5. **Within one's heart, reason, etc.; by true nature; basically: I know inside that he's not guilty. Inside, she's really very shy. (NON)**

6. **Slang. In prison. (NON) SPEECH.**

Noun: (PHYSICAL INSIDE), PERSON, PLACE OR THING:

7. The inner or internal part; interior: the inside of the house. **(PHYSICAL INSIDE)**

8. The inner side or surface: the inside of the hand; He pinned the money to the inside of his jacket. **(PHYSICAL OUTSIDE)**

9. Usually insides. Informal. The inner parts of the body, especially the stomach and intestines: The coffee scalded my insides. **(PHYSICAL INSIDE) BUT NON-PHYSICAL AS WELL ONE CAN'T TAKE A PICTURE?**

10. **A select or inner circle of power, prestige, etc.: a man on the inside. (NON)**

11. The shortest of several parallel, curving tracks or lanes; the part of an oval track closest to the inner rail: The horse came up fast on the inside. **(PHYSICAL INSIDE)**

12. **the inward nature, mind, feelings, etc. (NON)**

13. **Slang. Confidential or secret information. (NON)**

14. An inside passenger or place in a coach, carriage, etc. **(PHYSICAL INSIDE)**

Adjective:

15. situated or being "on or in" the inside; interior; internal: an inside seat. **(PHYSICAL INSIDE)**

16. **acting, employed, done, or originating within a building or place: He used to work on the dock but now he has an inside job. (NON)?**

17. **derived from the inner circle of those concerned in and having private knowledge of a situation: inside information. (NON)**

18. Baseball. (of a pitched ball) passing between home plate and the batter: The pitch was low and inside. **(PHYSICAL INSIDE) ON THE BLUE I ANSWERED IT THE WAY!**

Idioms: (NONPHYSICAL)

19. **Inside of, Informal. Within the space or period of: Our car broke down again inside of a mile. (NON) MEASURED SPACE?**

20. **Inside out (NON)**

21. With the inner side reversed to face the outside. **(PHYSICAL INSIDE)**

22. Thoroughly, completely: She knew the work inside out. (NON) COMPLETE!

Origin of Inside (NON):

Middle English word dating back to 1350–1400; see origin at in, side[1]

Synonyms for Inside:

23. Inside, interior both refer to the inner part or space within something. **Inside is a common word and is used with reference to things of any size**, small or large: the inside of a pocket. Interior, somewhat more formal, denotes the inner part or the space or regions within; it usually suggests considerable size or extent, and sometimes a richness of decoration: the interior of a country, of the earth, of a cathedral.

Antonyms for Inside:

24. for inside **outside, see it is everything in between in all ways!** MAINLY HOW THEY RELATE TO THE CENTER.

25. . Outside, exterior.

Our perception is incorrect because of the way we as humans are processing language. The correct direction is in-between from the inside to the outside and back to the center of itself. I think the world is spilt perfectly between inside and outside. Spiritually, the definitions break down to one God and to the part in us that is the same where we all unite to be **equal** as one race together, the human race. When we learn how to merge the **non-physical/physical and the spiritual/human with the inside/outside,** we can know God, love, truth, space and time. The merging is the universe's secret, which can be found in the center/middle of us and in language by what is overlooked. It stands to reason that when one finds it through love, one must be able to express it through and in writing. It will provide us all the answers embedded in the language. One must know God's truth to see that we are God, too.

Language is broken down between the inside and outside, narrowed down to the non-physical and physical and then tightened down to tie the spiritual inside and the human outside. Now, imagine what happens when we complete the word on the inside and outside using these factors in the correct order. When all words have the same precision in life's jigsaw puzzle from the way they interact together, all will be answered to make it whole in perfect sentences. When opposite words are across from each other **in** their proper places **on** the opposite ends of the stick, this adds to the meaning of a single word. Then, our perception will have to match with the word. The "parts" are next: the word is **split** by these pieces so that both sides have an inside verb and an outside noun. We can use any word that has the four main definitions for the app. The processes and patterns will be the same for any word. It seems as if all words relate to the whole. All the parts, pieces and sections of the rules and regulations break down from the whole perfectly, each piece, part and section going back to itself where the whole is never broken, just split, separated and divided properly and perfectly.

For any **single word,** the pieces, parts and sections of the word make it whole so it can be partitioned from the inside to the outside. This makes the word complete on one side and whole on the other, making the wholeness of the word. We can use **any word** for this purpose. Let's use **piece** and play with the process. Any word's meaning typically starts with a noun, verb or adjective. The first definition is usually the **noun** which is the outside meaning, or the visual. The second definition is typically a **verb** which is the inside meaning. **These are the hidden secrets! The mystical and invisible/intangible** are waiting to be visible or tangible and they are in plain sight, but are secret until all the pieces and parts in a word in the definition are together, working simultaneously to be one whole, perfect word. The definition, for the most part, has two or more definitions in it.

S.C.C.U. (Self, Community, Country, and Universe) partitioned from the inside and also on the outside that are broken down properly. How they relate together is key but look at it as if all is on the inside or on the outside. Be sure to look at how they are broken down "by the inside and outside" instead of all just inside of the S.C.C.U. or just the outside of the S.C.C.U. First, split the inside and then split the outside in half. **Then separate** by "what is" non-physical (inside) and physical (outside) and then **divide** by the spiritual inside and the human outside. The goal here is to first unite in the mind, which is all of us. The bodies will follow, and the soul will lead in an egalitarian society. God's plan is for us to know ourselves. The Universe is the key and holds all the correct answers. It is in plain sight, but it's not what we see; it's what we don't see, even though it is right in front of us.

There are two main parts to understanding our language as the pieces and parts are separated and put back together in itself to be made whole. We all miss how our language becomes whole. God is intangible as well as non-physical and humans are tangible and physical. The complete man and woman together are one human inside metaphysically making up a whole human. What make up the universe are things and living things and each have an inside and outside. Notice how God is intangible and non-physical. If he was visible or tangible this would be where he comes back to himself! He would be human... Notice how humans are tangible, visible and physical where it comes back to itself! This is the full circle - that which is both together the inside intangible, where non-physical and invisible is one side and the other side is the outside the human side tangible, physical and visible making up both sides or the full circle. And notice how the universe is made up of things and living things! Where this too is correct and comes back to itself, us. God is intangible and non-physical. Humans are tangible and physical. The universe is made up of things and living things and each of these comes back to itself. This goes deeper into explaining our language and how it separates and comes together with all the pieces. God is the perfect human and the perfect human is God where it comes back to itself and this explains the whole universe in writing. Non-physical is one side of the universe. We can try to live on the spiritual side alone if we choose because we are made up with both sides - spiritual and human sides - and so is the universe made up of both sides. Just as important to the physical side of the universe we do live on as well is the spiritual side, which is equally shared and explained through definitions from the definition I defined non-physical "'not relating or concerning the body" physical I Define 1. relating to the body 2. Relating to things perceived through the senses and opposed to the mind, tangible or concrete. I am guided by definitions of how the universe is broken down and how we participate in that. Men and women both have a spiritual side and both have a human side. The same as we (outside) are/our (inside) in language we have an inside and an outside the same as are language (us, our language and God are all the same).

The four secrets that are sacred (connected with God) make everything whole.

1) God and humans are the **NON-PHYSICAL Inside / PHYSICAL outside** 2) Men and women are the human outside and spiritual inside, 3) inside/outside, or one side, 4) **Non-physical/Spiritual inside/PHYSICAL/human outside** and outside / inside. **The first definition is** inside /inside and **the second definition is the** outside/outside. **The third definition is the** spiritual inside / **human outside** or one side and the fourth definition is the outside / inside or one side. These definitions, organized correctly, will pinpoint any truth. The four **definitions** are all linked together in a single word, simultaneously!

Timeless Wisdom App: Rubik's Cube of Knowledge.

Both the spiritual inside and the human outside are the center of both. Together, this will create the truth for any issue or subject, for anything and everything everywhere, to include its timing as well. All the knowledge in the world will be organized by one word which has the same patterns for all words when we get one completely right. Time and knowledge are centered together perfectly, united with the past, present and future and embedded in each definition when we know how to center the horizontal and vertical for accuracy of the present moment of the word.

Piece Definitions: The foundation in organized placement of completed words by definitions as part of the whole.

A) (spiritual inside) the children took turns piecing together each other's jigsaw puzzle (inside) assemble something from individual parts (outside) a portion of an object or of material, produced by cutting, tearing, or breaking the "whole" **(human outside) a piece of** cheese of something. **(in/**in out**/out).**

B) the children took turns piecing together each other's jigsaw puzzle, **a piece of** cheese a portion of an object or of material, produced by cutting, tearing, or breaking the **assemble something from individual parts (in/out/**out/in).

C) A portion of an object or of material, produced by cutting, tearing, or breaking the **assemble something from individual parts the children took turns piecing together each other's jigsaw puzzle, a piece of** cheese (out/in/ **In/ out).**

Three sides: Spiritual side

1) **A piece of** cheese the children took turns piecing together each other's jigsaw puzzle   (**human to** spiritual one side) **and vice versa** .

   A. The children took turns piecing together each other's jigsaw **a piece of** cheese

2) A portion of an object or of material, produced by cutting, tearing, or breaking the **assemble something from individual parts** (outside **to** Inside one side) **and vice versa**

A. Assemble something from individual parts a portion of an object or of material, produced by cutting, tearing, or breaking the ...assemble something from individual parts - **the children took turns piecing together each other's jigsaw puzzle.**

3) **The children took turns piecing together each other's jigsaw puzzle:** assemble something from individual parts a portion of an object or of material, produced by cutting, tearing, or breaking the) "whole **a piece of** cheese or something." (**in**/in red/ out/**out** blue) **and vise verse.**

A. **A piece of** cheese or something a portion of an object or of material, produced by cutting, tearing, or breaking the **assemble something from individual parts: the children took turns piecing together each other's jigsaw puzzle**

The definition's placement of the single word will define God's word in a set of words. What He says is the complete truth. We need to figure out how our language does this.

The pieces, synonyms and homonyms of the word Piece:

The word from the (out to in) outside opposite of the word **"piece"** is the word "whole." The inside double polar opposite word to "whole" outside in "**is all the parts and pieces**" (inside to out) is us and the universe. **The** inside **with a verb is the main part of a sentence together on the** outside **to make the word whole with a** noun completing **"wholeness"** and is described in an adjective **all inside and outside in four parts** in a single word. I don't know if this is true?

Piece: the children took turns piecing together each other's jigsaw puzzle: assemble something from individual parts (one side red). **Peace** freedom from disturbance; quiet and tranquility **you can while away an hour or two in peace and seclusion** (one side **blue human outside**). In some ways makes a complete word?

The word is a part of an anagram. How can a computer figure this out? Could be zeros and ones organized. Any other rules and regulations I'm missing?

Peace synonyms: tranquility, calm, restfulness, peace and quiet, "peacefulness", quiet, quietness.
Privacy, solitude.
Piece synonyms: law and order, lawfulness, order, "peacefulness", peaceableness, harmony, nonviolence.
The center is where the synonyms match perfectly on the word inside piece and outside peace is "peacefulness" to get to the center's center of peace inside and piece by piece peace on the outside.

When we piece something together on the inside, we become whole. "Peace," on the other hand can refer to peace on the outside world, as well as the inside world. Most words have something lacking in them, keeping them from being complete and whole.

Homonyms are words that sound alike, but that have different meanings. They have the same spelling, but their meanings are different.

There is an opposite word for each word on the inside and outside to make it whole. The patterns to complete the language are missing to make it whole in God's way, which is perfect.

When all words in the dictionary have the same precision in life's jigsaw puzzle by the way they interact together, all will be answered in perfect sentences the way we are to live. When opposite words are across from each other **in** their proper place **on** the opposite ends of the stick (up and down, **down and up**) to add to the meaning of a single word. We will have our perception match up with the word on what is **IN** and **ON** the inside to out, outside in and **in** to in, side to side **out to out, end to end, back to front, front to back**, all the "pieces" of the word are completed in this faze. The "parts" are next the word **split** by these pieces 1) inside and outside 2) **verb inside** and noun outside equal in the split in halve half on both sides **inside** a verb and **outside** a noun perfectly split 50% of all words meaning. Use any word that has the four main definitions as all do for the app using any word for this purpose example.

The word has a polar opposite. I think these are great examples as to why language is perfect; we should leave it in.

The oxymoron is inside of the word **ITSELF.** For the most part, each word has a noun on the outside. The human/outside part is split in half from the other side of the word, which is the inside or the verb. **When one recognizes all things and living things can be explained with the correct patterns of "ONE" word.**

This also shows how our language could be perfect if all ways lead to how to become one. Unfortunately, belief often gets in the way of knowing. The "divine" outside is the church (just God, not our interpretation of God) and a part of us inside the self is divine and in writing they are all the same. This is what 99% of people are missing. God, writing and the self are the same. We just need to see the way they are identical in all languages by definition. People have missed this for years; they don't see that we live in a perfect world and how it is up to us. God put this playbook in you to use your head and heart together as one. We and the universe are one after it comes back to itself. The system is right in front of us. Our language is the organized Bible with instructions when the definitions are complete and whole.

What can a language do with all words when they are together properly? We can know everything in time, understand love, know the honest truth, and explain God in all ways. This is an effort in togetherness, for people to help each other and ourselves for the future and our children's children. When the center's center of the definition is built, we have the correct foundation for learning with and from the **"whole."**

The word's whole meaning is in "**itself**" "**the law of identity.**" The word is defined and provided after the pieces, parts and sections show how a word comes back to itself from both ends to the middle inside of the center outside to unite the intangibles and tangibles, the visible and invisibles. This is the horizontal way of coming to the center from both ends back to itself in the center. The vertical way, from top to bottom and the bottom to the top, achieves completeness in the definition to the word, hopefully to make it whole and come back to **itself. The three words split, separate and divide** into pieces, parts and sections in any and all ways to make the completed whole "definition" in the word. When each word and each sentence work together flawlessly and are united with the **same correct** pattern, every word on the planet is on the same page. Languages work in the same way as people or God; once you understand language, you may understand yourself and God at the same time. I did it backwards, and it works in the same way. Everybody will understand God, us and language in writing from the inside out and the outside in. We will then know how to defend against disease and divorce by uniting in oneness because there is nothing we can't find the truth about on the outside from what we find on the inside.

The "word" is broken down from the "whole" and then "**split**" into one half, with a verb side and a noun. Nouns can be divided into two main categories: **proper** nouns and **common** nouns. The only difference is what's capitalized. Both nouns can be plural by adding suffixes at the end but still can explain everything in "time" as it happens with the right organization. God designed everything from fragments to come into one God in complete **"WHOLENESS."** Our perception takes a while to see the brilliance correctly as we do live in a perfect world. We already live in a perfect world and it's up to us to live it, learn it, love it and KNOW it. The word is "separated" by the inside and outside and is also **"divided"** by the spiritual inside and the **human outside.** This can be categorized into **seven basic groups.** 1) Pieces 2) Parts and 3) Sections **of** and **in** the word are the completed whole word on "one side" of and in **the human side which is the horizontal side that is completed after tying in the** physical side **of the word.** Using only one side is only part of any truth (spiritual side or human side) and it causes one to lie to themselves, usually without knowing; they just aren't seeing the correct processes to the whole truth. The correct "pieces and parts" help us to understand that the spiritual side is built in all the way up **on** the word and **split** all the way down **in** the word to the center. It is built all the way down in the word and **separated** on and in each side, all the way up in the word to the word's middle. It is spilt and separated, to be divided **in** one side **of** the word and to the center's center **on** the other one side **of** the word. **When the spiritual side (the vertical side) of the word's meaning ties in with the** non-physical side, **we are almost complete in all ways.** The center's middle of the universal truth to the millisecond of completeness is perfect in organized writing. It involves using few skills after what is correct is defined in one whole system, and "KNOWING" is merged with the skills of timeless wisdom with God's language skills. We can connect the dots to the perfect, whole, complete self but we need to put it in writing for our children's children.

The vertical side is the spiritual inside and it completes the whole word back to itself. The next four groups are: **4) Segment 5) Constant 6) Partitioned 7) Definition. This refers to the Whole word** once undivided, not separated or split. This is to KNOW the processes without a cog in the wheel to the center's middle of perfection to find the whole truth by what we find on the inside which is all the same in perfect sentences. The answers come back to themselves for the scientific proof. The same way we are God; everything comes back to oneself where the whole universe is one.

We start at the whole on the outside and break everything down from there. When we achieve perfection, we have no missing parts, members or elements in the organization of our language. We start on the inside, a complex unity organized of parts fitting or working together, with the outside as one in a coherent system with the complete amount to the entire system. We then have a whole word that is totally complete. We can leave it open for improvement by not shutting down thoughts.

Let's start another word because the patterns are the same for all words. I envision that the app will have all words complete with a perfect foundation type in the word and we will fill in the blanks. This will open up the possibilities to tighten down any truth. This will add on to the definitions and the understanding of the way it is split, separated and divided from the whole to see life's truth. **The sum of all the parts is equal to the whole. The way all the pieces and parts fit into itself is also the whole (the whole being self, God or any language).**

Verb inside 1. **Verb: part; 3rd person present: parts; past tense: parted; past participle: parted; gerund or present participle: parting** (of two things) move away from each other. **"his lips parted in a smile" and 2)** divide to leave a central space. **"at that moment the mist parted"**

Adverb noun 1. to some extent, partly (often used to contrast different parts of something)."the city is now part slum, part consumer paradise"

Are the adverbs in the definition out/in or **out**/in?

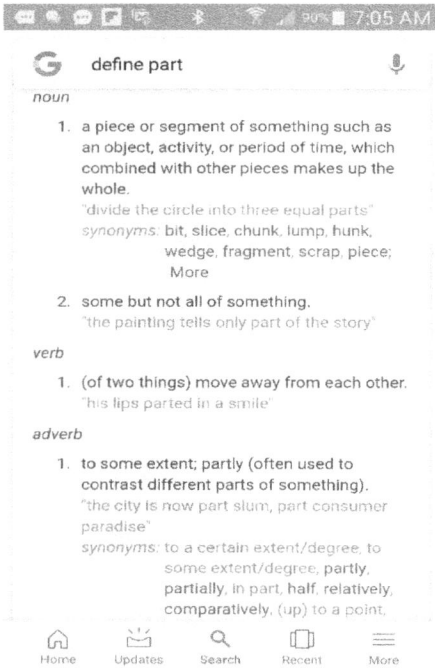

ONE SIDE has two or more definitions outside **noun** a word is the nouns (other than pronoun) used to identify any of a class of people, place, or thing **common noun,** or to name a particular one of these **proper nouns.** The part of the definition on the noun outside **for** the word **part** the **plural** noun outside 1. a piece or segment of something such as an object, activity, or period of time, which combined with other pieces makes up the whole. 1**"divide the circle into three equal parts.** 2. some but not all of something. 2**"the painting tells only part of the story"**

Each part **ONE SIDE has two or more definitions** inside a word is used as a verb (a word that is not conventionally used a verb typically a noun) "any English noun can be i (past tense), but some are more resistant than others". The word **part** inside the word is a "verb"; the definition is **in** the word of two things) move away from each other. **"his lips parted in a smile", 2ᵃ⁾** divide to leave a central space. **"at that moment the mist parted."**

Each **ONE SIDE has two or more definitions: adjective:** a word or phrase naming an attribute, added to or grammatically related to a noun to modify or describe it. The part of the definition to describe the word **on adjective**

definition for part: (inside) (outside). Add in later pronouns and the rest of the rules. When we complete this for the app:

Each Part **ONE SIDE has two or more definitions:** adverb Part a word or phrase that modifies or qualifies an adjective, verb, or other adverb or a word group, expressing a relation of place, time, circumstance, manner, cause, degree, etc. (e.g., *gently, quite, then, there*). noun 1. to some extent; partly (often used to contrast different parts of something)."the city is now part slum, part consumer paradise."

Now imagine in the app there is yellow with a word. We just change one word at the top and automatically it finds all the meaning of the in and out. The placement is organized by the non-physical and physical, the spiritual inside and **human outside.** In all ways, the rules and regulations work together as one and this will find any truth. The app will store every word to keep us from lying to ourselves. Using time lapse photography, it will store the completed definitions to make the language perfect and organized, just like how the perfect race is the human race. It will be reimaged with full academic completeness to redefine God as being in the self, and this will be explained in and by a language to make sure it is correct in the use of definitions split by nouns outside and verbs inside into a oxymoron's oxy (inside) and morons (outside) into the middle of the center so all the constants in each word is used. Non-physical (inside) physical (outside) intangible (inside) tangibles (outside) invisible (inside) visible (outside) it is what we don't know about the word to obtain God's word is what we should be working on together. Because when we "KNOW" we got it correct is when the "ONE" possible truth comes out after the process of elimination has been made.

The app will be a system that completes words and sentences for the whole center of truth in everybody, no matter the language, though English for now. It will use the non-physical part and everything by the physical part, where everywhere with time is explained together as being the same thing.

We will merge an online dictionary with definitions and all the rules and regulations to each word as it **splits** in half to find the inside verb and the other half, which is the outside noun. It splits into an oxymoron in **itself** and finds the polar opposite word to match. This will be done using the inside to outside opposite word in a sentence with the correct noun and verb for wholeness. The word will be complete with correct definition, using the physical and non-physical to **separate** the word by what is in writing or by whether a picture can be taken of it. The single word is then **divided** by what is human and spiritual. When we have the SSD right, all sides are split perfectly; add this back in because God is equal across the board. Meaning we/us are equal when we tighten them together, we will find the answers God has been praying for us to find .

There is only one reality based on the "truth." The question is, is it all right for people of the same sex to have an intimate, sexual relationship with each other? The reason why I'm asking isn't to know personally what you think, feel or believe it is ... And if you believe it's possible we are working against the universe. To be equal. We will use definitions for each truth for argument's sake. Let's see what we uncover.

There are no boundaries; we will discuss love, truth, the biological, and even God. What we all know to be true is that same sex couples can't procreate. Maybe they don't want kids but starting out with a justification is not the truth. So females typically have two of the same kinds of sex chromosomes, XX. Males typically have different kinds of sex chromosomes, XY. The exceptions are cases of XX males or XY females, or other syndromes.

Natural selection cannot explain homosexuality. But biology may be able to explain innate reasoning. Homosexuality is when an individual is sexually attracted to someone of their same gender. Males are referred to as being gay, while women are referred to as lesbians.

Men and women see things differently from the start and act from the opposite ends of emotions, using the sliding scale of growth. They must reach the center to ultimately see and understand the complete self and to make each soul whole. To be one is to see oneness from the inside to a high percentage of what is the same as God or self. The higher one goes in learning the five other senses, seeing, listening, thinking, believing and knowing, the closer they are to finding their complete self which is in the center of both sexes. The process is all the same for each sense to come back to itself by the use of a man and a woman. One can know this, but until all the senses are complete, they cannot see it. One hasn't made it to God until the emotions and the mind are complete. We usually overlook something, thinking we have put all the pieces together.

To know male and female, God and human, leaves no room for any deviations like LGBTTQQAIAAP, because this is clearly a human choice, nothing else. Now if, in fact, we can prove God is the perfect human on the ground (we need to know the Ground God inside and outside before we can know who God is in the sky - the truth about death on Earth and where we go would help in knowing God in the sky) and to help prove this use the LGBT communities to help make a case. God and human are a dichotomy and start from the opposite ends of the stick but the sliding scale ends up in the middle to connect and become complete to be one with the universe, where they end up being the same. Using God, language, and self to explain how everything comes together in the universe as one by bringing men and women together in all ways. It uses the same process as God and human because together men and women become one metaphysically to one human to connect to oneself and to be a God in knowledge. The man gets this knowledge naturally by being with a woman and vice versa, equally so. When timeless wisdom is implemented we live a life of Heaven on Earth. Following the wisdom and patterns of the universe, the opposites come around to one, tangible and intangible, physical and non-physical, men and women, God and human... polar opposite words put together. Breaking down the universe comes down to one thing... a child... and both sides of a same sex relationship can't do that. The truth is without justification: one side is a truth and a lie in place when the same sex is on the other side. We are spiritual on the inside, we are human on the outside...but we start from the opposite ends and learn to be a perfect human and grow to be or know God with the help of the opposite sex. Both are the truth, but one side is a lie when the same sex is together. The same when using language... on one side we use a noun and on the other side we use a verb. The nuggets and diamond are in the middle and this tells us the truth. All that is right and correct is not in the patterns of the universe.

We are both inside that which is to **"see"**, NOT BE metaphysical one male and female to the center of self is to each know God-self. The mind works differently based on gender, but it works the same when God status for both is achieved. Where does one receive this knowledge when with the same sex? The better chance to know God is with the opposite sex and the overall purpose of humanity is to know oneself by narrowing down to self, which is God. You can't reach the same non-physical or intangible part of the universe with the opposite sex because the gender is the same. The non-physical and intangible can only be changed by a growth of knowledge, getting to see how to live in the present moment. The spiritual side of our human side is literally written out and embedded in our dictionary. Everything is the same everywhere in time and our Bible is proof that it works backwards. The question is, are our bibles what God wanted them to be? This way is knowing God the human way. I am trying to show how we have all we need inside to find it. We needs to be with the opposite sex so we can know the part of the intangibles, to see with the mind what we are missing. If we have all we need inside, and God is within me, then I don't need the opposite sex to see it. But it is very difficult because men and women together don't even get it you may require a justification to be gay.

The gender thing is the biggest ingredient and a major key to defining God. The most misunderstood thing about God is that one needs to be God before one can know God. The proof is in the way everything goes together perfectly, starting with how God and humans are explained in an educated way. The way we as humans come back to ourselves, along with everything else, is required to be a complete God is to know oneself. This is physical, human and outside, horizontal to the center. The vertical part of the God/human is the non-physical or intangibles inside the spiritual to the middle of the center. The center of the vertical and horizontal makes us the completed, whole, centered god.

Yes, human is both God (inside) and human (outside) but I am God (spirit) first. God is also how everything works in perfect order of the inside and outside. People and things in the universe are in perfect order in writing. We can see this in how God is made up from a man and woman. The processes of one have to be the same where we look over what the difference is and miss what is the same. This is what it means to be asleep spiritually.

When you know God at that time, you can make that decision about love, as we can love any man, women or child we want to in the proper way. The guide to life is the organization of man, woman and child, the family. When only one side is applied (two women or two men being together) we are disrupting the flow of the universe because we are not equal and when only one side is used, spiritual or human, it is a direct lie to oneself. This is the same as a divorce or not getting over the need to be right or not getting over a fear all in the process to know God! Self can't see.

Men and women are important keys to know how God works. Look at it from the other way: start from the whole God and then the human god is split perfectly in half to a man and woman. We need to add on to God's perception. A small part of every human inside is God because he is multidimensional because he is divine and can't be split and we grow to see we are his equal.

The side you are on personally doesn't matter. The point is to get to an overall truth, the universal truth. This means working past your truth and my truth to find "THE" truth. These restrictions to the center make you equal to God and the same but different. We need to start with all the knowledge in the world and break it down. We have one word that comes back to itself on paper and we tie it into all the knowledge in the world. Let's start with the inside of the non-physical, the things you can't touch or take a picture of need to be in writing when it is whole. They are things, not a part of the body or concerning it. The polar opposite of non-physical is intangible (both can't be touched). They are both equal to the inside, but intangible can relate and concern the body. The polar opposite on the outside is tangible.
The world is spilt perfectly between the inside verb and outside noun. Spiritually, the definitions break down to see one God and to the part in us that is the same/God. One way we can see everything the world has to offer is by creating a universal Bible in which everything is broken down in the correct way. We can use patterns to make whole sentences, forming the universal truth with all the knowledge in the universe.

We can know God, Love, and Truth by language which is broken down between the inside and outside. It is then narrowed down by the non-physical and physical and tightened down correctly to tie spiritual inside and human outside. Then it squeezes the inside and outside. This will provide truth when the system works as if it was a well-oiled machine in which the universe reveals what it has to offer. Seeing this in one's mind is a process of elimination using the correct sides, starting from the whole to break it down in all ways. We miss or overlook what we don't know because we don't see both sides. The answers to life's problems are at the razor's edge of the inside and outside. Our minds just haven't been conditioned in this way yet.

The inside/spiritual means inside the human body. God resides in a part on the inside and is part of everything on the outside. Each side goes back in itself when displaying **outside/inside** for people or being human. When displaying non-physical/physical, the non-physical is inside things. The human **inside** is intangible, and the physical is the **outside** part of being human. But the outside part of the physical is the outside world and consists of things, not people. God is both things and a part of people. The center of God shows us how all things work to the center out, in us by language. This will define the inside and outside to the center and make God whole (He is always whole, but our perception shortens our views). God is more than we think. God is also instruction for everything inside and outside, and at the same time He is everything explained in writing using the twins. With the right teachings, it is in us to not overlook what is the same and miss what is different, but to be awake to notice and see what we "know" on the inside.

The definition gets spilt, separated and divided after the completed definition goes and comes back to itself in the **center,** meaning all the "perfect" parts in the definition make it whole. The parts and the whole are the **same** but **different (to put them together use the twins)** and add up to the same thing which is perfectly equal from both sides. It adds up to the center of the razor's edge, which is God, too. Now that it is whole, by using all the information and knowledge in the world, we will "**separate**" the perfect parts (because God can't be divided). The parts are perfect by definition and together they make it whole. The whole is in its meaning. **Up** at the top is overly agreeable and on the way **down** it is more agreed but further down it gets disagreeable. We become argumentative because of our feelings, and further down is even more argumentative. It is often fueled by belief. In the center is an honest agreement, reaching the razor's edge of both sides. The middle inside and the center outside form the center to find the universal truth. Centered between Love and Truth are all the answers to solve the world's problems with truth, guided in the center by love. This is done by breaking down all the knowledge as it comes back to itself (God, language and self). The system has all God's answers for the way to live in a heaven on Earth with all the instructions.

We just need to see to apply this. It is in the definition of the Definition. The definition comes back to **itself** and all words work the same in the patterns. All words come back to the self when one sees how it works.

The horizontal definition is nailed down to: if it's physical or tangible we can take a picture, if it's non- physical or intangible it needs to be in writing. This definition is vertical. If in fact you don't know, I would like to state it for the masses to fill in the blanks by using the interactive website www.yourname.Blog.\one. After we know the horizontal and vertical meaning we can seek what is in between in the plus sign to get closer to knowing everything.

dividing up, partitioning, separation, division, dividing, subdivision, splitting **(up),** 2. breaking up, 3. breakup how **and I don't know what this means yet in all definitions?**

synonyms: screen, (room) 1. Up 2. 3 off divider, (dividing) wall, barrier, panel
"room partitions"

The truth of all truths is when we have all the truths together in one word. This brings us close to the universal truth. The definition is split between the **non-physical** which are things not concerning or relating to the body and **intangibles,** which are things that are unable to be touched or grasped because they do not have a physical presence. The other side of the definition is the noun for the word. The tangible, physical outside things are the outside of an oxymoron. We are intended to use both sides and when we only use one side, we throw off the whole truth that will set us free. When people of the same sex are in a relationship, it can be hard to find truth naturally because it requires both sexes/sides to be equal. People who get a divorce don't "know" either, though they may think they do. Building a complete human on the inside is required before one knows who and what God is. People think they know, but they only have one part of the truth, and they are missing another part.

We as humans are the way inside. The Truth and the Light are layers of knowledge in us that make us God on the inside or all-knowing to be able to explain everything to the center. We should approach God differently and understand that the perfect God is human or really the perfect human is God. We need to know this in us first before we can "know" God in an educated way. The **non-physical** is the inside of the definition and the outside is in plain sight, marked with a 0 where the meaning is. Non-physical **things** and intangibles have to do with the living thing **inside**. On the other hand, the physical and outside things are tangible and a picture can be taken of them.

Let's break down the idea of the outside and inside. First, we will focus on the physical.

There is a physical (outside) and an intangible (inside). Things that are tangible are perceptible by touch. This also means they are things that can be seen; we could take a picture of them.

The first part of the definition of **physical** is an adjective related to the body as opposed to the mind (I consider this everything **on** one side **in** the **physical outside such as a body of water**) The second part of the definition refers to things perceived through the senses as opposed to the mind.(I consider this everything **on** one side or the other side **in** the outside of **"living things"**).

The **outside** includes physical things relating to the body as opposed to the mind (I consider this everything **on** the **outside** of living **human/animal things**). The second part of the definition refers to things perceived through the senses as opposed to the mind. (I consider everything on one side or the other side **on** the **outside** of living human things that have a physical presence). **Inside/spiritual** relates to the animal/human spirit or soul **outside** as opposed to material or physical things (I consider this everything **on** the **outside** of living people that has to do with the soul).

The polar opposite word fills in the gap to bridge the inner and outer. They come together in the center to the razor's edge from both sides of the definitions. All the parts and pieces can fit into the whole to make up one God. It is like a jigsaw puzzle; there is only one way to put it together.

Our world is full of dichotomies; gender differences, polar opposites and human/God differences. The world outside **on** relates **in** to the inside world to open **the third** world. This is how we see the laws of polarity and how it separates and divides from the whole by definition. The outside and inside both have a complete truth. We find the whole truth through how they relate to be equals in three separate worlds. The truth in life is for us all to uncover in the third world together, which is the universal truth! The processes and the patterns of time, truth, love, space and religions are organized into math, science and literature which are all centered on one purpose. The answers are between the sexes.

The world is made of three things, down to one, with everything working as it comes back to itself. The answer is not exciting, but it is cool if you see that it (God) and the "things" are the answer. By things, I am referring both to living things and inanimate things like a body of water. Both types of things have a physical presence. The soul **part of a human being's "things" is regarded as immortal on the inside and "sole"** is on the **outside, acting as a polar opposite word** meaning one and only. The spiritual definition relates to the religion or religious belief and this is self. The inside of things and the outside of things help us to see the difference in the center of **all** things which are the answers in life, and to see why everything is the same as life and God. What religious leaders need to "know" before they teach it is how things and living things come back to themselves. This is the proof that God's lost word, not the Bible, is backwards. When God put everything together originally, all the answers could be found through the inside and outside of the human body and the mind, and still can. The ancients figured this out, as we can see from the structures they built. Things and living things are the parts of the whole and now we don't even recognize the tool of God's instructions to know, not just believe. The body is the temple of itself individually and also **self is the temple in all religions collectively. And we are part of the God-self.** Do you see the patterns yet?

In each word, we have the process right once we find the missing link(s) **in** the inside where it seems as if all is God. But when we see how the patterns are the same in each of us, we should be able to match Einstein's theory of relativity **on** the outside and **in** the inside and see how it relates to relativity together on both sides where all is one. So, start with the word, then define it, then know what it is so you can go back because it is what you started with. By defining it in one of the same three ways it is the same but different. This is simple but not easy to see or understand, as it is for everything in writing, but it is easy to overlook. Or you can wait until it reveals itself to understand that the whole truth is when we see all three at the same time, so it doesn't change the meaning. The complex math problem is solved when we look at it in the correct way. We are manually breaking the app down and we are developing it as well. People would be just as confused as you by what you don't see because you "know" all this inside. We are organizing it in an educated way for the masses now, where you don't need to be smart – you just need to be open to see things in a different way to see how everything fits together. Again, what stops one from seeing the truth can be their conditioning or the way they think. Often, they think they know something when in reality they don't. Scholars have the best shot of being able to define God through the way words work.

First we need to know ourselves as well as God before we can come back to ourselves because that is what it means to be God before we "know" what and who God is. Otherwise, it is only a belief. Not a high percentage of people "know" who **God is. The way religious leaders perceive and teach about Him is only a part; we need to go further, deeper, higher and wider. He is part of us, making all humans equal to Him individually, but in a stronger way when we are united together. God is all things. This is "in" the universe and also "is" the universe. He created us with all the answers already inside of us. We are born to be equal together and with Him, and this is how we know the way things work. As you may have heard in church, "God is the way!" All things work only because He is the way things work for people and all things are a part of Him. A part of all things and living things and the instructions of the way they work together are also the reason why "God is the way". This is proven by language when we break it down.**

All people and things are truly one and are both the same and this defines God. This is a way to understand the truth about how the **mind** works as one or all together with God to be one and equal. The **body** is the guide to how the mind works (the temple) to be God. The **soul** works as one inside the mind and outside of the body to be one with the universe by the **energy** of God with His direction and the education that has the correct process, down to be the guide for all. The answers are written down through **language in their definitions.** Even God, when each thing comes back to itself, is the proof. What does it mean to come back to the self, as God is human? The best way to explain is by an example. A lot of times in the Bible, God is mentioned, but it could mean you or all people or both. God is **truth**. **Light** is energy, which is the same as God because God is energy too. **Life** is love, the same as how God is love, as well as light, life and truth. How do we define everything and everybody perfectly for our children's children? God can't be divided so we are all gods. We need to split, separate and divide from the whole or Him. Regarding looking into the perfect pieces and parts, start with looking at the other side of tangible things; focus on what is in the invisible part of the parallel universe where the things are the same but different, this forms that which is God and is the proof of itself. People are in between the spiritual side which is love, and human side which is truth.

When they come together, they are united in the center of the razor's edge for both sides. The system is inter-technology to find the truth God left for us to uncover by his word. When each side comes back to itself, the center of the system is written into the Rubik's Cube of Knowledge for our children. In the center is the perfect language, where every word comes back to itself and all the rules and regulations are correct and complete. The truth will set us free when it is seen in the correct way. Each thing comes back to itself and all the pieces and parts fit the same into the whole before we can see the whole (which is God). Until then, we have faith to bridge the gap until we "know." Otherwise, we make things up and lie to ourselves by telling part truths. This often spreads to others unintentionally because we don't see the whole. Churches for many years have conditioned us to believe in God rather than finding the way to "know" God in all ways. Or at least how to know the process to think, listen, believe and know to see inside and outside. I'm suggesting we add another way by using self (at least part of the inside of self) to all religions to help our perception to unite the truth and see how humanity is God's partner to learn from both religiously and non- religiously.

The equal and balanced center's middle is the midpoint and center of the three: 1) Non-physical and physical, 2) Spiritual and human and 3) Inside and outside. All these pieces, parts and sections add up to the whole no matter how we split, separate, divide and partition the whole. It is the same as the seven basic parts by definition: 1) Pieces 2) Parts 3) Sections **4) Segment 5) Constant 6) Partitioned 7) Definition**.

Using the word "Part" in the definition for a correct way: the parts are equal to the whole because we need the part to make it whole therefore it is the same in that way.
(**Inside** to inside**)**, (outside **to outside**) (outside to inside) (**spiritual** side to **human** side). Examples are:

C)   His lips parted in a smile 2. At that moment the mist parted 1. (of two things) move away from each other 2. Divide to leave a central space. 1. A piece or segment of something such as an object, activity, or period of time, which combined with other pieces makes up the whole. 2. Some but not all of something 1. **Divide** the circle into three equal parts. 2. The painting tells only part of the story. And vice versa.

A piece or segment of something such as an object, activity, or period of time, which combined with other pieces makes up the whole some but not all of something: **divide the circle into three equal parts; the painting tells only part of the story. His lips parted in a smile at that moment the mist parted** (of two things) move away from each other divide to leave a central space.

The four secrets that are sacred (connected with God) and that make everything whole to understand the main sections are: 1) God and human are **NON-PHYSICAL Inside** /PHYSICAL outside 2) Men and women are human outside and spiritual inside, 3) Inside/outside, or one side, 4) **Spiritual inside /PHYSICAL outside** and outside / inside. **The first definition is** inside /inside and **the second definition is the** outside/**outside. The third definition is** spiritual inside/**human outside** or one side and the fourth definition is outside / inside or one side. The four **definitions** are all linked together in a single word simultaneously.

Parts Definitions:

A) **His lips parted in a smile; at that moment the mist parted** (of two things) move away from each other divide to leave a central space a piece or segment of something such as an object, activity, or period of time, which combined with other pieces makes up the whole **divide the circle into three equal parts the painting tells only part of the story. (in/**in out/**out).**

B) **His lips parted in a smile; at that moment the mist parted: divide the circle into three equal parts the painting tells only part of the story** a piece or segment of something such as an object, activity, or period of time, which combined with other pieces makes up the whole (of two things) move away from each other divide to leave a central space. **(in/out/**out/in**).**

C) A piece or segment of something such as an object, activity, or period of time, which combined with other pieces makes up the whole (of two things) move away from each other divide to leave a central space **His lips parted in a smile; at that moment the mist parted divide the circle into three equal parts the painting tells only part of the story.** (out/in/ **In/ out**).

Three sides: And vice versa

> **1) The circle into three equal parts the painting tells only part of the story:** his lips parted in a smile; at that moment the mist parted. (**human to** spiritual one side) **and vice versa.**
>
> **A)** His lips parted in a smile; at that moment the mist parted; **the circle into three equal parts the painting tells only part of the story.** (one side to one side or side to side).

D) A piece or segment of something such as an object, activity, or period of time, which combined with other pieces makes up the whole (of two things) move away from each other divide to leave a central space (outside **to Inside** one side) **and vice versa**.

E) (of two things) move away from each other divide to leave a central space a piece or segment of something such as an object, activity, or period of time, which combined with other pieces makes up the whole.

F) **His lips parted in a smile at that moment the mist parted** (of two things) move away from each other divide to leave a central space a piece or segment of something such as an object, activity, or period of time, which combined with other pieces makes up the whole **the circle into three equal parts the painting tells only part of the story.** (in/in red/ out/out blue) **and vise verse.**

G) **The circle into three equal parts the painting tells only part of the story** a piece or segment of something such as an object, activity, or period of time, which combined with other pieces makes up the whole (of two things) move away from each other divide to leave a central space **his lips parted in a smile at that moment the mist parted.**

The parts, synonyms and homonyms of the word Part:

The opposite of the word **"part"** is the word "whole" on the inside. The inside double polar opposite word to "whole" outside in **"is all the parts and pieces"** inside to outside be the "whole" inside us and outside the universe.

The inside **with a** verb **and an** adverb **is the main part of a sentence together on the** outside **to make the word whole with a** noun. **"Wholeness"** is described in an **adjective altogether with the inside four parts** in a single word.

Part **The circle into three equal parts the painting tells only part of the story his lips parted in a smile at that moment the mist parted.** (one side **blue/ red**). **Whole** all of; entire "he spent the whole day walking" used to emphasize the novelty or distinctness of something **"the man who's given a whole new meaning to the term "cowboy."** (one side **blue human outside**).

Part synonyms: bit, slice, chunk, lump, hunk, wedge, fragment, scrap, **piece**; portion, proportion, percentage, fraction "the last part of the cake"
Whole synonyms: entire, complete, full, unabridged, uncut, noun intact, in one **piece**, unbroken; undamaged, unmarked, perfect. Entity, unit, body, discrete item, ensemble, all

every part, the lot, the sum, the sum total, the entirety "**the whole** of the year" "a single whole" "the whole report"

The center is where the synonyms match perfectly outside **in** the word "part" and **on** the inside to the word "whole" the centers center is **"Piece"**.

Synonyms are inside and outside **meanings.**
Homonyms are outside and inside. They are words that sound alike but have different meanings. They have the same spelling but different meanings and origins (e.g., pole[1] and pole[2]); homograph 1. Bass" fish" 2. Bass "drums" plural nouns. Homophones 1. Buy, by, bye. *Preposition, adverb and noun. Use when needed.*

Antonym: outside and inside meanings of words a word opposite in meaning to another (e.g., *bad* and *good*).

When opposite words are across from each other **in** their proper place **on** the opposite ends of the stick in the centers center (up and down, down and up) to add to the meaning of a single word.

The opposite word of **part** is **whole.**

(**Antonym**) The front to back of the word **part** on the outside of the opposite word **whole** to the inside to complete the word from back to front but slides from each part you **"KNOW "**on the inside to the wholeness we have on the outside.

Breaking down word Definition far enough to come back itself:

Listening, think(ing), believing, seeing, knowing.	Person, place or thing
VERB Intangibles other five senses. Tangibles	**NOUN**
Oxy	**moron**
0 **NON-PHYSICAL.** Writing	o PHYSICAL Picture

SECTION:

noun

noun: section; plural noun: sections

Instructions for the next steps are also in the definitions. Example: the system for any **single word,** the pieces, parts and the sections of the word to make it whole are partitioned back to itself and this makes the word complete. I'm demonstrating the patterns around the single word. We can use **any word** for this purpose; let's use **section.**   Use the example to your left, or a dictionary. For each **section, ONE SIDE has two or more definitions.** We now have two adjectives, **two** verbs and two nouns. 1. Any of the more or less distinct parts into which something is or may be divided or from which it is made up. **"arrange orange sections on a platter"** 2. A distinct group within a larger body of people or things. **"the children's section of the library".** Blue is the outside world and the human world by definition and one side of the truth.

G   Define sectioned

DICTIONARY

Enter a word, e.g. "pie"

sec·tioned
/'sekSH(ə)nd/ ◀ͦ)

adjective
adjective: sectioned

1. made or divided into a separate sections.
   "the sleeping area of a sectioned tent"

2. **BRITISH**
   having been committed compulsorily to a psychiatric hospital in accordance with a section of a mental health act.
   "a sectioned patient has to gain permission before leaving"

sec·tion
/'sekSH(ə)n/ ◀ͦ)

verb

Home Updates Search Recent More

G   section

noun

1. any of the more or less distinct parts into which something is or may be divided or from which it is made up.
   "arrange orange sections on a platter"
   synonyms: part, piece, bit, segment, component, division, portion, element, unit, constituent
   "the separate sections of a train"

2. a distinct group within a larger body of people or things.
   "the children's section of the library"
   synonyms: department, area, part, division
   "the reference section of the library"

verb

1. divide into sections.
   "she began to section the grapefruit"

2. **BRITISH**
   commit (someone) compulsorily to a psychiatric hospital in accordance with a section of a mental health act.
   "should she be sectioned?"

Home Updates Search Recent More

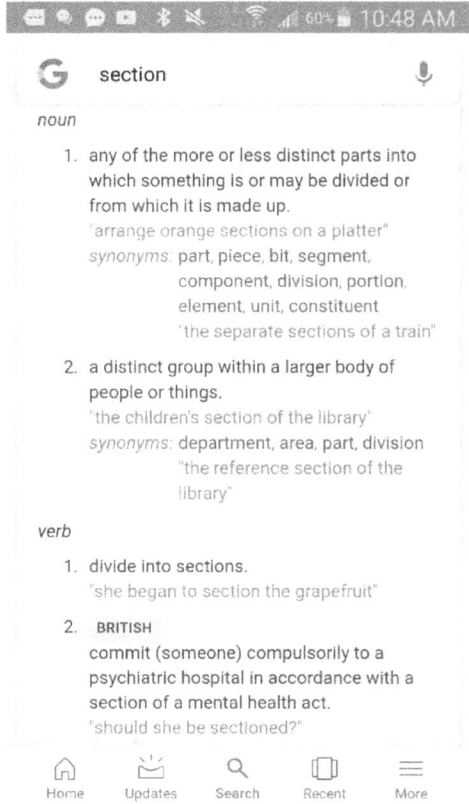

Verb inside 1. third person present: sections 1. Divide into sections. **"she began to section the grapefruit"; " separate an area from a larger one" parts of the curved balcony had been sectioned off with wrought-iron grilles"** Biology cut (animal or plant tissue) into thin slices for microscopic examination. Surgery divide by cutting." **It is common veterinary practice to section the nerves to the hoof of a limping horse".**

1. British commit (someone) compulsorily to a psychiatric hospital in accordance with a section of a mental health act. **"should she be sectioned?".**

Adjective the center **1.** made or divided into a separate sections. **"the sleeping area of a sectioned tent"** British having been committed compulsorily to a psychiatric hospital in accordance with a section of a mental health act **"a sectioned patient has to gain permission before leaving".**

Remember this this the third world, a world by "itself".

One world by itself is part of the truth.

Chapter Thirteen:

Our Perfect Language, Isn't One

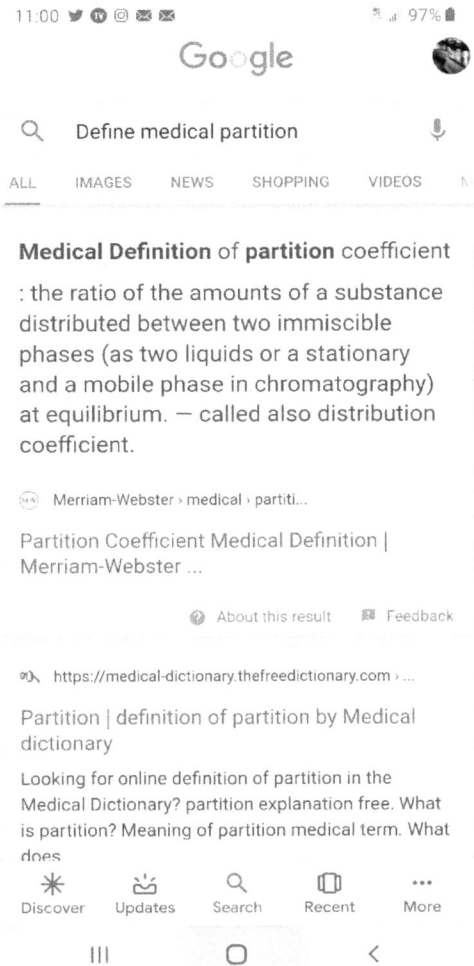

The constants, like gravity or the sun in life are the same as the constants in writing. We have to **split, separate and divide** from the whole to have infinite partitions down to liquid to explain everything... it's the way we process the information. The way we process is the same as the way we think, listen, believe and know and to find both sides of "what is," is the truth to the center of the middle. As to liquid of any and all types our language brought me to this medical definition of partition coefficient efficiency using two liquids. We will know when we use the correct processes guided by the universe to connect the jigsaw puzzle in life how everything fits perfectly together down to liquid. Once everything is connected, physical and non-physical, intangible and tangible, spiritual and human/animal, things and living things, using science and religion. This can all be explained through philosophy in language using the twins, after we have connected all the polar opposite words by definition placement. We can connect the visible and invisible universe when everything comes back together as one to itself and then the universe and us will unite. We as a people will have identified the proper and correct rules and regulations to split between spiritual and human, using the inside and outside to the middle of the center. Using language leads us to the correct pieces, parts, sections, segment, constants, and partitions so we get the correct definitions until we obtain the whole! People missed what the term "God is the whole and everything" means. God is the "way," to "know," "understand", and to "see" how everything works naturally in the universe. We are God when we follow his lead correctly because we are identical (we are human when we don't follow and there's consequences to that). People with the mind of God connect on Facebook to "global stabilized energy. com LLC." or www.yourname.blog. The mind can't see how the middle of the center is hit between all these "ways." In language it shaves the definitions down simultaneously to the one truth, guiding us to see our inter inteligence, showing us the correct processes to see the one for future generations to put in the Rubik's Cube of Knowledge so we can live Heaven on Earth. Once we acknowledge "our" (inside) and "are" (outside) truth and tie them together we will have the same truth and it can be verified through language and self. An example: "of" is part of the whole in language and everything means whole, complete, entire in language. To describe language is how self comes back to itself, the tangible and intangible universe, both sides of language, us and God in everything can connect together to unite. In your mind the constants standing still like each has a permanent pillar. The words and conversations go around the pillars and the definitions direct these three words and the conversation together (split, separate, divided) by how they interact up or down and by the way they relate to the definition. The way the universe works in the non-physical realm is we live in that world or the physical world explaining our mistakes by men and women, and human and God merging to the center of the universe to see we are all one by design. Used the correct way, the constants are perfect from the wholeness to become parts of the whole. We are able to see how we are to live because the answers are in the one truth using the correct formula of God's word.

Instructions for the next steps are also in the definitions. Example: the pieces, parts and sections of the word make it whole and being partitioned back to itself makes the word complete. I'm demonstrating the patterns around the single word. We can use **any word** for this purpose; let's use Constant.

Adjective: constant

occurring continuously over a period of time.

"the pain is constant"

Synonyms: continual, continuous, persistent, sustained, around/round-the-clock.

ceaseless, unceasing, perpetual, incessant, never-ending, eternal, endless, unabating, nonstop, unrelieved.

interminable, unremitting, relentless

"the constant background noise"

steadfast, steady, resolute, determined, tenacious, dogged, unwavering, unflagging

"constant vigilance"

Antonyms: fitful, inconstant

remaining the same over a period of time.

"the company has kept its prices fairly constant"

Synonyms: consistent, regular, steady, uniform, even, invariable, unvarying, unchanging, undeviating, unfluctuating

"a constant speed"

Antonyms: variable

(of a person) unchangingly faithful and dependable.

Synonyms: faithful, loyal, devoted, true, fast, firm, unswerving; More steadfast, staunch, dependable, trustworthy, trusty, reliable, dedicated, committed

"a constant friend"

Antonyms: fickle

the pain is constant; the constant background noise; constant vigilance; the company has kept it

prices fairly constant; a constant speed a constant friend

Noun: constant; plural noun: **constants**

a situation or state of affairs that does not change.

"the condition of struggle remained a constant"

Synonyms: unchanging factor, given

"dread of cancer has been a constant"

Mathematics

A quantity or parameter that does not change its value whatever the value of the variables, under a

given set of conditions.

Physics

A number expressing a relation or property that remains the same in all circumstances, or for the same substance under the same conditions.

Occurring continuously over a period of time. **"the pain is constant"** a situation or state of affairs that   does not change **"the condition of struggle remained a constant."** Mathematics: a quantity or parameter that does not change its value whatever the value of the variables, under a given set of conditions. a number expressing a relation or property that remains the same in all circumstances, or for the same substance under the same conditions.

A number expressing a relation or property that remains the same in all circumstances, or for the same substance under the same condition the pain is constant the condition of struggle remained a constant a situation or state of affairs that does not change a quantity or parameter that does not change its value whatever the value of the variables, under a given set of conditions

EVERYTHING GOES THROUGH THE CONSTANTS VERTICALLY one way and **HORIZONTALLY** in the other to pinpoint the one truth.

Verb **Split**

A number expressing a relation or property that remains the same in all circumstances, or for the same substance under the same condition: **The pain is constant; the condition of struggle remained a constant light squeezed through a small split in the curtain I could never do a split before** a tear, or fissure in something especially down the middle or along the grain a situation or state of affairs that does not change (in gymnastics and dance) an act of leaping in the air or sitting down with the legs straight and at right angles to the upright body, one in front and the other behind, in one at each side; **the ice cracked and heaved and split lets split up and find the other two** break or cause to break forcibly into parts, especially into halves or along the grain (with reference to a group of people) divide into two or more groups **a quantity or parameter that does not change its value whatever the value of the variables, under a given set of conditions**

Noun **Separates**

A number expressing a relation or property that remains the same in all circumstances, or for the same substance under the same condition: **The pain is constant this raises two separate issues** things forming unit by themselves, in particular a situation or state of affairs that does not change **police were trying to separate two rioting mobs the milk had separated into curds and whey** cause to move or be apart divide or cause to divide into constituent or distinct elements **a quantity or parameter that does not change its value whatever the value of the variables, under a given set of conditions**

Verb Divide

Consumer magazines can be divided into a number of different categories: the question had divided Frenchmen since the Revolution; separate or be separated into parts disagree or cause to disagree; a wide divergence between two groups, typically producing tension or hostility a situation or state of affairs that does not change; **there was still a profound cultural; The pain is constant; divide between the condition of struggle remained a constant** the parties **a quantity or parameter that does not change its value whatever the value of the variables, under a given set of conditions**

G partition 🎤

par·ti·tion
/pär'tiSH(ə)n/ ◄))

noun

1. (especially with reference to a country with
separate areas of government) the action
or state of dividing or being divided into
parts.
"the country's partition into separate states"
synonyms: dividing up, partitioning,
separation, division, dividing,
subdivision, splitting (up),
breaking up, breakup
"the partition of India"

verb

1. divide into parts.
"an agreement was reached to partition the
country"
synonyms: divide (up), subdivide, separate,
split (up), break up; More

Feedback

Next, let's use the word **partition.** I think Church and State go together perfectly using language to tell us how the word partition is a key factor to proving this scientifically and religiously, because justice on the inside refers to knowing the skills of timeless wisdom to prevent divorce, racism and disease which is "knowing self" (Love on the inside with no fear) - the part of our spiritual side that is exactly the same we are born with - and together we can formulate the patterns of the truth narrowed down to one truth in our minds first.

The definition is a NOUN: partition 1.

(especially with reference to a country with separate areas of government) the action or state of dividing or being divided into parts. **"the country's partition into separate states."** SYNONYMS: breakup "the partition of India" a structure dividing a space into two parts, especially a light interior wall plural noun: partitions, SYNONYMS: screen, (room) divider, (dividing) wall, barrier, panel "room partitions." In chemistry, the distribution of a solute between two immiscible or slightly miscible solvents in contact with one another, in accordance with its differing solubility in each. Computing each of a number of portions into which some operating systems divide memory or storage.

SYNONYM

🔍 partition

1. partition (n.)

a vertical structure that divides or separates (as a wall divides one room from another)

Synonyms:

| brattice | wall | screen |

| bulkhead | construction | divider |

| structure |

Antonyms:

VERB: partition; 3rd person present: partitions; past tense: partitioned; past participle: partitioned; gerund or present participle: partitioning 1. divide into parts. **"an agreement was reached to partition the country."** SYNONYMS: divide (up), subdivide, separate, split (up), break up; share (out), parcel out "the resolution partitioned Poland" divide (a room) into smaller rooms or areas by erecting partitions. The hall was partitioned to contain the noise of the computers. "SYNNYMS: subdivide, divide (up); more separate (off), section off, screen off "the huge hall was partitioned" separate a part of a room from the rest by erecting a partition. "Partition off part of a large bedroom to create a small bathroom" Poland, India.

Why are there synonyms on both sides **human outside (noun)** and **spiritual inside (verb)**? Oh, I get it - humanity just hasn't put together how everything is the **"same"** but different like a verb and a noun.

The same with synonyms and antonyms, which are the vertical structure to the spiritual side that life offers by how we separate and divide.

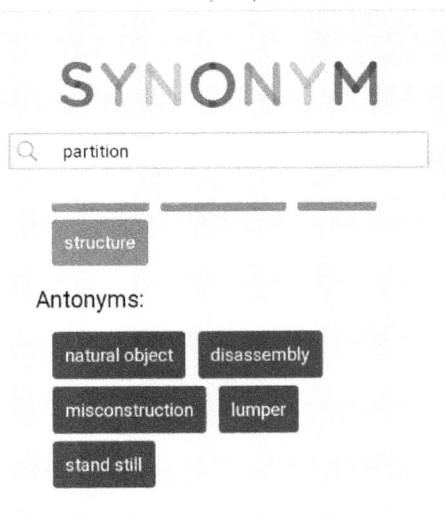

SYNONYM

partition

structure

Antonyms:

natural object   disassembly

misconstruction   lumper

stand still

A) (especially with reference to a country with separate areas of government) the action or state of dividing or being divided into parts **the country's partition into separate states** divide into parts **an agreement was reached to partition the country**

Divide into parts - **an agreement was reached to partition the country** (especially with reference to a country with separate areas of government); the action or state of dividing or being divided into parts; **the country's partition into separate states** (in/in out/**out**).

B) **an agreement was reached to partition the country; the country's partition into separate states** (especially with reference to a country with separate areas of government) the action or state of dividing or being divided into parts; divide into parts **(in/in/out/out/out/in)**.

C) (especially with reference to a country with separate areas of government) the action or state of dividing or being divided into parts; divide into parts; **an agreement was reached to partition the** country; **the country's partition into separate states** (out/in/ **In/ out**).

Three sides: And vice versa

SYNONYM

Q partition

2. partition (n.)

(anatomy) a structure that separates areas in an organism

Synonyms:

body part   septum

Antonyms:

ride   join   connect

- **the country's partition into separate states; an agreement was reached to partition the country** (human/spiritual one side) **and vice versa.**

- **an agreement was reached to partition the country; the country's partition into separate states** (one side to one side or side to side).

(especially with reference to a country with separate areas of government); the action or state of dividing or being divided into parts divide into parts (outside **to Inside** one side) **and vice versa**.

- divide into parts (especially with reference to a country with separate areas of government); the action or state of dividing or being divided into parts

- divide into parts (especially with reference to a country with separate areas of government); the action or state of dividing or being divided into parts; **the country's partition into separate states** (in/in red/ out/out blue) **and vise verse.**

- **the country's partition into separate states** (especially with reference to a country with separate areas of government); the action or state of dividing or being divided into parts divide into parts **an agreement was reached to partition the country out/**out/in/in

SYNONYM

Q   partition

SYNONYM

Q   partition

3. partition (n.)

the act of dividing or partitioning; separation by the creation of a boundary that divides or keeps apart

Synonyms:

division   partitioning

subdivision   sectionalization

segmentation   septation

zoning   sectionalisation

separation

4. partition (v.)

separate or apportion into sections

Synonyms:

divide   zone   separate

separate off   screen off

Antonyms:

Cryptogamia   Phanerogamae

end   misconception   beginning

Somehow, the vertical way!

SYNONYM

Q   partition

5. partition (n.)

(computer science) the part of a hard disk that is dedicated to a particular operating system or application and accessed as a single unit

Synonyms:

computer memory unit

Antonyms:

attach   stay

SYNONYM

Q   partition

6. partition (v.)

divide into parts, pieces, or sections

Synonyms:

pound   divide   separate   part

partition off   pound off

Antonyms:

middle   synthesis   union

continuity   joint

Partition *1. NOUN*

(especially with reference to a country with separate areas of government); the action or state of dividing or being divided into parts.

"the country's partition into separate states"

SYNONYMS:

1. dividing up, partitioning, separation, division, dividing, subdivision, splitting **(up),** 2) breaking up, 3) breakup

"the partition of India"

a. a structure dividing a space into two parts, especially a light interior wall.

PLURAL NOUN: partitions 1) Share (out)2) parcel out

SYNONYMS:

een, OFF (room) 1. Up divider, (dividing) 2. 3 off walls, barrier, panel

"NOUN: partitions"

VERB:

3rd person present: partitions

divide into parts.

"an agreement was reached to partition the country"

SYNONYMS:

divide (up), subdivide, separate, split (up), break up.

Share (**out**), parcel **out** 3. up 2. **out** 1. partitioned

"the resolution partitioned Poland"

o **divide** (a room) into smaller rooms or areas by erecting partitions. words describing **(NON-PHYSICAL INSIDE)**

"the hall was partitioned to contain the noise of the computers"

Subdivide, divide (up); 1. Up, 2. 3

SYNONYMS: separate (off), section off, screen off

"the huge hall was partitioned"

- ○ Separate a part of a room from the rest by erecting a partition. words describing (NON-PHYSICAL INSIDE)

"partition off part of a large bedroom to create a small bathroom"

an agreement was reached to partition the country; divide into parts the country's partition into separate states (especially with reference to a country with separate areas of government) the action or state of dividing or being divided into parts.

The definition of "definition" is broken down to plural nouns of an antonym and synonym. The definition is how it comes back to itself.

One side is the same but different. Women are light Red and men are light blue. The word in the definition is on the human side with a sliding scale horizontally from the center **out/in and** in/out in all ways. One side antonym and one side synonyms **split** equal in all ways (just as and just is) in half down the center and up the middle to be itself after we complete the whole (word).

- • One side is different but the same **as** the spiritual side with the sliding scale, but vertical from the middle is a midpoint. Before one knows that God exists, they can only believe. What I see at the center of the + sign spiritual inside and **human outside, veridical** and men **and women** horizontal is the whole truth all of Love, **time** and space the big part of knowing God and the truth literally. Noun: **definition**; plural noun: **definitions** a statement of the exact meaning of a word, especially in a dictionary...**a).** an exact statement or description of the nature, scope, or meaning of something. To understand it further is to see the other side to make it whole.

Poetry is the result of basic polar opposites. It is when you take two things that don't seem alike but that are paradoxical.

Google   G   word definition or TV de

🔍 :e between the middle a   Television | Definition of
                               Television by Merriam-Webster
ALL   SHOPPING   IMAGES   NEWS   Merriam-Webster › dictionary › televi...

As nouns the **difference**   Definition of television. 1 : an
between middle and **center** is   electronic system of transmitting
that **middle** is a **centre**,   transient images of fixed or moving
midpoint while **center** is the   objects together with sound over a
point **in the** interior **of** a circle   wire or through space by apparatus
or sphere that is equidistant   that converts light and sound into
from all points on the   electrical waves and reconverts them
circumference.   into visible light rays and audible
                                        sound.

What is the difference between   Tv | Definition of Tv by Merriam-
the center and the middle? -   Webster
Quora   Merriam-Webster › dictionary › TV

🏠 Home 👑 Updates 🔍 Search ▢ Recent ≡ More   🏠 Home 👑 Updates 🔍 Search ▢ Recent ≡ More

◁   ○   ▢   ◁   ○   ▢

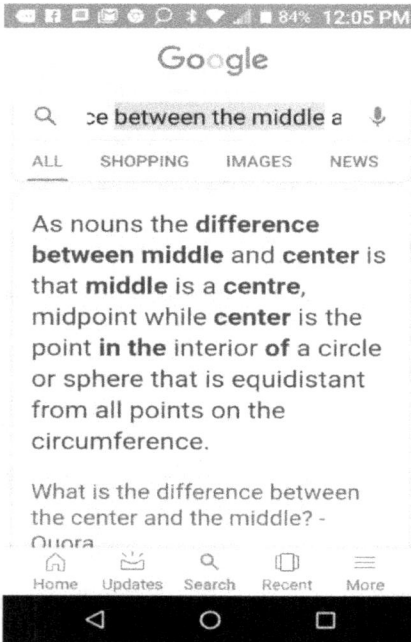

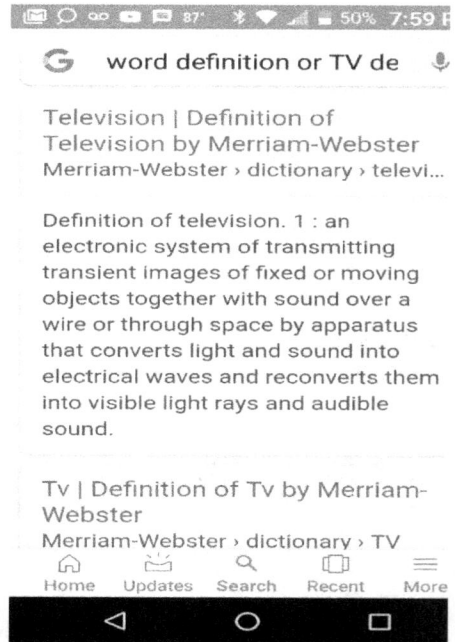

meaning, denotation, sense; More

interpretation, explanation, elucidation,

SYNONYMS:

description, clarification, illustration

"the definition of "intelligence""

c)   the action or process of defining something the degree of distinctness
      in outline of an object, image, or sound, especially of an image in a
      photograph or on a screen; the capacity of an instrument or device for
      making images distinct in outline. **"we've been pleased with the
      definition of this TV".**

SYNONYMS:

> clarity, visibility, sharpness, crispness, acuteness; More resolution, focus, contrast.

> The truth lies between the inside equidistant to the outside because we live in a perfectly symmetric world.

"the definition of the picture" **Consummate Constant = spiritual side** of "dimensional" definition (add to all definitions) **showing a high degree of skill to be perfect, complete, supreme and flawless when synonyms become mixing in to each word.** This is our perception of what a God is. The only definition is on the spiritual side (consummate). When we bring together our spiritual and human sides, doesn't this make us God (or a god)? In the end, it is seamlessly organized by definition. The instruction is in the definitions. Follow the patterns; it is simple but not easy. **Homograph; plural noun:**

Each of two or more words spelled the same but not necessarily pronounced the same and having different meanings and origins (e.g., bow[1] and bow[2]).

HOMOPHONES: 1. Buy, by, bye. *Preposition, adverb and noun.*

PREPOSITION: **plural noun:** prepositions

1. a word governing, and usually preceding, a noun or pronoun and **expressing a relation to another word** or element in the clause, as in **"the man *on* the platform,"** "she arrived *after* dinner," "what did you do it *for* ?".

ANTONYM: noun - Linguistics a word opposite in meaning to another (e.g., bad and good)

Google

definition of word and a definiti

ALL   SHOPPING   NEWS   IMAGES   VIDEO

A **hologram** is an image created by a photographic projection of a recording of a light field rather than an image formed by some sort of lens. It appears as a three-dimensional representation on a two-dimensional object, which can be seen without intermediate optics such as goggles or glasses.

What is a Hologram? - Definition from ...
Techopedia › definition › hologram

About this result   Feedback

PEOPLE ALSO ASK

Home   Updates   Search   Recent   More

ANTONYM: "**plural noun**": antonyms

SYNONYMS: plural noun: synonyms

Definition *NOUN*

noun: **definition**; plural noun: **definitions**

1. 1.

a statement of the exact meaning of a word, especially in a dictionary.

> ○ an exact statement or description of the nature, scope, or meaning of something. Writing

> meaning, denotation, sense; More

> SYNONYMS: interpretation, explanation, elucidation, description, clarification, illustration

> "the definition of "intelligence""

2. the action or process of defining something. Writing2.

the degree of distinctness in outline of an object, image, or sound, especially of an image in a photograph or on a screen.

MORE resolution, focus, contrast "the definition of the picture"

> clarity, visibility, sharpness, crispness, acuteness; More

SYNONYMS: resolution, focus, contrast

> "the definition of the picture"

> ○ the capacity of an instrument or device for making images distinct in outline. picture

"we've been pleased with the definition of this TV"

(especially with reference to a country with separate areas of government); the action or state of dividing or being divided into parts.

"the country's partition into separate states"

SYNONYMS:
1. dividing up, partitioning, separation, division, dividing, subdivision, splitting (up), 2. breaking up, 3. breakup

"the partition of India"

b. a structure dividing a space into two parts, especially a light interior wall. 1) Share (out)?

PLURAL NOUN: partitions 2) parcel out?

2X screen, (room) 1. Up 2. 3 off divider, (dividing) wall, barrier, panel

"room partitions"

VERB:

3rd person present: partitions

1. 1.

divide into parts.

"an agreement was reached to partition the country"

SYNONYMS:
divide (up), subdivide, separate, split (up), break up; Share (**out**), parcel **out** 3. up 2. **out** 1. partitioned

"the resolution partitioned Poland"

o **divide** (a room) into smaller rooms or areas by erecting **partitions.** writing

"the hall was partitioned to contain the noise of the computers"

subdivide, divide (up); **1**. Up, **2**. 3 off

SYNONYMS: separate (**off**), section **off**, screen **off**

"the huge hall was partitioned"

○ **separate** a part of a room from the rest **by erecting a partition.**
Writing

"partition off part of a large bedroom to create a small bathroom"

A synonym is a word or phrase that means exactly or nearly the same as another word or phrase in the same language. For example, shut is a synonym of close.

SYNONYMS: alternate, substitute, alternative, equivalent, euphemism.

a. "'harsh' may be used as synonym for 'oppressive'
b. a person or thing so closely associated with a particular quality or idea that the mention of their name calls it to mind. **c.** "the Victorian age" is a synonym for sexual puritanism

NOUNS ONLY on the outside! But from the Antonym and Synonym; with the; "plural noun": and under the definition of definition.

Here is what caught the right verb for me! 1. "The definition of intelligence" 2. "Our definition of what constitutes poetry" 3. #2 in the definition of definition 4) **"the Victorian age" is a synonym for sexual puritanism**

VERB: **consummate**; 3rd person present: **consummates**; past tense: **consummated**; past participle: **consummated**; gerund or present participle: **consummating.**

make (a marriage or relationship) complete by having sexual intercourse.

"his first wife refused to consummate their marriage"

> o   complete (a transaction or attempt); make perfect. **writing**

"his scheme of colonization was consummated through bloodshed"

SYNONYMS: complete, conclude, finish, accomplish, achieve; More

execute, carry out, perform

up, **wrap** up; 2 ups?

"the deal was finally consummated"

ADJECTIVE: **consummate**

showing a high degree of skill and flair; complete o perfect.

"she dressed with consummate elegance"

SYNONYMS: supreme, superb, superlative, superior, accomplished, expert, proficient, skillful, skilled, masterly, master, first-class, talented, gifted, polished, practiced, perfect, ultimate; More

complete, total, utter, absolute, pure;

exemplary, archetypal

"his consummate skill"

Definition defined: But the truth is, in what formula is it defined?

a statement of the exact meaning of a word, especially in a dictionary... an exact statement or description of the nature, scope, or meaning of something - **our definition of what constitutes poetry;** the action or process of defining something; the degree of distinctness in outline of an object, image, or sound, especially of an image in a photograph or on a screen; the capacity of an instrument or device for making images distinct in outline; **we've been pleased with the definition of this TV; In Biology -** a taxonomic name that has the same application as another, especially one that has been superseded and is no longer valid

Consummate defined:

make (a marriage or relationship) complete by having sexual intercourse; **his first wife refused to consummate their marriage;** complete (a transaction or attempt); make perfect **his scheme of colonization was consummated through bloodshed**

showing a high degree of skill and flair; complete or perfect.
"she dressed with consummate elegance"

Whole

ADJECTIVE. whole

1. all of; entire.

spent the whole day walking SYNONYMS:	entire, complete, full, unabridged, uncut
	"the whole report" the meaning in the parentheses is the guide somehow?
ANTONYMS:	Incomplete

- used to emphasize a large extent or number. Writing nonphysical.

G Define whole 🎤

adjective

1. all of; entire.
   'he spent the whole day walking'
   synonyms: entire, complete, full, unabridged, uncut
   'the whole report'

2. in an unbroken or undamaged state; in one piece.
   'owls usually swallow their prey whole'
   synonyms: intact, in one piece, unbroken;
   More

noun

1. a thing that is complete in itself.
   'the subjects of the curriculum form a coherent whole'
   synonyms: entity, unit, body, discrete item, ensemble
   'a single whole'

2. all of something.
   'the effects will last for the whole of his life'
   synonyms: all, every part, the lot, the sum, the sum total, the entirety
   'the whole of the year'

⌂   ⌣   🔍   📖   ☰
Home   Updates   Search   Recent   More

"whole shelves in libraries are devoted to the subject" what is this?? It's more than an example.

2.   all of; entire

in an unbroken or undamaged state; in one piece.

"owls usually swallow their prey whole"

intact, in one piece, unbroken.

SYNONYMS: undamaged, unmarked, perfect

"they unearthed a whole humanoid skull"

- (of milk, blood, or other substances) with no part removed. Picture. Physical.

- healthy. Writing. Nonphysical.

"all people should be whole in body, mind, and spirit." What does mean??? Both inside and outside! These are the universe's secrets that are sacred and can be found by the correct spiritual guide, grounded.

*NOUN: **whole**; plural noun: **wholes**; noun: **the whole***

1. 1.

a thing that is complete in itself. The definition of a sentence when it is completed and whole.

"The subjects of the curriculum form a coherent whole" means the system.

SYNONYMS:
entity, unit, body, discrete item, ensemble

"a single whole" each and everything becomes whole in itself.

2. 2.

all of something.

"the effects will last for the whole of his life." What is the same!

SYNONYMS: All, every part, the lot, the sum, the sum total, the entirety

"the whole of the year"

ADVERB: **whole**

1. 1.

used to emphasize the novelty or distinctness of something.

"the man who's given a whole new meaning to the term 'cowboy.'"

He spent the whole day walking; owls usually swallow their prey whole; **the subjects of the curriculum form a coherent whole; the effects will last for the whole of his life** all of; entire in an unbroken or undamaged state; in one piece a thing that is complete in itself all of something **the man who's given a whole new meaning to the term cowboy;** used to emphasize the novelty or distinctness of something

I'm demonstrating the patterns around the single word but we can use any word in the place of **piece, use split.** Use the Google example to your left, or a dictionary. Any word's meaning typically starts with a noun, verb or adjective. The first definition is the NOUN **outside.** The first inside is a verb on the inside. **1$^{st\ inside}$**. break or cause to break forcibly into parts, especially into halves or along the grain. **Underneath that the next sentence in parenthesis is (spiritual inside) "the ice cracked and heaved and split" 2$^{nd\ inside}$ VERB:** (with reference to a group of people) divide into two or more groups. **"let's split up and find the other two" (spiritual inside).**

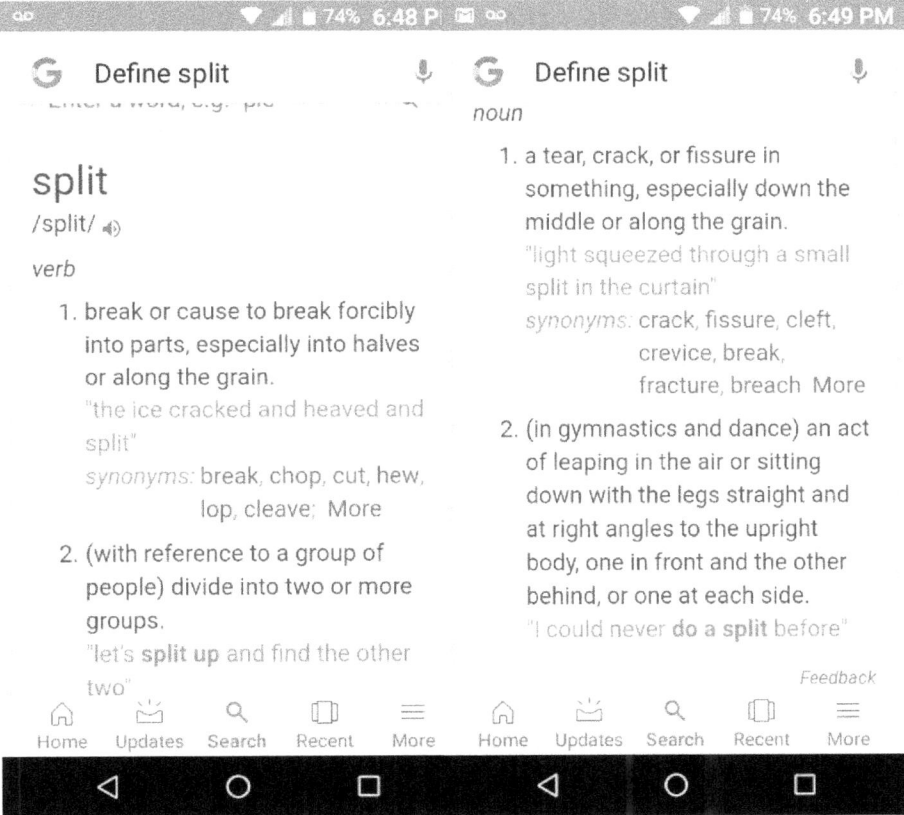

The **1$^{st\ definition\ outside}$** on the left typically a verb but as you can see a **noun 1.** a tear, or fissure in something especially down the middle or a along the grain. **(human outside) "light squeezed through a small split in the curtain."** 2. (in gymnastics and dance) an act of leaping in the air or sitting down with the legs straight and at right angles to the upright body, one in front and the other behind, in one at each side. **"I could never do a split before" (human outside).**

1st noun Each split **ONE SIDE has two definitions** outside **noun** - words are the nouns (other than pronoun) used to identify any of a class of people, place, or thing **common noun,** or to name a particular one of these **proper nouns.** The part of the definition on the noun outside for the word split. a tear, or fissure in something especially down the middle or along the grain.(**outside**)

2nd noun Each split **ONE SIDE has two definitions** outside **noun** The part of the definition on the noun outside for the word split ." (in gymnastics and dance) an act of leaping in the air or sitting down with the legs straight and at right angles to the upright body, one in front and the other behind, in one at each side." (**outside tying in the two definitions outside human**) "**a piece of** cheese" or anything.

1st verb Each split **ONE SIDE has two definitions** inside a word is used as a **verb** (a word that is not conventionally used a verb typically a noun) "any English noun can be verbed (past tense), but some are more resistant than others". The word split inside the word is a "verb" the definition break or cause to break forcibly into parts, especially into halves or along the grain (the **spiritual inside** is beneath) "**the ice cracked and heaved and split**" (inside to **inside**).

2nd verb Maybe we need a different red! Each split **ONE SIDE has two definitions** inside; a word is used as a **verb** (a word that is not conventionally used as a verb typically a noun) "any English noun can be verbed (past tense), but some are more resistant than others". The word split inside the word is a "verb" - the definition (with reference to a group of people) divide into two or more groups. (the **spiritual inside** is beneath) "**lets split up and find the other two**" (inside to **inside**).

Each split **ONE SIDE has two definitions: adjective,** a word or phrase naming an attribute, added to or grammatically related to a noun to modify or describe it. The part of the definition to describe the word **on adjective definition for :** (**inside**) When we complete this for the app, we will add in later adjectives, pronouns and the rest of the rules.

Using the parts in a correct way (inside/inside to **inside/inside**), (**inside to outside**), (**outside to outside**), (side to side). (**spiritual inside**) a tear, or fissure in something, especially down the middle or along the grain; (in gymnastics and dance) an act of leaping in the air or sitting down with the legs straight and at right angles to the upright body, one in front and the other behind, in one at each side; break or cause to break forcibly into parts, especially into halves or along the grain 2$^{nd\ verb}$(with reference to a group of people) divide into two or more groups **"light squeezed through a small split in the curtain"** **"I could never do a split before"** "the ice cracked and heaved and split" "lets split up and find the other two" (outside to **outside**) (inside/inside) to(inside/inside) (Each side **spirit**/ **human**) and (one side outside **/inside**

Split Definitions:

A) **the ice cracked and heaved and split; let's split up and find the other two;** break or cause to break forcibly into parts, especially into halves or along the grain (with reference to a group of people) divide into two or more groups; **light squeezed through a small split in the curtain; I could never do a split before** (in/in/in/in out/**out**/out/out).

B) **the ice cracked and heaved and split; let's split up and find the other two; light squeezed through a small split in the curtain; I could never do a split before;** a tear, or fissure in something especially down the middle or along the grain; (in gymnastics and dance) an act of leaping in the air or sitting down with the legs straight and at right angles to the upright body, one in front and the other behind, in one at each side; break or cause to break forcibly into parts, especially into halves or along the grain; (with reference to a group of people) divide into two or more groups **(in/out/**out/in).

C) a tear, or fissure in something especially down the middle or along the grain; (in gymnastics and dance) an act of leaping in the air or sitting down with the legs straight and at right angles to the upright body, one in front and the other behind, in one at each side; break or cause to break forcibly into parts, especially into halves or along the grain; (with reference to a group of people) divide into two or more groups **the ice cracked and heaved and split; let's split up and find the other two; light squeezed through a small split in the curtain; I could never do a split before** (out/in/ **In/ out).**

D) **the ice cracked and heaved and split; let's split up and find the other two; light squeezed through a small split in the curtain; I could never do a split before;** break or cause to break forcibly into parts, especially into halves or along the grain; (with reference to a group of people) divide into two or more groups; a tear, or fissure in something especially down the middle or along the grain; (in gymnastics and dance) an act of leaping in the air or sitting down with the legs straight and at right angles to the upright body, one in front and the other behind, in one at each side (**In/ out/** in/out). **No incomplete works here – let's split up and find the other two.**

E) **light squeezed through a small split in the curtain; I could never do a split before; the ice cracked and heaved and split; let's split up and find the other two (human to** spiritual one side).

F) a tear, or fissure in something especially down the middle or along the grain; (in gymnastics and dance) an act of leaping in the air or sitting down with the legs straight and at right angles to the upright body, one in front and the other behind, in one at each side; break or cause to break forcibly into parts, especially into halves or along the grain; (with reference to a group of people) divide into two or more groups (outside **to Inside** one side).

The pieces, synonyms and homonyms of the word Split

The word from the (out to in) outside opposite of the word **"split"** is the word "halves." A plural form of half 1. to the extent of half the inside double opposite word to "whole" outside in **is all the parts and pieces are whole** (inside to out) is us and the universe. **The inside with a verb is the main part of a sentence together on the** outside **to make the word whole with a** noun completing **"wholeness"** is described in an **adjective all inside and outside in four parts** in a single word. (I think?? So far)

Split synonyms: verb **and** noun

split synonyms: verb.	break, chop, cut, hew, lop, cleave, snap, crack "the ax split the wood" break apart, fracture, rupture, fissure, snap, come apart, splinter
split synonyms: noun:	crack, fissure, cleft, crevice, break, fracture, breach "a split in the rock face" rip, tear, cut, rent, slash, slit "a split in the curtain"
Cracked synonyms:	chipped, broken, crazed, fractured, splintered, shattered, split.

Adjective: damaged, defective, flawed, imperfect
                        "a cracked cup"

The center is where the synonyms match perfectly on the word inside split and outside cracked is **"cracked and split"** and vice versa to get to the center's center.

- Homonyms are words **"to become cracked or split."** Each of two words having the same **pronunciation but different "meanings"**, origins, or spelling (e.g., to, too, and two); a homophone.

Split: **the ice cracked and heaved and split** (one side spiritual inside). Cracked "the old pipes were cracked and leaking" (one side **human outside**) (**spiritual inside/ human outside**)

The opposite word **meaning** inside or spiritual and outside or human! **Split.**

(**Homonyms**) The, end of one side of the word **split** on one end spiritual the **ice cracked and heaved and split** in halves on the other half at the further end of the human side in the word the old pipes were **cracked** and leaking" from the other end but slides from each end to end you **"KNOW "**on the inside and outside are the same to wholeness.

The pieces and parts of God in the wholeness of everything, to everywhere and everybody perfectly fit together, broken down into one language by one God after we complete one word back to itself.

The four secrets that are sacred (connected with God) the base to understand the main sections are 1) God and human is **NON PHYSICAL Inside** /PHYSICAL outside 2) Men and women is human outside and spiritual inside, 3) inside/outside, or one side, 4) Spiritual inside /**PHYSICAL outside** and outside / inside. **The 1st definition is** inside /inside, and **the 2nd definition is the** outside/**outside** 3rd definition spiritual inside / **human outside** or one side and 4th definition outside / inside or one side. The four **definitions** are all linked together in a single word simultaneously of **"split"**: the ice cracked and heaved and split lets split up and find the other two break or cause to break forcibly into parts, especially into halves or along the grain (with reference to a group of people) divide into two or more groups light squeezed through a small split in the curtain I could never do a split before. (**in/in**/in/in out/**out**/**out**/out).

What are the **Sections** divisions? Separations partitions divisions splits.... Let define them:

1. (Verb split) 1ˢᵗ verb break or cause to break forcibly into parts, especially into halves or along the grain. **(Spiritual inside) "the ice cracked and heaved and split" 2ⁿᵈ ˢⁱᵈᵉ verb** (with reference to a group of people) divide into two or more groups. **"let's split up and find the other two" (spiritual inside).** The **noun 1.** a tear, or fissure in something especially down the middle or a along the grain. **(human outside) "light squeezed through a small split in the curtain"** (Noun split) 2. (in gymnastics and dance) an act of leaping in the air or sitting down with the legs straight and at right angles to the upright body, one in front and the other behind, in one at each side. **"I could never do a split before" (human outside)**.

2. (noun: separates) things forming unit by themselves, in particular; (verb, **separates)** cause to move or be apart **""police were trying to separate two rioting mobs"** (2. Verb) divide or cause to divide into constituent or distinct elements. **"the milk had separated into curds and whey (adjective, separate forming or viewed as a unit apart or by itself "this raises two separate issues".** The **"word"** is complete when the **pieces** are partitioned correctly how the word is **split, separated** and **divided** in **itself** with all the **pieces** in any and all ways to make the completed whole "word".

3. (Verb: **divide)**; 3rd person present: **divides**; past tense: **divided**; past participle: **divided**; gerund or present participle: **dividing** 1. Separate or be separated into parts **"consumer magazines can be divided into a number of different categories"** 2 verb disagree or cause to disagree. **"the question had divided Frenchmen since the Revolution"** (noun: **divide)**; plural noun: divides a wide divergence between two groups, typically producing tension or hostility. **"there was still a profound cultural divide between** the parties"

Verb **Split**

light squeezed through a small split in the curtain; I could never do a split before; a tear, or fissure in something especially down the middle or along the grain; (in gymnastics and dance) an act of leaping in the air or sitting down with the legs straight and at right angles to the upright body, one in front and the other behind, in one at each side; **the ice cracked and heaved and split;**

let's split up and find the other two; break or cause to break forcibly into parts, especially into halves or along the grain (with reference to a group of people) divide into two or more groups

Noun **Separates**

this raises two separate issues: things forming unit by themselves, in particular **police were trying to separate two rioting mobs; the milk had separated into curds and whey;** cause to move or be apart; divide or cause to divide into constituent or distinct elements

Verb Divide

consumer magazines can be divided into a number of different categories; the question had divided Frenchmen since the Revolution; separate or be separated into parts disagree or cause to disagree a wide divergence between two groups, typically producing tension or hostility **there was still a profound** cultural **divide between** the parties.

Each piece of **ONE SIDE has two definitions in the word.** The outside **noun** is a word, the nouns (other than pronoun) used to identify any of a class of people, place, or thing **common noun,** or to name a particular one of these proper nouns. The part of the definition on the noun outside for the word **Consummate** - no definition here.

Each piece of **ONE SIDE has two definitions** inside a word is used as a **verb** (a word that is not conventionally used as a verb, typically a noun) "any English noun can be verbed (past tense), but some are more resistant than others". The word **consummate** inside the word is a "verb" the definition: (**outside human) make (a marriage or relationship) complete by having sexual intercourse.** (inside) "his first wife refused to consummate their marriage"

Each piece **ONE SIDE has two definitions:** adjective is a word or phrase naming an attribute, added to or grammatically related to a noun to modify or describe it. The part of the definition to describe the word **consummate: (inside) showing a high degree of skill and flair; complete or perfect** (outside) "she dressed with consummate elegance"

Using the parts in a correct way inside to inside, outside to **outside,** side to side, here are some parts of the definition:

A) **Showing a high degree of skill and flair; complete or** his first wife refused to consummate their marriage she dressed with consummate elegance; **make (a marriage or relationship) complete by having sexual intercourse (in/**in out**/out).**

B) **Showing a high degree of skill and flair; complete or make (a marriage or relationship) complete by having sexual intercourse;** she dressed with consummate elegance; his first wife refused to consummate their marriage. **In/out/**out/in

C) She dressed with consummate elegance; his first wife refused to consummate their marriage; **showing a high degree of skill and flair; complete or make (a marriage or relationship) complete by having sexual intercourse.** Out/in/ **In/ out**

D) **Showing a high degree of skill and flair; complete or make (a marriage or relationship) complete by having sexual intercourse** his first wife refused to consummate their marriage; she dressed with consummate elegance. **In/ out/** in/out

One Side of the definition in the word

The 1st definition is inside / **inside** and the 2nd definition is the outside/**outside** 3rd **Inside /outside** and 4th outside / inside. 5th outside/. The four main parts of definitions are all linked together for all words in place.

(Homonyms) The front to back of the word **piece** on the **inside** spelled differently to the **outside** sound the same as the word back to front **none** •
The word from the (out to in) outside opposite of the word **consummate** is the word **"incomplete"**. The inside double polar opposite word to "incomplete" outside in **"complete"** (inside to out) is us and the universe. The whole circuit or circle is complete; an incomplete is the whole.

The whole complete language consummated together (the twins in language) correctly defines "GOD" in education because He is "all," "everything" and the "way." Our own perception is holding us back to the correct knowledge because we are the way through self, language and God to be everything and the "all" of self the exact mirror image of God which is us. The intellectual challenge to life meets in the center of the human side and the middle of the spiritual side together faith is for the human side to gain the knowledge to be one God or one with God both have the same results.

Inside Red + A-truth = a-t, working with two letters words. [Define at; unstressed uh t, it (this is to define at: in, on, or near: to stand at the door; at the bottom of the barrel or in a time.)

Blue + A- truth = a-t, Purple inside a-t + outside a-t + the truth of how Blue/Red relate = the truth. t.t. or   and it could be purple?

Blue and   make   Green = outside laws: Physics, Philosophy and mathematics etc. How outside Law are relative to the way they relate to the inside spiritual laws balancing inside and outside.

          Red = Orange = inside laws: The spiritual laws do they relate with the outside Laws is it relative?

Purple is both a world of one, blue is a world of one or red is a world of one = tt is the 3rd world of one and (inside) our/are (outside) laws (in writing or communication) on the outside in is a world of one. (a-t), the laws on the inside out are a world of one (a-t) Orange = both worlds of one. = tt + a-t + a-t =??   r = 4t? The question is the orange inside laws are the skills of wisdom are the spiritual laws?

The secondary colors are Purple - the way red and blue, Green and Orange possibly the way green and orange relate to the inside/outside laws

1) Inside | 2) outside, 3) inner/outer 4) outer/ inner, 5) outside/inside
                              Red is (A) equal truth all the inside is a world of one. / Blue is (A) equal truth, the outside world of one. The purple inner/outer is a world of one of one, so in what world to be inside the non-physical |outside the physical, inner/outer.

This is to look for the different ways of our perceptions for us to see what the process is to break down the truth of truth is, one is the outside (Blue + Green = outside laws) or one is the inside what is is (two i's, is to be) the same but different is to (Red = Orange = inside laws) see all that is/are possible in every and all ways at the same time makes up another world of perception on its own. The   is elusive, unknown and is the bound, brains and designer with the plan that is constant and doesn't move that is laid out but covered for us to see from within to fine, then uncover the parts of the truth and share them.

This is a way to imagine the breakdown of the universe and worlds, by the way we relate and live as a humanity, by the way we are tied to Earth. We can look at the God thing in a different way, using the Mind, Body and Spirit/Soul. These are just for illustration purposes. By using the inside world as the Mind, the outside world for the Body, the Spirit can be used for both inside world and/or the outside world representing the 3rd world. The Soul, while we are still alive, uses us to see all of the collective ways to perceive what is inside or outside, inside/outside (part or degrees of each) inside/outside !! in/ne /   .
These are the inner combinations, l is the law of the outside polar, the n is the inside, the next n is how inside and outside relate, the e is the inner spiritual laws, the   is all and every at the same time = inne .

The crowd will participate through the ***sharing of thought*** for the self, community and country. The Mind is the Universal Intelligence and is the inner parts. The center of a human is inside to inside. There are many different degrees of perception where one sees it the way they perceive it to be (outside world).

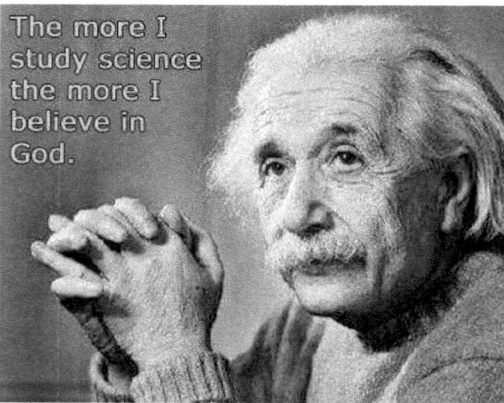
The more I study science the more I believe in God.

The big God and/or Cosmos may be you. Maybe, with the wisdom of the crowd, we can enhance our use from the inside of us that will help make it better. Together we will find simple brilliance, the center of "being knowledgeable." The world outside is relative to the inside world by the way they relate. The understanding of both worlds alone can help eliminate or reduce many addictions. This is the 3rd world. The outside and inside relate – it is not seen, but it is always there. Until both are understood, and the simplicity is not overlooked, it will fail to be seen. I believe in humanity to see how all the patterns are the same but different but also come to one truth..

The proper truth depends on what world you are in or on (ducks or universes). Each world shows a proper truth; they seem proper because of the perspective they are being seen from. The worlds, looked at in the proper way, will help to reveal the 3rd world. You see it from the inside out or from the outside in. It is like starting from different ends. This is like each has a sliding scale from one world (inside) back to the other side, the outside world, then showing the center of the inner and the outer world, revealing the 3rd world. None of the worlds can see anything but themselves (same as Ducks and Universes). The 3rd world can't see anything but itself. Seeing how they relate with each other gives a person with the right perspective the growth to see from a bird's eye view how the inside/spiritual world works perfectly together, like a puzzle. The human world outside works perfectly against the other worlds. When one understands the portal, they can see life's beauty (the perfectly symmetrical world). The correct teaching works from the center out on a subtonic level. This is a form of knowledge. When the inside and outside worlds are balanced, this makes one knowledgeable.

The English language can illustrate how we are all one, starting from one-, two-, three-, and four-letter words. The educated side of the human (outside) knows this part, but it is still only one part - the outside. Once we see how the small words form a sentence, we will understand how the relationships work for the inside world as well.

Mind. All and everything on the inside of us and the inside of the world in the universe.

Metaphysical: (Inside). The Mind, feelings, emotions, thoughts, beliefs, and the act of knowing space and time.

Me, we are all ME's one says who is Bob. (if you were Bob, you'd say that would be ME). All me [Your name]

- The Universal intelligence is the inner Mind of God and us. The world of the human outside is the same as the physical Universe and is still separate. We are able to exist and be on either world non-physical or physical. The world of spirit is not what one thinks; it is more like the counterpart of how pi relates to everything that is relative to the outside world.

A simple way to say what this means; As a human we can either "live outside" on the human, physical side of the world (outside our bodies), and/or we can choose to "live inside," in the non-physical side, the spiritual world (from the inside). To be or not to be is the question? If it's to be from the right (non-physical side) everything on the spiritual side, and you know what that means when you are over the need to be right. A perfect example of this is President Trump, who is not over the need to be right. There is no right and wrong when it comes to which side you're living on- the non-physical world or the physical world and when you know to live on both equally you can be over the need to be right. Do you know what is the right side of though? It is knowing how to let the bad ones dissipate.

Is to be in the physical world to exist on and in the now? To be or not to be is the question to live in the non-physical world.

Is to be ▌physical 'or non-physical | Not to be is the question.

'Inside' that is if it is to be that is to be on the 'right of what is the need to get over right. That is a need for sure, where there is no right or wrong to see what world it is it is not to fear without act on thought by choice of good thoughts with wanting to understand what it is to be on the right of how to chose what are thoughts right side wrong watch disappear this is to be which way, this the right one to see for sure.

The science smalls are the nucleus 'to' (find is to believe) an atom and quirks. There are 12 things smaller than the atom. etc. We now have three spheres = 9 with one sphere more is 4 = 12, we also have 12 partitions. Still working this A, E ,I,O,U...down at the bottom. Read Red separately from Black and purple as if they are working together in different ways. The same with blue.

The statement to the One Mind 'is that or that is' in all of us inside and outside, inner and outer has a polar opposite starting with ('of' means part of the whole) "of" / "to"(the balance way the laws work together) (to 'find') 'to means to define emotion to a particular location' [is to] 'believe') the (inside/outside) get one to the designer (of, [is to?] {('Be' to 'know') [is to] [is (is, is now) to] (each world inside sees at the same time from different ways to the outside, this is part of or all the whole making up the third world? I think so far) 'is to' know now}. Is (now) to (find) be (know) of what that 'is to be right the right of what is 'is' getting over the need to be right - that is a need for sure the need to be right the' need is to get over is right 'to be on the side is to the right or wrong (know truth) We (is the inside of US is to Know of which way is the right that is to know for sure the way [is to] see into the truth from the outside in to Me Myself and I. And the inside out to the inside of the Mind Body and Soul. To listen to our bodies in silence will provide all the answers to know what love is. {(if, it), (on, in), (as, at) is there 7? (Is it 'to'??)} Starting at two letters then three and so on then back to one letter. Example: the first two letters: One = One world inside plus one world outside = US is outside and WE are inside representing one, a world of its own UI and God. Starting with one letter like I AM inside and am I outside is a polar inner and outer.

Is if 'it is' to be 'is to' be on the right side 'of what is', is to get over the need to be right, that is a need for sure, as their is no right or wrong when seeking a divine power from red or blue worlds.

[Is if] the possibilities of the non-physical world inside of us [is if] we took everything out of the non- physical would we be left with only the energy of our senses, then it doesn't matter if the inner and outer physical side of us can share the same space or not? Then [it is] we are the same in the (outside) physical world and inside the non-physical world [it is to be] or not to be means to know which world is to be on non-physical or physical world.

Is (now) to (find) be (know) or not to be! is (A) (not the question? (is 'a' (the) where Shakespeare just thought he was done (like me many many, many times)? He stopped which side spirt/non- physical or physical/human. Then next what is the need to be right 'of is' to get over 'the need' to be right of the truth of this of is for us after we know something now at this time 'of' after the word know triggered that lead me to how did I know what is next, the logical question: how do I know which way is the right! Then to the right 'of is' to get over the need.

This opens up the 3rd world only if you are open to growth and the window of seeing is not blocked by cloudy thoughts, beliefs and/or judgment. The world on the inside is the same but different from the world on the outside. This is the balanced center that leads to the portal. A clear way to see this is to dismiss any bad thoughts and let the good ones malinger no matter what.

Self can refer to one individual, or to everyone at the same time. The most important and complete element on the planet is us. We are made to continuously emulate the workings of the universe. By connecting science as the outside of a human and religion as the inside, both start at the opposite ends of the stick. Ultimately, they come to the middle at an equal rate. Emotions and logic, men and women, God and human, and Universe and Humanity are all centered equally. Everything fits together perfectly and is the system as it is up to us to uncover the plan is to become one God, one love and one truth together. Life's plan is to unite the self and through this we will solve all human conditioning problems and relationship problems that come up.

Everything in time and space is one complete God that cannot be divided, whether you see it, believe it or not. God is the complete puzzle; He made the puzzle and controls how it works and how it goes together. We miss things and don't see the whole because we are human. This is how we unite to become stronger. Together we push out unintentional evil so we can eventually see the whole to become one.

Love and truth are the complete truth and this is what it means to know the God-self first. The second is to protect the nucleus of the family by the playbook of their child. One has to see for themselves, but it is so easy to overlook or miss things, or not see at all. This leads to a misunderstanding, or only having a part of the truth. This can cause us to unintentionally lie to ourselves. That is why we have such high divorce rates. We are oblivious to the depth of the whole Universal truth. Most pain and suffering comes from human's lack of education. We don't know that we are God and have all the necessary skills within us, but we just need to be taught the correct way to tap into them.

The deeper one knows the God thing, the more complex it is for outsiders who have not had a transformation to see. But it is easier to understand from the inside, for those who have had a transformation. People try to figure things out from the outside in, and rarely do they try to see the whole truth. The people that are oblivious are mostly everyday people. Ninety-nine percent of them are not aware that both sides, inside and outside, each have a complete truth. Each pattern follows the universe's makeup and the issues are the same. In the end, this makes up the whole truth, which is God, love and self.

God is the perfect unity of all things, connecting all the systems into one big machine that operates perfectly without a component out of place. We are included as part of the masters of the machine. This means we can see how all everything works in unity together like a puzzle. The guide to the universe is broken down into many playbooks.

Thirty years ago, I asked a friend if he believed in God. He said that he wants to believe, but he didn't understand why there is so much pain and suffering in the world. It was a question I couldn't answer for myself for many years. I wonder if the pain and suffering in the world comes from a lack of knowing and being able to learn the skills of Timeless Wisdom. We know that using the skills can reduce pain and suffering tremendously. Though the cause of pain and suffering is us, it is not necessarily our fault. It occurs because we don't understand and are not aware of how things truly work from the inside.

In some ways, we look at our parents as gods until we ourselves become adults. As we get older, we no longer believe our parents are gods, but we usually understand that they did what they could with what they had. We understand that they may not have known everything about what it means to be human. They acted in the way they were conditioned to. In a Tony Robbins documentary, he discussed the idea that the pain our parents give us can either stay with us or leave us. We have seen over time that parenting in the wrong way can damage a child, and this often manifests when they are an adult. This often happens because the parents didn't use the skills of the past. They didn't know what now can be explained through the symbolic divine that exists within each one of us. They didn't have the skills of timeless wisdom. We may find out that the skills of timeless wisdom are the same in all people and that they are the God part which is the same in all of us. What does that mean? The processes of the skills don't change over time (they are timeless). Life's plan doesn't change; it remains for us to uncover what is on the inside. Every generation should take what they have learned and add it to the timeless wisdom. We now are to put the operations in sync to a laser focus, narrowing down the nuggets of information into order. Our **_Purpose_** is for us to discover constants, and to see what is relative. $E = mc2$ where c is the speed of light to the outside of Global stabilized energy to the energy. **_That is_** why our energy relates to all within us to Global stabilized energy from inside as our outside. It is stable like gravity.

Let's look at the same thing in a different way. What if God, love and the truth are the same, just in a different way and they all end up the same inside each one of us way down deep? What would that look like? The reason why is inside of us. We need to see collectively, organize and operate what we know in a more efficient, effective way. This will provide results of what inter-technology can really do collectively. The inside world and outside world of oneself are separate and exist on their own, like a sliding scale. The vertical scale goes from believing to knowing, from God to human and the center is the Rubik's Cube of Knowledge, explaining balanced love, God and the truth after we see past the barricade and through the portal and the past present and future perhaps are the same, with the right knowledge. In some ways, our conscience is to unintentionally mislead science. The answers may lie between the lines of our subconscious (which is the inside) and then our conscience (outside) as we think our minds want to work as one for ourselves, then together as one. We do, but it's the way we follow the relationship of just one side or the other. The answers lie between the inside to the inside or the outside to the outside. We as humanity have put together different parts of the portal to make it whole. We just have to let our minds see and go to the depth of understanding in the sacred part of what we find down deep in ourselves. This may be in our soul or spirit. We need to peel away layers of the human side and at the same time layers of the spiritual inside to understand that what is between the lines is another level or dimension as part of the truth. We will find that inside each of us is a connection if we want to use it. I think self-help is the way of tying religion and the law together. We just need to change the perception of what is godly. The thing that is the hardest to recognize is the easiest to see. We often overlook this because we think that it can't possibly be that simple. But being smart isn't about reading and writing; those are tools. It is about the way one sees and understands.

Inside   The mind = UI. Universal Intelligences. = This is one Universe.

Outside   The body = Universe, Earth and Human, = One place to live.

Inside /outside The soul = unity, One spirit inside and outside in communications.

Outside/ Inside/ Center.   The connection between the World and Humanities sub-tonic connection is God and self.

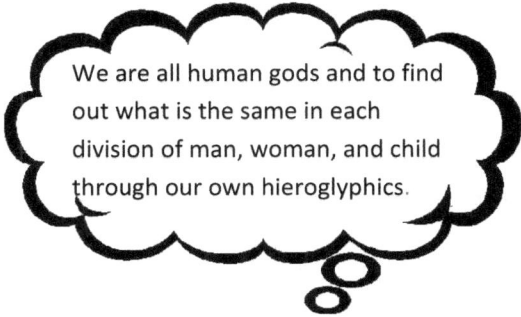

We are all human gods and to find out what is the same in each division of man, woman, and child through our own hieroglyphics.

Chapter Fourteen:

Mary Baker Eddy
Related Emails

While I was waiting for my manuscript to get professionally edited my brother-in-law TJ gave me a book, because he said what I wrote has already been done! I said "really?" But the book was published in 1875 and in my mind, I said, "The author was a female. She was divorced, too, and her book turned into the God thing like mine did?" He was wrong, but I can understand, because when one follows love we see and seek the truth.

I read the book that TJ gave me, which was "Science and Health with Keys to the Scriptures", by Mary Baker Eddy, published in 1875. It SOLD OVER 8 MILLION COPIES. I think him giving me the book was the best help someone could have possibly given me because even though I'm not a religious man the book TJ gave me was about his religion. What this did was enhanced her work where the main body of her work was to prevent the human race from the ailments of "The Human Conditioning" by learning how and what to "believe" through Christ Jesus's work, using faith and his knowledge. As I was reading the book, I sent Tj and my editor (Keidi) updates which I will post here; Tj was on point - it showed how to believe and who to follow. And mine was the "SAME" for different reasons but could end up accomplishing the same thing to my amazement and if there is a possibility to help, then I say explore any and all options to cure human conditioning. What she (MBE) Mary Baker Eddy believes is absolutely correct for the most part, for what I believe is true. For example: both TJ's parents were Christian Scientists as well but died because they held on to a belief backed by "FAITH" (if you know then you don't need faith) that wasn't true from no fault of MBE. The fact is it's not about what you believe or even what you think you know but "what is true." The whole truth is the answer (it's simple but we overlook it). What we "KNOW" may not be the answer unless it is the truth for sure, beyond a shadow of a doubt. Only God's word is designed to get to a series of truths to find the whole truth though the correct formula of the process that works for any and all problems at the same time.

By the end of the emails and letters you should see the process to know the formula. It is simple but not easy and my 2nd editor didn't get it but Tj did. These emails and letters are unedited and my writing is poor so may be hard to understand but if you read the whole book you would have a better chance to understand because the whole book has been edited.

A series of emails I sent regarding the Mary Baker Eddy book follow, and should add insight into the matter of religion. In addition, they may help explain a portion of the process that went in to editing an early version of the book:

From TJ:

July 2, 2019:

KEVIN BEFORE YOU GO ANY FURTHER I NEED YOU TO READ MRS. EDDY'S MAJOR WORK "SCIENCE AND HEALTH WITH KEY TO THE SCRIPTURES" AS YOU WILL FIND WHAT YOU HAVE BEEN WORKING ON FOR YEARS HAS ALREADY BEEN DONE BY HER AND AT THE BACK OF THE BOOK ARE 100 PAGES DEVOTED TO SHARING HOW PEOPLE WERE HEALED JUST BY READING IT. BUT IT ABSOLUTELY LAYS OUT THE TRUTH AND HOW IT RELATES TO ALL THINGS AND HOW GOD IS REFLECTED BY AND IN ALL OF US. I HAVE EXTRA COPIES AT HOME BUT PLEASE TAKE A WEEK AND READ IT BEFORE YOU GO ANY FUTHER SO YOU GET WHERE SHE IS COMING FROM AND YOU WILL FIND YOU ARE COMING FROM THE SAME PLACE. PLUS, SHE IS MUCH EASIER TO UNDERSTAND THAN YOU ARE SO THERE'S THAT TOO. BUT READ IT FROM COVER TO COVER AND YOU WILL SEE SHE WAS HUNDREDS OF YEARS AHEAD OF HER TIME HERE ON EARTH WHICH IS WHY SO MANY DON'T UNDERSTAND LIKE YOUR BROTHER SCOTT. HE THINKS SHE FOUNDED A CULT WHICH SHE DID NOT DO!!! SHE JUST WANTED PEOPLE TO KNOW GOD AND HAVE A RELATIONSHIP WITH HIM/HER.

Tj,

This is the conversation I'm having with my editor now!

No response needed just includes where I am in the book and some opinions....

Keidi,

I will need to read my book again; as I said you have some mad skills and right now I need to see how these 4 or 5 important points make it back in or how they need to be detailed because the first time I think you overlooked them (the very points I thought should go to the pros) and here is an example: My brother-in-law asked me to read this book "Science and Health with Key to the Scriptures" by Mary Baker Eddy. Published in 1875. He said I should read this because he thinks what I'm writing has already been done. I am 220 pages in, and so far, he is right. All the answers that are correct are without error - God through Love and Truth guided by spiritual and mass (mine is spiritual and human between them is the truth finder - the law and the proof to know, not just believe). She said the Truth makes no laws to regulate sickness, sin and death for these are the unknown to Truth and should not be recognized as reality. She is correct until a deeper Truth is found (that which I did) a way to graduate from believing to "KNOWING" the proof is in our language between the middle of the center at the razor's edge of nouns and in verbs in writing when you have the correct ingredients. Together with the right sentences for understanding when the rules and regulations are done correctly (humanity is not doing it the right way now, including you). I am just trying to introduce something new. She also indicates the fruit of the knowledge tree is without error but failed to see she was on the right track but we as the people can put that together without error, because the perfect human is God. The point of the language, self and God in the book all come back to themselves making them the same as all "one", in the universe, of one!

Let's see where you are when you finish?

With respect, Kevin

07-25

Keidi,

Here are some things that should make it back in the book. Some can be used for the truth for what I'm after or could be used for the pros. This is just what the book I'm reading pulled out of me. I thought you should be aware of it. The master said "if a kingdom divided against itself, that kingdom cannot stand".

Starting with self we as humans are naturally divided because of our spiritual side - that which is immortal (mind, non-physical, intangible, "verb", polar opposite inside words comes back to itself, five inside senses thinking, listening, believing, seeing, knowing) and our human side that which is mortal (body, physical, tangible, "noun" polar opposite outside words, self, outside senses). These sides when merged correctly in the center equal the truth, and we find the answers for life and in life and is "God's Word", literally. Shows how humanity is all "KNOWING" through each language predicated the language has an inside part and an outside part to break it down to explain how God is everything everywhere and the way everything works. As I said it starts with "self" or (Same as God) God. One of the same if you put self behind or in front of each religion, because to "SEE" God's image one needs to connect the inside and outside of a human but also see and understand the dichotomies of male and female to apply to oneself. One half is love, the other half is truth and together are all the perfect answers from the center (truth) and the middle (love). Jesus said: "For whosoever shall do the will of my Father which is in heaven the same is my brother, and sister, and mother." The error in this is we think we are NOT the same as the human God "Jesus" because if we were the same there would be one religion throughout the world by adding "self" to every religion. One God in heaven our Father and the rest are relatives human Gods all the same a part that has god in us.(page 267). One need not have faith when we have mastered the formula to the center of all "KNOWING" that which becomes knowledge without error using a language when it becomes perfect as "God's word" (the truth is covered by error) we need to strip away error by hitting the middle of spiritual truth and the center of human truth.

The pieces and part I thought were explained in my book until it got edited: the term Christ, or Jesus the Christ (to give the full and proper translation of the Greek) may be rendered "Jesus the anointed" Jesus the God- crowned or "the divinely royal man", as it is said of him in the first chapter of Hebrews:-(page 313). The point is definition without error when the parts are properly placed the truth can't help but come out. I found the formula that reveals "GOD'S WORD" for the English language. Along with the way "YOU" look at things your relationship with ourselves directed to be the perfect human (not to be perfect but to know the skills of timeless wisdom perfectly) God and you are schooled the same. With this the relationship with the one you had babies with can stand together by choice until we figure out how death works. "Jesus gave us a glimpse of that." Jesus said, "He that believeth on me, (not in me) the works that I do shall he do also" (page 326). We are human Gods too with the right training taking away error. Jesus walked on water and maybe we can get there too! When we hit the height of spirituality? Maybe in the definitions somewhere where placed in the correct order vertically loop and the right way horizontal between what is matter (human) and spirit with correct rules and regulations. An example: The human (matter) side is pretty self-explanatory because it is tangible and a noun. But the spiritual side is intangible and a verb - the unknown side, God. But can be explained by and in language from the correct separation from the inside and outside of language. To "see" from the outside is by our eyes and to "see" by the inside is our minds to understand the polar opposite words "see" in all ways together complete the word to make it whole when it comes back to itself. One word whole and all complete - the perfect scientific proof to uncover "the Holy Ghost or spirit" by uncovering the other side of the word to complete it to make whole to come back to itself. You're right only one copy should be sent to the pros and it should be earth shattering by what I uncovered "the best of the best."

Thanks
Kevin

p.s. half way through the book!

On Fri, Jul 26, 2019 at 9:23 AM

Actually, this really helped! Inadvertently I am showing how what she says is true and the formula that makes it so, with definitive proof by what I uncovered. Read what I sent my editor and see if what I am doing is coming together? Up to page 350 with some details below. Thank you; it gives me a point of reference.

08-12

Kevin,

That's funny you mention page 468 because I was actually going to refer you back to that page and let you know the scientific statement of being near the top of the page right above the definition of substance that is the core foundational statement of everything Mrs. Eddy preached from and healed from right there so go back to page 468 and re-read and memorize this scientific statement of being because that is the core of our entire religion. And oh, by the way Kevin, it's a wonderful healing prayer as well so if you're ever in need like I've been with this stupid car accident you pray that prayer and it brings about healing immediately

Sent from my iPhone TJ

Jesus said "I and my Father are one"--- that is, one in quality, not in quantity. I demonstrated how all things and living things become "ONE" even matter and spirit. Explained by language put everything the same but differentness in both sides of everything. But how everything is split, separated and divided from the whole, or God image. What is the most important is how the twins, brothers in language explains how everything is the same and separated and divided. This is where I enhanced Dyer's work! Where humans are just the same, (Dyer says) but also the same as everything because it all comes to one, or back to itself. Matter and energy, love and truth, God and everything, even you. When you understand God, He and you are One! "Truth and love" are one, "time and space" are one "another one goes here." "Perfect Love casteth out fear" as they cannot share the same space for the truth our children need to be aware and educated correctly for a union to stand; divorce is pointless when one knows the skills of timeless wisdom. Originally this whole project started because I said to my ex-wife "someday somebody will prove divorce is wrong and pointless" for the majority and can be worked out when children are involved. I didn't know 25 years later it would be me to uncover with scientific proof but moreover this would lead me to explain myself, God as one with humanity and the formula to and in life and I'm still not religious so I'm thinking religion has it wrong. But Jesus is the same as us we are one and we are seeing it wrong because as our own children we love like gods and since God is love our children are gods, too. I have never felt as much pain as when my ex-wife absconded with our three children in the dark of the night to live across country for the kids to grow up without their real father; the law didn't even protect me and we had joint custody (get joint primary physical custody). As you know I never did anything wrong when we were married never hit or cheated on her, provided well and just loved her. I maybe went to the bar too much, but I was young. I went four or five times a month, but I didn't even like getting drunk and did nothing that couldn't have been worked out. When the pain is so great, we seek comfort in God's love when the greatest love I have ever known is gone and too little to talk. Well, the oldest was five but it's not the same, she wouldn't let me talk to them anyway. I keep seeking what is love; I wanted to understand it from my ex, my children and even God, I came from a good family so I understood that love, and when I tie into the truth I really dug deep and started to explain my 1st family. But also, we are God's children so that makes us relatives part god and part human because we come from the original source and He made us, right? As the family is key to understanding "God" and how all things and people work, they start the process to life and in life is family really; how everything works was God's goal and still is shared with language and self are the "SAME" but differentness. I found out how to consummate a marriage "spiritually"; it is to make a god-child and interact together, share that child as God's equal is having the same equality as being equally the same as Man and woman metaphysically together as "ONE" to God (the only reason why same-sex relationships don't fit) have the best relationship possible by choice from the correct education God provides and a rough copy of the formula is in my book. I found the education was with self; what it is to be a God is "KNOWING" what it is to be true to oneself, humanly, is to have sex to consummate a marriage we all know how to do this married or not.

Our parents take us to church but the church really doesn't know this they just have their priorities mixed up; where the children grow into adults love and truth start all over again on their own but demonstrate the perfect world together in the center after you see both sides of self! This is where humanity has lost sight of God correctly when we live as adults in the scientific world where all becomes "one" with self or "oneself" is God (all people together is one self) and our neighbor using the right formula we start living heaven on earth with the right relationships is only with the opposite sex to spouses and our children: this is where one finds the truth because the truth is immortal, always right! The human side is error but not always because it sees some truth and is mortal that's why the nucleus family pulls God's plan together automatically when followed properly. Page 468 -what is substance? Answer-- Substance is that which is eternal and incapable of discord and decay. Truth, Life and Love are substance, as the scriptures use this word in Hebrew: "The substance of things hoped for, the evidence of things not seen" Spirit, the synonym of mind, Soul or God, is the only real substance. The formula to have scientific proof and God's word the same word will change writing for ever without error and now ready to cure disease when the formula is reveled.

08-12

I went back and reread the scientific statement of being! (Wow, you realize the core of your religion is the whole basis of my book). She did it better because she writes far better than I do, but the basis is the same and when you read my completed book you will understand how she and I are exactly on the same page. But even though she articulates it better than I, the patterns are the same for me to go a few steps deeper and people will understand the reasoning without error (because it is the truth). I hope my editor recognizes and understands the details of where I go deeper and is able to make sense of it and puts an understanding on paper to "KNOW" not just believe. An example - what we can do if Jesus was a human God the same as all of us, we would have one religion; one God is oneself or all of self together (our numbers would be much greater). Language is able to explain without error the intangibles of God, Love and the Truth in writing to scientific perfection with God's blessing. I pointed it out to the editor I hope she puts it back in. I would rather have the formula put in her words, so people understand it. So, all things of substance can be explained the same way in the same patterns when tying together the intangibles and tangibles inside and outside to make language whole perfect (God's mind). I just explain God if you don't understand I will try to break it out.

08-15

Thank you Tj – it should be clearer now?

The world needs to know "ONESELF" is God individually defined by [Your Name] God all together by all of "SELF" (you and everybody else together) is when humanity unites all of self (Language discreetly and directly defines God individually and all together at the same time is one God all of self). Page 535 - When will man pass through the open gates of Christian Science into the heaven of Soul, into the heritage of the first born among men? Truth is indeed "the way" (I think there is an error in her thinking by the way she and I are following the truth because the way is "self" individually (God) and "self all together" is everybody and is one complete God and from His perspective only one God. The scientific proof is when "self" the intangible part completes the whole word with the tangible part and commence the entire self, inside and outside means humanity, God and oneself. Continuous with every birth and death, humanity being "directed by language" for perfect knowledge to understand with all the answers guided in between the center of "LOVE" and the middle of "TRUTH" to know everything perfectly without error.

In language, is where we see the scientific proof because the God that I imagine run science and when they are equal, we live up to who God made us to be, His equal. When the intangible with the polar opposite words with the rules and regulations all go through one word (not the other way around), and it comes back to itself to be whole! And what makes it complete is by connecting the inside "intangible" word and outside "tangible" word together (this process will explain everything, the unknowns even the holy spirit when all words are entirely consummated without error). One must first understand how to separate each word into an oxymoron; "oxy" spiritual side of the word and "moron" human side of the word also the definition in the dictionary for the word to split up for nouns which are human and verbs which are spiritual and how they are divided. The answer to God's word which is only the truth becomes his voice when we get each part correct we'll have mastered His system in language; language will guide us to get there (because God is the way) to hear His voice. Perfect means the human Condition is healed - no disease, no poverty, no divorce, live a life in perfect harmony with the one you had babies with in love and truth with the right skills and when "SELF" becomes God we love our neighbor, when God becomes "SELF" we love our neighbor as if they were ourselves! Because we all know what it is to be the same God because it just is "The perfect human with total and complete KNOWLEDGE" of the God-self inside and out is God and in order to see this "all ways at the same time" need to be seen and understood correctly. So, all knowledge a part we don't know is can we come back to life and if so for how long? Or do life and death come together in any way or can we get our youth back? My question is: will this truth finder answer these questions?

Answer to the gates: When we drop Christian at the gates! We are left with science we now include the whole world in one religion "SELF" humans are part spiritual (God) and part human we stand exactly the same as Jesus Christ a human God, we need to catch up to his teachings and not misunderstand them so we can do what he did (he is NOT interested in being praised). It matters not what we are "So you thinketh you shall be." We are "Children of God" direct relatives to and from God we can justify in any way. The immortal side to see truth when taught correctly how to see perfection and the human sides both are a truth; without one you don't have the whole truth but it's the way the sides get to the center of the middle without getting lost, overlooked or confused so use the guide between human and spiritual to see truth to weed out error (an enhancement to MBE).

This formula when complete, and when it gets the blessing of all the other pros (religious, spiritual and academic leaders) it is exciting because to "KNOW" God exists or He did when we are born with a part of Him inside us, now believing in God has an end to "KNOW" and understand everything from things to living things through the direction of language, self and equal to God mathematically are "one" as demonstrated in my book. How the world is explained by one child "YOURS" and Jesus is just an example of what humans are capable of when the spiritual side is fully tapped into. How (your) the child is God and the guide to keep mom and dad to stay together the definition of love comes from equality and the truth! Is all the correct answers (your) child driven through the relationship starting with "self", God? And the other person/god that helped make that God-child the other parents both should be skilled properly in timeless wisdom, language and God-self. When an individual sees there is only "one" correct reality and it is God's plan! Accurately to perfection. Because the universe operates as a mirror image of human correctness; to work perfectly it needs to be equal and perfect for checks and balances to take place. For no disease to exist or poverty AND IT STARTS WITH self individually and THE ONE YOU HAD BABIES WITH collectively for the Community when we are down to less than 5% divorce rate by choice not fear or religion by being equal to each other male, female and God we will have mastered God-self and truly "KNOW" God and His plan (God, Self, language, child, adult, humanity to work in unison) and how to have relationships with each without error we will progress to living heaven on earth, humanities and personal collective goal of what should be the same.

On Mon, Sep 16, 2019, 6:32 PM TJ < wrote:

Read your email and wow that's a lot to take in again can you have Keidi break it into bite size pieces so folks can digest it in little pieces? Also read the letter below and you have a couple of spelling errors and grammar errors so can you have her redo before you send it to him?! Would be wise on your part I think just my two cents.

Sent from my iPhone TJ CLU CHFC

On Sep 16, 2019, at 1:36 PM, Kc Patt <kcpattison@gmail.com> wrote:

Hello Keidi,

I think after reading this and then the Morgan Freeman letter attached we should talk about the ending as the letter is more the end of the book with all the other content I sent you.

Hi another thought!,

How can we unite the world together starting with the pros and the public using social media and other outlets of media to get on the same page? A solid foundation led by truth that is backed up is what we have. How God and "self" is/are the same thing, individually separated by yourself labeled by [Your Name] along with all of "self" meaning everybody or humanity is God too, so it matters not what one thinks, believes or knows because it just is...the truth! "SELF" From God's perspective there is only one God because he made us!!! With the help of his adult human gods or his children to have children and to make families but nevertheless equal to him as his partner. The breakthrough into explaining God through language and everything else that exists correctly is where words come back to itself each word is the proof spelled out scientifically. Such as where the second "self" completes the entire word how is spelled out 1st part of self is us individually the 2nd part of self is us too but collectively both explain God perfectly down to "one" God because we are born with a part of God in us and the definitions come back to itself. When we complete the entire dictionary with this formula we will have figured out God's word and when we complete sentences with this formula will hear God's voice to know the truth to eventually "KNOW" every "thing" and "living thing" and how everything works in the universe. The relationships with "self" - remember "God and self" are the same thing because God is the perfect human. An example: is Jesus a human god we are equal to? The churches got it wrong and are holding us back from great things. Our Father, whether physical form or not, made the inner workings, intangibles and non-physical etc. parts of the universe in his image identical to the human conditioning (the proof science, religion and academics missed) both sides outer working, tangibles and all physical things go together are explained by nouns in writing perfectly for how humans and God go together in the universe inner workings are separated by intangibles and non-physical stuff is explained by verbs in writing together are one (too much irrefutable proof to be wrong) but first separate this way by the inside and outside then divide by spiritual and human then split by verbs and nouns for us to unite our self and put in writing don't worry they are all the same if it fits perfectly its correct. The one you had babies with made another god hopefully still with undoubtedly the most important relationship to master. Because when we find piece by piece together on the inside to be whole in our God-self or spiritual side and our human side become are "ONE" we are in and at peace. This reflects the outside for our communities to unite and become one. Now 50% of us or more have been through a divorce unfair to our K.I.D.S. we need to "Keep Innocent Dreams Safe". We all have a spiritual side and that side is intangible and identical to God's perfection in his invisible image (illustrated by the universe) that makes us all the same. The other side is human tangible that gives us our individuality and imperfection, putting both sides together is the fight within self; we must first "know" how to split, separate and divide "language, self and the human god" and "KNOW" how it comes each back to itself. But how to solve that fight within is to understand it! To become a god add the knowledge of the opposite sex and know the patterns of the universe they will provide answers as it operates as a mirror image of humans correctness the human body and the intangible universe among many other things.

Humanely to consummate a marriage is to have sex and spiritually consummate one is to have a god child together something nobody else can give you the possibility of a perfect life or close as it gets (I think my mom had that life; she is 78 years old).   The child has always provided God's knowledge to tap into as the glue to God and to keep a marriage together in a happy environment and when those skills are mastered by using timeless wisdom and inter technology (God) by using truth and love are the correct answers to life in the center to unite. We as humanity, when we achieve a high percentage of togetherness and unite through education, amazing things will happen like happiness, inside and out by the way you look at things the things you look at change. "Justice inside and outside." This means humanity is understanding God's game plan; it is under our control to live heaven on earth with life having little or no diseases, no mental health issues and inside the body all works perfectly - our thinking, believing and knowing skills... work down to what just is.... the truth by what operates in the middle of spiritual and the central part of human for the best outcome. The work that will been done on the inside by a change of focus will help the planet to achieve "Global stabilizedenergy.com " on the outside it will provide us with little to no crime, and no mass shooting, churches will dismantle beliefs that are in error and the world will have one religion with the ability to all know the correct intent of Jesus's work is for self! (an example: Love your neighbor like your "SELF"). Answer - because we are the same spiritually with rules and regulations before we help others be trained correctly spiritually and humanly together. Where the truth will set you free. The science is how everything fits together perfectly when the right methodology is used all correct rules and regulations are used in the right way each word is completed and used properly with the formula in sentences to hear God's voice. The proof without error is in a perfect language and how everything fits perfectly and mathematically together like a puzzle. When we have this correct without error it will be "God's way" or his plan and language will tell us truth.... what is. When scientific proof and God are equal and have equality therefore an understanding to start with stands for everybody.

I needed your two cents. Thank you for reading and giving me your input. I had Andrea come over to help edit that letter to Morgan Freeman before I sent it but that changed because I thought one had to read the letter to understand the ending of the book. But I was wrong it is the ending of the book to understand the first part of the book and the last part of the book together is the formula for the truth and not a letter to be sent. Basically in short there are four parts to the truth. 1. Man 2. Women 3.God 4.Human

The truth works in unison to the center at the same time all together to be the one and only truth to everything in the universe (understanding the patterns and formula). MBE nailed a vertical truth between God and human, and another vertical truth between human and spiritual, basically the other way. But she didn't acknowledge the horizontal truth of man and woman making up one perfect human to be God. Basically, in a human being we have a spiritual side which is God. What connects God is man and woman together as one; both start at opposite sides of the stick and when they meet at the center with that knowledge on both sides we are "ONE" complete human the perfect God. We have a human side that is in error but can see the truth. Each side is a truth; one side without the other is part of the truth (an unintentional lie, justification, overlooking, not seen, being oblivious to the truth) but not the whole truth. Basically, the book teaches the horizontal truth and the vertical truth and creates a plus sign and in the center is "THE" rock solid truth from science or by God one of the same answers when it is correct. The human truth - what is the spiritual truth? It is the same when they meet correctly like in a puzzle using the right formula. MBE had the formula right with a few adjustments but she just needed to go deeper which is why she wasn't able to cure all human conditioning. Because together we need to cure relationships mainly with self and all the other problems at the same time; the system needs to be perfect so everything will be perfect... basically know and understand God's plan perfectly. I hope that helps?

09-20 (actually a personal matter about funding for editing)

Well that's a shame that she's wanting to charge more gosh darn money but geez you got to get her to read the emails so she gets the point she has to be able to draw this to a conclusion successfully because you and I both know if she screws up the last 5% the whole book is toast because in my opinion the last part of the book - that last 5% - is the most important of the whole book because it drives home the point you're trying to make to everybody who reads it.

09-29

Tj, my editor either doesn't understand or has not read the emails from me to you. But nevertheless, as you can see, she's focused on wanting more money and not answering my emails. The truth is if she had read the emails, she would have been trying to negotiate how much she could retain as a percentage of selling the book. Basically, any editor can finish the book, she understands 95% but not the end. You my friend understand 5% - the end - but how it becomes reality is the "TRUTH" what you don't see only because you haven't read the book. The truth in the now truth in life for life for our children's children and God's truth is in every partial to complete truth guided by the 4 truths man, woman, God, human truths on the cover of the book how each one works we can split, separate and divided all together as "ONE" truth for anything and everything. This process of the patterns and the system are the same for everything that makes God perfect. Humanity needs to see we are the beneficiary to learn the correct way.

Kevin

09-20

True.

She answered an email with one word "Yes" she did read our emails. I hope she outlines the 4 truths because we can get to any truth in the universe (all of us) with this formula. I will take a picture of the cover I sent to Jennifer. The book can potentially be the next Bible or the upgraded one using this formula with the truth that can set us free using God's word, literally. With that being said wouldn't you want a percentage of the book that has the potential to do great things rather than risk the measly editing dollars? I have enhanced all the professionals' work over the last 25 years with this (she has agreed); the answers are just as impressive to how I enhanced or can work together with MBE. I can get the pros to come to me now I was very hard on her for the first edit because the first edit she cut way too much out either because my writing sucks (as I know it is) and/or she just didn't understand it, same thing really, that she's finishing up by next week the 2nd edit. I will send you over the letter I drafted for her to edit to send to the pros where I enhance their work 3 months ago. I asked her to put what she cut out back in that had to do with the pros and how I enhance them. She has some mean writing skills but used them in the wrong way do you think it's possible she doesn't understand? Well we won't know until next week because the truth is she didn't understand on the first edit and now it just takes clarifying I think maybe possibly and it also explains what she cut out, thanks to you giving me that MBE book. And I think to edit mine right to capture everything correctly she needs to redo the whole edit because now she sees my whole intent and everything comes together from what I wrote in those emails as it is all the same thing! But what she sees now or understands should have helped complete it.

I started writing this letter to Morgan Freeman and when you read the letter it is the end of the book by how it ties down the truth together in the early part of the truth if it wasn't cut out? After reading that book (MBE) and writing what it pulled out of me it seems that whatever is cut out could be dangerous especially, with this letter. I had another book recommended - Joseph Smith; some Mormon book may pull out another chunk to make it easier to understand other sections like for the "church" goers that are seeking God on the outside and the "spiritual" group seeking God on the inside this may tie down the part so it will not be cut out accidentally and the academics will understand how and why that knowledge become "ONE." I think to prove it works gays are the reason - same sex relationships show how it isn't in God's plan only because A) The same side doesn't fit in the plan how the Universe works together with humans and it

all fits together perfectly into "ONE". B). The same side isn't equal either, making it uneven to "KNOW" God because C). Everything fits into "ONE." Meaning we "KNOW" everything inside us but we just don't "see" it; that is why we "think we know" when we don't "KNOW" to see the truth (this messes a lot of things up). Did you follow me there? This has nothing to do with gays themselves the "teachings" over time will prevent the ones seeking love for the wrong masculine or feminine choice the exceptional levels humanity can make up when divorce by choice is less than 5% by the right teaching with the correct "knowledge." When we haven't been using God's system! It is now time to enhance to change to the making the perfect
system!

Hello

I hope the light is bright and made it back in the book with great detail as to the formula in language tie in the horizontal and vertical truths making "ONE" (outlining how "one" works) answer for each thing by the way of the correct process to the middle of the center in the plus sign to pinpoint the right perfect answer. The truth is "God" - how everything works God's way because He is the right way and our instructions how we should see and behave understand the truth first for everything we as humanity figure out together using the universe, language and how things come back to self for each truth. Once we have the whole entire truth the ones that choose to live out of the truth can, but what will the penalty be? I'm assuming not to be set free. This way after we work for the answers to define truth, we can be set free if and when it is the real truth. Example: The human body is defined by breasts, vagina and a penis; all can be altered surgically except the hip structure making them the permanent female gender to society or the male hips is the truth! One can lie to themselves to convince other genders that this is interchangeable and acceptable, but the truth is not hidden and altering doesn't fit in His plan. When archaeologists find the skeleton the bone structure dictates a male or female and this cannot be altered so there is only one truth; the rest is lying to ourselves. So altering one's body, changing one's sex and gay relationships or divorce don't fit so far. I can help with divorce but it involves God (again I'm not a religious man but I do not think God is either) and the way you are lying to yourself not knowing God or oneself as it is all the "same" for humanity. The universe has all the answers and I will give you the formula even though they are within you. The way we are using religion is keeping us from the correct answers or the whole truth by unknowingly lying to our self. The church should be running the country alongside the politician because the plan in the end is to provide justice inside and out for all of "self" worldwide to be one nation under God using his spiritual laws combined with human laws. This is all in the dictionary in the definitions and God lead me from the "LOVE" I lost in the middle of love by the center of "TRUTH" together helped me see the whole truth to the love I have now. Completing "self" first is to unite a male and female together inside (all the pros missed) you to be god along with uniting the spiritual and human side inside you after you "know" how they work together. We have completed "oneself" (not really, don't get confused because self has all the answers inside, too, because we are some mixture of the spiritual side Perfect Image) and ready to be trained for a union with a spouse to fit perfectly when we start with "SELF" everybody in "one" mind to work the same spiritually God's way, we all live in "one" body the universe and "one" soul together to be perfectly the same in equality for a egalitarian society with self, which is to come back to self when we have the right knowledge to live in this perfect world together. We can unite and grow the world if we have a perfect understanding of how "self" works inside the community. Is the relationship between spouses two self's as "one" and outside the Country is everybody all of self to become "ONE"? The human gods are or have made another god as they will materialized in time with the same quest to better humanity unless we hand the universe over in a knowledgeable way.

What I think the answer is - when "self", the relationship of both spouses, is complete, all the knowledge of knowing God which is the perfect human or "knowing self" is to understand the four truths and how we get to the "one" truth, is in this formula. The closest a man and a woman can get is a simultaneous orgasm and then have a child (explains the universe in total to be intelligent things work from the center out using God's instructions). A whole human is a man and a woman complete together equals a God in oneself with perfectly taught educated "LOVE" without fear; this is why God is love when we learn to control the fear of fear we experience the equality of the same "LOVE" as God to become soul mates when we understand how the whole truth works. How self is us individually as well as humanity together we are "ONE" Which "LOVE and "TRUTH" are "ONE" the answers to everything and is the perfect way to know God for humanity to be equal by the standards of the universe to experience for no racism, divorce and disease.

We now can get the pros to come to us with the way we define "all knowing" and get down to the truth for relationships between any man or woman with a child, by both doing work inside can make god status and have an overall happy marriage. What the human condition is exposed to, and basically everything this book has the worth to use God's power to benefit humanity in the correct way and grow inter technology exponentially. What do you think it will take to make this the best piece the best it can be? Reedit the original manuscript and just cut out duplication.

Summary:

Once we consummate the split, each side comes back to itself in everything, and the 3rd world opens up.

The constants, like gravity or the sun in life are the same as the constants in writing. We have to **split, separate and divide** from the whole to have infinite partitions down to liquid [YBA1] [kk2] to explain everything. It's the way we process the information. The way we process is the same to everything - the way we think, listen, believe and know is to find (outside) and fine (inside) both sides of "what is" is the truth to the center (human, outside) of the middle (spiritual, inside) follow the writing by sides. As to liquid of any and all types, our language brought me to this medical definition of partition coefficient efficiency using two liquids. We will know when we use the correct processes guided by the universe to connect the jigsaw puzzle in life of how everything fits perfectly together, down to liquid. Once everything is connected - physical and non-physical, intangible and tangible, spiritual and human/ animal, things and living things, science and religion can be explained through philosophy in language using the twins in both sides in writing after we have connected all the polar opposite words by definition placement. We can connect the visible and invisible universe when everything comes back together as one to itself the universe and we will unite.

We as a people will have identified the proper and correct rules and regulations to split between spiritual and human, using the inside & outside to divide in the middle of the center to separate. By using language this leads us to the correct pieces, parts, sections, segment, constants, to partitions and gets the correct definitions by definition until we obtain the whole (the answers to perfection you are looking for in a specific thing or living thing). To everything and anything to include the cure for any and all disease by the definition placement "God is the whole and everything " people missed what it means - God is the "way" to "know", "understand", and to "see" how everything works naturally in the universe. We are missing tapping into the most intellectual form of intelligence there is – us, when we are God. We are God when we follow his lead because we are identical (we are human when we don't follow and there's consequences to that) people with the mind of

God. Connect on Facebook to "Global Stabilized Energy LLC." globalstabilizedenergy.com or www.yourname.blog Liquid and compare quirks in things smaller than an atom and we can explain them but now we can explain how everything connects. The mind can't see how once the middle of the center is hit between all these "ways" in language; it shaves the definitions down simultaneously to the one truth guiding us to see our inter intelligence when you see the formula work simultaneously you will see why the mind doesn't see the truth to each and everything: why divorce, disease and having gay love has all the answers in the wrong way too! The answers are in the middle of the center and the center of the middle is the correct answer to each and everything when we write the new universal bible for the world with this formula that is revealed down below.

Now, as to the letters to the pros that I've talked about in the book:

The first thing we need to do is unite the professionals by solidifying that God is self or at least a part of Him and all of our self is everybody to see that Humanity is "One" whole God that needs to unite to be equal to the one God that can't be divided. We as the human gods are separated by [Your Name]. We have nailed down by language what is the same but the differentness (the twins) to go between the human side of us and the spiritual side of us to be correct and master the jigsaw puzzle of life. For example, pros like Dr. John Gray: to further his work on the gender differences, start from the opposite ends but when connected in the middle of the center, male and female will unite in one person their self, inside making a complete human ready to see and be the perfect God. After one has grown up spiritually/inside with all the skills and back down, grounded, where everything lines up scientifically back to itself with the correct knowledge. Once the dichotomies are complete between male and female and (emotional, mental, physical and spiritual) are connected we are then knowledgeable and the same, whole, humans that are not only the same but are equal to God, on the inside to know self (God), not just to believe but to KNOW for sure, as Oprah would say! We all will not only know God (self is first all that which is the same) but through him we will see how everything else works and is connected literally **INSIDE** us waiting to see how things work. Through the confirmation of words, we can "know" everything when the language is correct and perfect by the rules and regulations as they are not now. Through the definition in our dictionaries in each of our perfect languages when all is complete, we will tell the story of God's plan using his word. How it's done is explained in the book "The human race is God too and also he is [Your Name]" as he is the other side of "self" and the scientific proof to that is when it comes back to "itself."

I am asking for the minds to come together and unite in the book so that when we build our course guided by professionals to deliver a course on the portal, on God's word, on God's plan and how humanity is all knowing (chapter). This has been explained in the book as well.

Another example of a pro is Deepak Chopra, who wrote "You are the universe." In his early years, what stuck with me was the difference between selfish and selfless. Selfish being on the human outside and selfless being on the spiritual inside. "The rose" was a symbolism he used to explain a series of events regarding how light bulbs one at a time turned everything on inside. The recent derivative of the word "whole" is "Holy", which helped me see a different light on spirituality, how to make it "whole" and complete in writing what is holy (God because He is intangible and to make whole He needs the counterpart the tangible) can be made complete and made whole and put in writing as truth to know God. This also helped me see the intangible meaning of spiritual or the other part or side to tangibles that make each picture whole and complete for everything to make sense. This furthers Deepak's work in that everything in the universe has its counterpart and when together, the whole makes complete sense (spiritual and human, life and death). Each part works perfectly, independently, as a truth or together as one! Together or apart as if it were the religion for humanity we haven't uncovered yet, the religion is how humans all work the same perfectly through our differences in life but possibly when language is perfectly correct and every cog has been taken out are we to know death too in all ways, not just believe? It would be nice to see if we get there.

The king of polar opposite words is Tony Robbins. Over the last 30 years he has captivated audiences by finding polar opposite words, the inside and outside, to words that go together perfectly and that started the detection of how language is perfect to explain life. Tony's work has been an inspiration for me to see the intangibles (spiritual) to complete each picture to be whole and to make total sense of how language fits together from the inside to the outside and back to the center with each side having its own truth to make that truth multi-dimensional with a specific pattern that holds true for everybody to be and see God's word. But by throwing in the other set of senses, listening, thinking, believing, knowing and seeing, Eckhart Tolle mastered these skills and shared this with humanity.   Dr. Wayne Dyer mastering, in his early years, the knowing skill (knowing what the word KNOW means in all ways) created a wealth of wisdom out of ordinary knowledge.   In his lifetime, he was the seeker of light, love and truth in timeless wisdom. I went to see him 25 years ago in Phoenix, AZ and in his talk, he said that we are all the "same" (understanding this is somewhat complex). It took me 25 years and I was hoping to do this in his lifetime to further his work as the student becomes the teacher. We as humans are all KNOWING even in the light - the same as God - and we as living "things" are the same as "things" that do not eat making the universe and us all one of the same.   The proof is in the twins in writing where the tangibles and intangible comes back to itself to make it whole. God is only part holy because to be complete with everything it/he is "WHOLE" only his image is broken apart and each "part" is perfect; all parts are/is in the jigsaw puzzle to put together correctly using His guide. This is the scientific proof like in a math problem where you know how to check your answer to see if the method is perfect. We have uncovered a new science for proving spiritual things. We know they are intangible, so the methods to know what they mean are in words. Part of the process making them tangible is for each word to be whole. To know what is hidden in each word and sentence. In addition to sending the book to the pros to enhance, I will also send to other pros to enhance like Bruce Lipton, Gregg Braden and Joe Dispenza, the scientists, for confirmation for uncovering science's new methods that prove the existence of spirituality but more importantly how to "KNOW" not just believe it's always been there I just uncovered it. My work is also an extension of Eckhart Tolle's work. When all the different pieces are understood we mustn't reinvent the wheel of all the professionals. We must honor what has been uncovered correctly, even in part, so we can properly piece the jigsaw puzzle of life together to make A Rubik's Cube of Knowledge.

Oprah has been the one that has tried to make sense of all these pros and came close in her 26 episodes in 2015. I am here to further that for God, Love and Truth! Love and truth are polar opposites. They fit perfectly together and have the correct answers and questions "to and in" everything when they meet in the **middle** "of and in" the **center** (not seeing this is the laws of thought), **the excluded middle, The Law of Identity -** A is A Everything is the same as itself: follow the language patterns into itself a word, words and definitions to see life's pattern. **The Law of Non- Contradiction -** NOT (A and not A) Explained under paradox and oxymoron. Nothing can both exist and not exist at the same time and in the same respect; or no statement is both true and false. **Everything is the same as itself**; or a statement cannot not remain the same and change its truth value. Where God lies in perfection every time! God is much smarter than we think. It doesn't matter what you think, believe or know, it "just is"! And knowing what that is inside of us because everything ties and fits together in the universe perfectly and we are God in that way to "KNOW" and "SEE" how all the knowledge in the universe works but the catch is, we need to do this together and unite "the way" to know and show everything with the proof "by and in our writing" guided by the dictionaries our families and self to know everything we want with perfectly whole truth. All of this is in the rules and regulations of one word NOT us trying to stuff each word into the rules and regulations; we are to have all the rules and regulations flow into each word (change the way the mind looks at it). The perfection of us knowing how all this works together will reduce disease and have fair justice, on the inside (church is supposed to guide us to the perfect human that which is God) and outside, the law should do! Both together the right way will unite "SELF" bringing God together to you using this knowledge and if you don't get it, re-read the book and if you don't get it I will ask the pros. And I will ask them to help me write "an online course." Remember we know everything inside but how do we get to it? Together with the right teaching on the outside I will teach the pros what myself and all of them together know and possibly what they don't know. This will replace wanting a divorce or wanting to be gay for living heaven on earth for our children, children living united, solving or at least putting a big dent in the world's human problems (human conditioning).

To do this the world needs to know that knowing God is, to know the self-first, on the inside, before we can know God on the outside, which now is believing not "KNOWING", and that it or he (God) is the same for all of us. The overall "truth" for all of us can be put together by "love" (love and truth in the middle of the center where God lives and comes back to itself) and/or science to see where all of the pros are correct and how we put them together, with my book, to see where everything fits perfectly. I propose to make one social media account for all, naming it "Global Stabilized Energy.com", and build a monthly subscription splitting it up by how many pros (and non-profits) it takes to get through the portal for the normal person, providing them with the Rubik's Cube of Knowledge in timeless wisdom! That which is the same for everybody, God. As an uneducated and non-religious man, I am able to see the patterns the pros laid down and have expanded that through the inside where we know everything, using the collective mind. I will tell the pros - In the event you are interested in helping, I will go through the manuscript and pick out where you can help or you can read to see where I have possibly enhanced your work and where you can make my piece better. For clarity, my book has Howard Schultz saying make sure it's big and then he said make sure it's bigger and then the final thing he said is make sure it is even bigger than that, then I make sure it's even bigger than that. My question: is this big enough? GOD, I would like the pros to be my partner. I think Oprah should take the lead.

The original manuscript can be downloaded at GlobalStabilizedEnergy.com/yourname or you can wait until the professional editor is finished. I need to warn you that my writing is terrible but please don't let that deter you from understanding what is meant here. Let the book angel do her magic for the masses. Please DM me @kc underscore patt @kc_patt or call me at @Globalstabilize on twitter or email kcpattison@gmail.com and kc@Globalstabilizedenergy.com

The following pages contain suggested letters to be sent to select professionals in their field:

To: Oprah Winfrey

Dear Oprah Winfrey,

About five years ago I watched your 26 television episodes on God, and immediately afterwards I called John Gray to voice my opinion on where I felt you needed to go deeper! I have been writing a book since then and just got my final edit and proofread back. My family thinks I went off the deep end. My support system consists of no one that knows God correctly but there are still old business partners. Through the years, though, I've lost touch with three of them. Since those episodes aired, I have uncovered much more in my writing. I thought this book was for the masses but after all the professional editors, I realized it is for the professionals, like the spiritual leaders and the professors in universities around the world to tie in the religious leaders to form one religion for the whole world - self. The goal is to show how everything goes together perfectly like a puzzle, and this can and will be explained in language using the twins to explain God. Thinking back to when I interviewed John Gray 20 some years ago for my documentary "Divorce in Modern America. Nobody Wins", I recall distinctly asking him a question about the "skills" but he at the time was unable to answer. The skills I was referring to were the same as Eckhart Tolle wrote about. For years now I thought everybody that went through the portal or big "Aha moment" "knew" the God thing and had all the skills, but I was wrong.

I suspect Gayle King is a sleeper and "KNOWS" the God thing, too, by the way she interviews people (I could be wrong) and she is the person to help me explain how church and state go together in God's perspective. The skills of a marriage are not only the key to understanding self individually as a God (One love) and choosing to share that skilled love with your spouse (without fear) of the opposite sex but also the key to understanding all of self (everybody) as

One God, to unite the world. The key where you needed to go deeper is the process to the "One truth" where God is the only way to "KNOW", not just believe. It starts with the parallel universe, where one side is invisible, intangible, non-physical and spiritual and can be explained in language by a verb. The other side is visible, tangible, physical and human, explained in language by a noun. The middle of the spiritual side and the center of the human side are all the answers in the universe - the perfect correctness in God's image for us to know everything all the way down to the "One truth" for any single issue (all the human conditioning ailments) like the Coronavirus. We need to perfect a language.

First, let's start with English. Some suggestions are in the book and the patterns are the same as the universe - one side spiritual and the other side human, split by the twins in language to put both sides together in the center for the correct answer and this questions that which is provable to be "God's Word."

I watched the interview you did with Wayne Dyer where he took a year to do the Dao (Daoism). But that seemed to me like a wrong turn for him, because as the leader in spirituality, he was responsible for me learning what the word "know" meant 25 years ago, along with where you need to die while you are still alive spiritually, among many other things. SELF is the answer as we know, not another religion, SELF is the unknown religion to unite the world. I may be speaking out of turn because I don't know much about the Dao (ask Howard Schultz if that's big enough to define God and uniting the world?). I know now we overlook "self", because churches need to go deeper into the spiritual part and the human part. They need to be equal to reveal the perfect answers to the God thing in our own language, to show truth about God's word. To know everything in this universe is in the right formula as explained in my book. One of the closest people to get there was Deepak Chopra, when he held up the rose. A bunch of light bulbs turned on for me. Deepak also said recently that "holy" is a derivative of "whole", meaning God, but I'm sure he didn't see it that way. It set me up to see things like 'of' means part of the whole and the whole is God. By following His lead, we need "to see" things all ways for how we overlook things where the universe and things go together perfectly, and language was the key to show when it came back to itself.

Anthony Robbins is the king of polar opposite words but I'm sure he doesn't know one side of each word is spiritual and the other side is human. The same principles go into language, self and gender differences (the abstract way of how "self" ties everything together to itself whether it is God, self or language), with an added twist - the inside and the outside enhance our rules and regulations. A key to helping with a big part of a perfect language is that when we have the perfect language it will explain God in every way, with us as His equal when we do it His way that resides in us. The other person that explains God best is you, by listening to all the pros but mainly yourself to seek the truth. By digging a little deeper you will find all the answers! An example of this is where God, love and the truth are correct, but the truth is, it's "One God", "One Love" and "One Truth." This holds all the answers and questions between them perfectly in the present moment in time. The present moment in time or the continuous now for everything in the universe and in life. The scientific proof is when God, language and/or self, come back to itself to make it perfect.

I tried to explain this concept in my book, but the editors kept cutting it out because they didn't understand. But after I enhanced Mary Baker Eddy's book SCIENCE AND HEALTH WITH KEY TO THE SCRIPTURES, I also realize now, how I enhanced John Gray's book MEN ARE FROM MARS AND WOMEN ARE FROM VENUS by the four truth's 1) Male, 2) Female, 3) Human, and 4) God. This enables anyone to get to the "One whole truth," for each issue. Anyway, the four professional editors I have hired to help with the structure keep deleting what they think is duplication but really it is the same but different on one "end", back to front and front to back on the other "side" (see God in all ways the end and side) inside out to outside. In reality this just leads us to the center of ONE (the same patterns as Men and Women that make up a whole human equal to a God) in a box where God directs us to live seeing things in all ways for each issue using the correct perspective.

Ultimately the center stone to unite humanity in equality and knowledge is the center of spirituality and humanity, both collectively and individually. This is the key to our universe. Solving the never-ending journey of the perfect system we live in is not to overlook what we have inside us, by using the right teachings. I learned from my divorce and the right way though the professionals and now have enhanced many of the pro's work that we all have within us....finding what is exactly the same is the God part of us, in us, to establish how we are God's mirror image. I would like you to read the book and comment, and if possible, round up the pros or my teachers on a Facebook talk so the student can become the teacher! It is too bad Wayne in his lifetime didn't see this. This can show all of us how we can join with the Pope to form one religion, self. At some point this book or the one the pros put together with me could top the sale of the Bible because it is down to "what is ", not what one believes or knows.

Peace,

Kevin C. Pattison Kcpattison@gmail.com Global**stabilized**energy.com

Website not done

To: John Gray

Dear John,

If you'll remember, about 5 years ago we had a conversation about the 26 television episodes that Oprah ran, asking some really tough questions about God. We had both had watched this. I had expressed thoughts about how I felt she was missing the "truth" and "gender differences", whereas you agreed that God, love and the truth are really all major components in life. Although this has reached a new depth for everything to be explained in the universe by "One God, One love and One truth" together, using the formula of One word, that which is "God's Word" when uncovered the correct way. I expressed my desire to write a book and as I remember, you mentioned through our short conversation, that I was attempting to do it all - explain the whole, everything through the mind, body and soul, humanity and the universe with the power up, as all we have is a belief. I did what we discussed, but it turned out to be much more! I have communicated with you on Twitter -- kc_patt (kcunderscorepatt) - since I feel you are one of my teachers. As it turns out, I have enhanced all my teacher's work!

I began writing the book shortly after speaking to you and worked on it until today. I am now ready to publish, after three complete professional edits, but in the process the editors cut out way too much. However, I made some amazing discoveries that not only enhanced Oprah's work but yours as well, in areas such as gender differences and their sameness but differentness, in "self" as a dichotomy inside to explain God as a whole. I've done this in part by the twins in language, explaining that the complete human comes together when the gender differences become "ONE" inside. As such, it will provide more understanding as the components come together.

Regarding Deepak Chopra and Eckhart Tolle along with the other pros, I have bettered how their work comes together as well, by showing how everything works perfectly together like in a jigsaw puzzle. So, the book has pretty much taken on a life of its own and I've discovered things deeper than my teachers, which I didn't even know existed by the way it goes together. In the process, I've become what Oprah described as a trailblazer because of the major discoveries.

I've also enhanced Tony Robbins regarding what he keeps on doing with the words (the spiritual side and the human side). This ties in perfectly into language, I'm sure he is unaware of what I uncovered. And Wayne Dyer said we are all the same....as a lighthouse, but his extension is how things and living things are the same explained by the twins in language. It isn't the Dao (Daoism) or another religion, I may be speaking out of turn because I don't know the Dao, but it is our self; and if self is another religion, and then so be it. The One truth is overlooked because it is a formula of one person: Male, Female, God, Human. These go together with "One God", "One Love" and "One Truth."

Dyer was alive when I started this book. I will show how *things* are the same as *living things* as well, by the spiritual side of language together with the other side of language - the human side. Together they are called the twins in language where anything can be explained down to One truth. They are defined by the differentness in the dictionary, where the word definition is shown by how the single word goes together simultaneously, as if it is an oxymoron in one word to show how spiritual side and our human side go together. I want to get this in the hands of my teachers and all the professionals because together with what I have uncovered it is the next step to unite the world through knowledge. This is done by using God or his plan that is in each of us when the teachings are right and our perception is correct, if we don't overlook things or let the mind or emotions take over in our self and stay asleep and unaware of the One truth for each issue, One God where "language, self and God explain everything in and on the Universe, and One love for life by choice because people understand the "KNOWLEDGE" of how it is when we can improve marriages. When both know self before marriage, this will unite the world and allow us to live in peace, because all the skills are the same in timeless wisdom when it comes to marriage, with little differences to unite the world (the churches should know this).

You and I met about 23 years ago. I came to your house in Van Nuys California to interview you for a project I did titled "Nobody Wins - Divorce in Modern America." You can Google it - my video clip is at the end and I'm shown with my kids back in the 90's. I just watched it - you look good! I won some national awards for the project even though it didn't turn out the way I wanted it to. The clip can be found at https://www.youtube.com/watch?v=cXJpfW3yUsY . I remember I asked you about "the skills" and at the time you were unable to answer. (Now Eckhart Tolle has been writing about "the skills" for years).

This book is truly an extension of that documentary we did, and I have truly advanced the theories of the pros now 25 years later. That child you see me with is my younger son, now 27 years old. I haven't spoken to him for years due to the divorce and his living across the country. But nothing can break the bond, so I thought. I missed the childhood of all of my children, spent a ton of money tied up in the legal system – just in an effort to try to see them, but what I miss most is all of us together. To know that our kids' love is made from the love I had with their mother, and that love never ends spiritually is something I've learned – that the God part of us is to know self-first = the Godself. I've realized how we are Gods, starting with the children and us as children – the perfect ingredient of the "now" to keep mom and dad together when using the Universe correctly with all the knowledge in the universe backing it up (that is why "SELF" is the religion). This knowledge leads me to how *self* individually and self is *everybody at the same time* is God multi-dimensionally and is explained perfectly in language using *"God's Word."* This is what's next - understanding what and how the formula to God's Word works.

I would be honored if you would comment as one of my teachers, in the book. I read your book Men are from Mars and Women are from Venus, after I got divorced in 1995, and that was the springboard to how the pros and I can now get the divorce rate down below 10% and help marriages stay together by making a choice for our children. By using the correct knowledge of God, it will spill into our churches when the program is built on "KNOWING GOD", not what people believe! The scientific proof is when the scholars see how everything comes back to itself as I explain in the book.

I must say I only wish I could write as well as you, but this is the best I could do (I hope between my teachers all can see what I have uncovered). I would like for you to endorse the book or read the summary. The simple principle is that a complete human is a God (the knowledge of a Male and Female together inside is a complete human in one person). The vertical truth is God, with a complete human, and is the spiritual side of a person or half of the truth. The human side of a person is the horizontal truth or the other half. One truth without the other is a lie to self. This looks at the genders Male and

Female separately and explores the other half of the truth yet still makes a complete human side. Through this formula the 4 truths (Male, Female, God, Human) work simultaneously as one truth. I found that the perfect language is God's Word - to know how each side of a word has a spiritual side and a human side to explain everything in the Universe, We look at this by how one word works in between One God, One Love and One truth. When you use the dictionary correctly it is in the definitions, which I explained in the book. I am hopeful you will see how to unite the leaders and help in this quest to ultimately unite the world using the religious, academic and spiritual leaders as one.

Sincerely,

Kevin C. Pattison

Globalstabilizedenergy.com

Kc@globalstabilizedenergy.com

kcpattison@gmail.com

To: Morgan Freeman

Dear Mr. Morgan Freeman:

I am a fan of the work you did around the world, about God. And, I just viewed a movie you did "Lean on Me" back in 1989. That was the inspiration to write to you, because what you said in the movie could very well get people on the right path to God in the correct way. The teachers you were speaking to said it's not the kid's fault. it's all your fault; if the test scores are not adequate you need to work together and unite to get it done.

When it comes to God, beliefs separate us. But if there was a way to "know" God and if we all work together, self and humanity can "KNOW" God. Because "SELF" and humanity are "ONE" for "ALL" and it is all up to us to unite to be ONE GOD together. The goal here is to HEAL FOLK FROM ALL DISEASES AND PAINS THAT THE HUMAN CONDITION IS EXPOSED TO! I got this idea from a book I was reading while I was waiting for my book to finish getting edited, because the person that gave it to me said the book I wrote has already been done but it was published in 1875 - "SCIENCE AND HEALTH WITH KEYS TO THE SCRIPTURES" by Mary Baker Eddy. I read that book with the intent to see what it pulled out of me to give a good closing for the editors to understand. I also hoped to enhance her work like I did with the other pros, with a letter I wrote to them, but I ended putting the material in the book to. It looks like I can do the same with this one, too.

To fix this we can start with lining up the "ONE" and only God - the "Universe" - with the human God (the actions of the universe and people are the same exact image) to show the correctness of being and how God works as the Universe. His image is identical to match perfectly without error all of what it is to be human and how it all works correctly and perfectly in the scientific proof in everything (almost like backing up the Bible). This continues down to proving the counter of a double negative. The way we live points out where it is wrong, because it doesn't fit in God's plan, the same as with same sex relationships, as it is clear even in the Bible page 127 - LEVITICUS 22 - "You shall not lie with a male as with a woman; such a thing is an abomination." God tells us what we want to know but it requires both sides, a man and woman, to see that the total, whole, entire truth "spiritual and human" is "A" Vertical truth. Male and female is "A" horizontal truth and both truths together are a plus sign is the overall or whole truth. The center of the truth is our actions, using the exact process in the book all the way to know "GOD" to know the "ONE" thing that is the right answer for anything to everything we do.

Opposite sides of the truth guide one to God, when men and women together combined that "knowledge" of themselves into "ONE." This has the answers to solving the human condition/problem. The human behavior dictates what is right and what is wrong (this is in the first part of the book); the Bible is only a guide. What I uncovered is how to "listen" to God's voice through his creation of the perfect language, piecing the right formula together in life and love. The spiritual and human side of the truth combined that "knowledge" evenly and equally to "ONE" and will solve relationship problems (God's, self, spouse, child and family, even political). If the truth doesn't fit together it isn't in God's plan and therefore it is not right, even if you made it to God status. God makes it available for everybody to see different ways than the Bible, but this way is perfect with no justification, using the dictionary with each definition of the vertical and horizontal truth. This is how everything comes down to "ONE" thing and fits perfectly for the right answer!!

What allows "DISEASE, DIVORCE and premature DEATH" to happen is humanity "NOT KNOWING" the perfect union with "SELF" individually inside and outside, the spiritual and human parts. Even though you may pray, meditate or even think about God, that he is the perfect side of you and if the light bulb isn't on, you're flying blind but is in "ONESELF"! Or the spiritual part, Answers to [Your Name] humanly and God spiritually unite both sides of self individually before you marry (parents have some work to do). The perfect relationship is the one involving the person you had babies with because the child is god and explains God and it is easier if you both "KNOW SELF" before you had kids no matter where you were brought up (churches have some work to do). Humanity is the same when all of "SELF" has the same knowledge where everything comes down to "ONE" answer in writing, using the correct formula in language. Then, married people everywhere will all have the skills perfected in "ONESELF" more so than not to live a life of heaven on earth to point out the bad. At this point we all can love our neighbor the same as our "SELF" because it is the correct education when one knows how to love back to itself or oneself; it is the same love or the ways for each person to know. This is not for us to be perfect, but to "KNOW" that the perfection in the system is what we miss in family. An example to uncover is what we miss, like Tony Robbins already "knows" God and most of the skills as he is a pro to be god along with the other pros that are god too, but he is missing the nucleus of the family which is part of what he got over to see God, with his real dad's ego (edging God out) Thanksgiving video.

Oprah didn't have to have a child to know why a child is "ONE" god, but she needs to be shown that to truly know that what it feels like to have your own child can't be taught. John Gray nailed the differences of one part, but the other part is how men and women with their "knowledge" together makes "ONE" human god. Deepak Chopra needs to be taught how to put religion and science together to be "ONE." The science guys need to be taught how science is God's proxy but comes together as "ONE." When divorce, racism, being sexually satisfied and all human conditions are managed and under control, it is at a miniscule level by the correct education and then we will have accomplished life's goal for our children ...children growing in a perfect environment to make what is wrong better and livable or right. We can give our kids something of substance in the right way. The next thing is to bridge life and death to "ONE."

I wrote a book, in editing now, focused on the concept that "The human race is God too! Also, He is [Your Name] SELF. " God and "SELF" are the same thing as you know, and so is all of "SELF", meaning everybody is one God (all of self could mean all of one person or all of self can mean everybody or both) when we see things the same way at the same time. This is how humanity unites when we have one picture of Global Stabilized Energy.com LLC. Love, truth and God. I suggest we put "SELF" in each religion and then we can at this point at least - to" KNOW" how to love our neighbor because we are the same. People can use my book to get there. In God's way I show how the perfect world works, using no belief or thinking we know but using the skills of The Rubik's Cube of Knowledge in life and language correctly with the right formula. This will guide us directly to What is... the truth to use God's voice in the perfect language that ties in why everything happens for a reason and what that reason is.

I would like you to distribute my book to every place you go around the world after it gets finished, but first I would like you and the pros like Deepak Chopra, Oprah Winfrey, Tony Robbins and John Gray to comment in the book anywhere you/they want before it gets done editing, or the opinions could be placed in the book, published on the last or front page of the book regarding what you thought of it or both could be done, for that matter. God is within you and is what you can or can't see but when you look at God as everything you "SEE" the universe with everything in it and how everything works. Then you take the whole universe and split it up, separate all the pieces, parts, sectors and partitions and divide them up from the parallel universe to divide up God or the universe because He can't be broken up. God made us and Him equal but it is hard to see when you look at itself or oneself; when it is complete we see "GOD-SELF" and human side are "ONE" and can see from Universe the almighty and you or self together they are "ONE."

Any rabbi, minister or priest or those in Eastern religion are seeking God on the outside. Which is noble, but one must first "KNOW" God from the inside to really "KNOW" God the right way.

I will leave you with this: we may have created our own division by religion where we just need to explain the Messiah by what we "KNOW" not by what we believe. The Messiah is both a savior and liberator for a group or the son of God, nevertheless people are "human" leaders and are the same. Both will come back if the age of Global Universal peace is not accomplished. "The annunciation of a set of rules applying to the relationships between states" (this is the definition under annunciation following language for Gods instruction). The Messiah in Christianity is the son of God (so are all of us - the same sons of God worldwide) I can prove this in my original manuscript explaining how Jesus and us are actually the same, (we). We have the same abilities if we climb to the height of spirituality.

The height of spirituality lives with our children and the answer is in the middle of the center in both of us. The person that helped make that God-child that all of our self's are to know inside justice to form the outside justice all together for universal peace to materialize. Because Christians believe, they do not "know", the prophecies in the Old Testament were fulfilled by his mission - death and Resurrection. What if he was trying to tell us that life and death work together, moving the box completely out of the way in our thinking to go further than out of the box thinking. Let's bring all the pros and religious people and the academics of the world together to see if it is possible to somehow put life and death together as "ONE" to see how they could go together. The point is - it's possible Jesus didn't take our sins away - that's something the church made up and built on and most people now believe, He was the king of the Jews but only on the last day of his crucifixion. I propose this because churches missed language in God's Word that directs us how to think, but it missed "oneself" individually and self all together as one God and 1.3 billion Catholics and another 1 billion Christians and 1.3 billion Islam and another 1.1 billion people in other religions are led to part of the truth because it doesn't make sense for everybody. My entire theory makes sense. If Islam is missing language, too, in God's word as well, the answers are all in between the spiritual side and human Side. I did my book through love and truth and that will unite the world by all other people's love. And it will help people understand love and truth the way God meant it, because the center of love and truth is something self does together when self-come back to "itself".

Sincerely,

Kevin C. Pattison

YourName.blog

Globalstabilizedenergy.com

Global stabilized energy LLC. FACE BOOK

kc@Globalstabilizedenergy.com

kcpattison@gmail.com

To: Gayle King

Dear Gayle King,

Nelson Mandela said it! "It is impossible until you get it done." Bernie Sanders quoted this during a debate, as well. Mandela also wrote a book about self. Not comparing myself to him, but I also wrote one, proving self is also God. I sent you the cover when I was developing it and now, I have completed the book.

I believe you help those in politics by showing God's equality, to see where God has its place from self and is directly related to politics. From this, to Oprah, and from the pros in spirituality to all churches, the point is that just by going a little deeper to understand the connection with over 5 billion people, the belief is that we will come together with One religion, "SELF." Just put self in front or back of any religion without asking them to change. From the political outlook, you can participate in showing how the plan is already there to run a country - we just need to uncover it and follow the plan. I am assuming you "know" the God thing too, only because you're such good friends with Oprah.

By us putting together the pros like Deepak Chopra, Eckhart Tolle, John Gray and Tony Robbins and all the people that found God from the inside, we can meet with the Pope to explain God through education. If we put everybody together using my book as a guide, we can examine not faith or belief but the "inside" spirituality - God where we and He are the same. We can explore how the human race is God too! Also, He is [Your Name] - in other words, we can all place our own name in the brackets and see that on the inside where God is, is the perfect human. But our job is to connect the perfect human to God for humanity to know the system as to who God is on the outside. Then we see that, inside to the outside and back to the center, is the one multi-dimensional God.

I enhanced what Oprah did by showing that Church and State go together perfectly. Again, I may not have covered it all in the book because it wasn't what I was focused on at the time, but it goes a little deeper, for clarity. One

Love, One Truth and One God - the answers in between these are guidelines to running a country correctly, when God's skills are put together inside us the right way, with self. Perfect language is God's word and the correct guide (I'm using English because it's all I know). I have some suggestions in my book on how to get there. I started writing this book after Oprah did 26 episodes, which aired in 2015, asking tough questions about God. I would like to explain it to you, how God is the most important teacher we have, and it is up to us to uncover Him together. I would like you to see the formula to the four truths and how they go together with One God, One love and One truth.

What I'm asking you to do, as a reporter, is to read the book or at least the summary before I publish it, and comment on it so I get it in the final edit. And, if you can, would you please forward this, and the book, to all six of the professionals I've listed, to similarly make a comment. I have not only enhanced all of the pros, but also enhanced elements of the book "Science and Health with Keys to the Scriptures" by Mary Baker Eddy, published in 1875

Sincerely,

Kevin C. Pattison

Globalstabilizedenergy.com

Kc@globalstabilizedenergy.com

kcpattison@gmail.com

For the Professor,

The first thing we need to do is to unite the professionals in the field of spirituality or certain other fields by solidifying what part of God's whole they have nailed down to be correct and have mastered in the jigsaw puzzle of life. For example, let's consider a pro like Dr. John Gray, where the goal would be to further his work of the gender differences and how they start from the opposite ends, but when connected, are in the middle of the spiritual side and in the center of the human side. Male and female will unite in one person - their self – inside, making a complete human ready to see and be the perfect God metaphysically!

After one has grown up spiritually on the inside, with all the skills, and has gone back down, grounded, where everything lines up scientifically, one goes back to itself with the correct knowledge. Once the dichotomies (emotional, mental, physical and spiritual) are connected and complete we are then knowledgeable - the same, whole, humans that are not only the same but are equal to God, on the inside. This shows us how to know self (God), not just to believe but to KNOW for sure, as Oprah would say! We will all not only know God (that self is first, all that which is the same) but through him we will see how everything else works and is connected literally **INSIDE** us, waiting to see how things work. To know God is a formula, not faith or a belief in Him, it is in the use of language.

Through the confirmation of words, we can "know" everything when the language is correct and perfect by the rules and regulations, as they are not correct now. Through the definition in our dictionaries in each of our perfect languages when all is complete, we will tell the story of God's plan using his word. How it's done is explained in the book. "The human race is God too! And also, He is [Your Name]" as he begins with "self." Place your own name in the brackets because it applies to each of us, and the scientific proof to that is when God comes back to "itself" and both sides are equal - one whole way, where everything lines up perfectly. This only works if you see things the way they are, because we know everything if we don't overlook, miss things or make them up. We see things differently than they are when using the uneducated judgment of our own perspective.

I am asking for the great minds to come together and unite (the spiritual, religious and academic leaders) in how God educations works correctly. In my book, it shows how we come together so that when we build our course on God to deliver on the portal and we find self – a course on God's word, on God's plan and how humanity is all knowing (explained in chapter 13 of my book) we will see that we are equal to God because He made us in His image, with the universe as a guide to knowing how things and living things work. We can then use this in our everyday lives.

Another example of a pro is Deepak Chopra, who wrote "YOU ARE THE UNIVERSE", and many other books. I think the title should be "You Are the Universe of One", because in his early years, what stuck with me was the difference between selfish and selfless. Selfish refers to being on the human outside and selfless refers to being on the spiritual inside. Over the years this concept has become clearer to a universal truth. Example: on this paper, or while reading the book out loud, one might mispronounce a word. One might say from the spiritual side of one's self - it's ok, he only has a high school education - he doesn't "know." But the human side says, 'he has a degree, he should 'know' – isn't the spiritual side better?" "The rose" was a symbolism Chopra used to explain a series of events such as how light bulbs one at a time turned everything on inside. The recent derivative of the word "whole" is "Holy", which helped me see a different light on spirituality and how to make it "whole" and complete in writing. This also helped me see the intangible meaning of spiritual or the other part or side these tangibles make each picture whole and complete for everything to make sense. This furthers Chopra's work in that everything in the universe has its counterpart and when together, the whole makes complete sense - spiritual and human, (life and death some day). Each part works perfectly, independently, as a truth or works together as one! Whether together or apart as if it were the religion for humanity, we haven't uncovered yet. But religion is how humans all work the same perfectly through our differences in life but possibility when we see correctly, we can know death too, not just believe.

The king of polar opposite words is Tony Robbins. Over the last 30 years he has captivated audiences by finding polar opposite words, the inside and outside. These are words that go together perfectly and that started the detection of how language is perfect, in terms of explaining life. Robbins' work has been an inspiration for me to see the intangibles (spiritual) to complete each picture to be whole, and to make total sense of how language fits together from the inside to the outside and back to the center, with each side having its own truth, to make that truth multi-dimensional with a specific pattern that holds true for everybody to be and see God's word. But by throwing in the other set of senses - listening, thinking, believing, knowing and seeing, another pro, Eckhart Tolle, mastered these skills and shared this with humanity. Dr. Wayne Dyer mastered in his early years the knowing skill (knowing what the word KNOW means in all ways) and created a wealth of wisdom out of ordinary knowledge. In his lifetime, he was the seeker of light, love and truth in timeless wisdom. I went to see him 25 years ago in Phoenix, AZ and in his talk, he said that we are all the "same" (understanding this is somewhat complex). It took me 25 years and I was hoping to do this in his lifetime to further his work as the student becomes the teacher, since I am now ready.

We as humans are all KNOWING, in the light or not, the same as God and we as "living things" are the same as "things" that do not eat, making the universe and us all one and the same. The proof is in the twins in writing in the book where the tangible and intangible come back to itself to make it whole. God is only part holy because to be complete with everything it/he is "WHOLE", showing how things work. That is why he is the way. This is the scientific proof like in a math problem where you know how to check your answer. The method is perfect. We have uncovered a new science for proving spiritual things. In addition to sending the book to the pros I mention here, to enhance, I will also send the book to other pros to see if their work was enhanced in any way, because we are in this together.

These additional pros may include Bruce Lipton, Gregg Braden and Joe Dispenza, the scientists, for confirmation on uncovering science's new methods that prove the existence of spirituality for One truth for each issue now can be explained by the parallel universe theory (as mentioned in the book) in writing to "know" God. But more important: how to "KNOW" everything, not just believe, that it's always been there, and I just uncovered it by seeing it a different way. My work is also an extension of Eckhart Tolle's work stating simply that when you know yourself you love your neighbor as much as yourself (the correct "knowledge" is love God's guide to self or your neighbor and life is the same, to know). The skills he teaches are the same in self as in timeless wisdom that should be used in a marriage for both people because the same skills work for that with little adjustment to help unite the world. When all the different pieces and parts are understood about self, we mustn't reinvent the wheel of all the professionals now and over the years because they hold parts of the correct knowledge to know God. We must honor what has been uncovered correctly, even in part, so we can properly piece the jigsaw puzzle of life together for "The Rubik's Cube of Knowledge". I think Oprah and I would make a great team.

Oprah has been the one that has tried to make sense of all these pros, and she came close to doing this in 26 episodes she aired in 2015. I am here to further state that, for "God, Love and Truth!" But to explain everything in the universe it is "One Love", "One God" and "One Truth." In between these are all the answers. Literally. and they show how we are to behave with Love and truth (which are polar opposites) but together at the same time this shows the one answer, when we use the four truths "Male, Female, God, Human." They fit perfectly together and have the correct answers and questions "to and in." Everything is revealed when they meet in the **middle** "of spirituality and in" the **center in humanity (**not seeing this involves the laws of thought**, and the excluded middle, The Law of Identity -** A is A = Everything is the same as itself). We must follow the language patterns of a word, words and definitions, to see life patterns. We must examine **The Law of Non-contradiction -** NOT (A and not A). This can be explained under paradox and oxymoron. Nothing can both exist and not exist at the same time and in the same respect; no statement is both true and false. **Everything is the same as itself**; a statement cannot not remain the same and change its truth value. This is where God lies in perfection every time! God is much smarter than we think (here is where the academic or professor is needed to help explain God in knowledge even if he doesn't know himself because He is the education). It doesn't matter what one or you think, believe or know, it just is, if it is God's way! Because It is right.

Because everything ties and fits in together perfectly and God is "the way" to know and show everything with the proof "by and in our writing", guided by the dictionaries in our own language, when each word is whole and is complete when it comes back to itself. Our families and our self, and especially our own children are the core to GOD and the universal **one Bible** through each language. All of this is in the rules and regulations of one word - NOT us trying to stuff each word into the rules and regulations, but it is all the rules and regs fit into one word. The perfection of us knowing how all this works together will reduce disease and mental health issues and we will have fair justice, on the inside (what churches are supposed to do!) It can help run a country and outside, the law should do as well! Both will reduce divorce and allow us to have one another's soul mates by choice. This is the pattern for living heaven on earth. It is to benefit our children, where children are living united, thereby solving or at least putting a big dent in the world's human problems by the way we behave together when we use the four truths.

To do this the world needs to know that knowing God is this: to know the self first, on the inside, before we can know God on the outside, which now is believing, not "KNOWING"; we must learn that it or he (God) is the same for all of us inside. The overall "truth for all of us can be put together by love" (love and truth in the middle of the center where God lives and comes back to itself) and/or science. The goal is to see where all of the pros are correct and how we put them together, using my book to make a master, to see where everything fits perfectly. I propose to make one social media account for all, naming it "Global Stabilized Energy.com", and build a monthly subscription, splitting it up by how many pros (and non-profits and churches) it takes to get through the portal for the normal person, providing them with the Rubik's Cube of Knowledge in timeless wisdom! That which is the same for everybody, God. As an uneducated, dyslexic and non-religious man, I am able to see the patterns the pros laid down and have expanded that knowledge through the inside where the church meets up perfectly over the 25 years where the correct education is the way, so we know everything using the collective mind down to one mind. In the event you are interested in helping, you can read the book to see the broad scope to add where it comes together and you can make the piece better when you add your two cents' worth.

The original manuscript can be downloaded at www.Global**Stabilized**Energy.com/yourname or you can wait until the professional editor is done. Please DM me @kc_patt or @Globalstabilize on twitter or email kcpattison@gmail.com and kc@Globalstabilizedenergy.com. to clarify.

Peace,

Kevin C. Pattison

Letter for an annulment to Catholic Diocese of Phoenix:

I've just written a book that, I believe, looks at God and religion, as well as all of humanity, and I'd like to share it, and my theories with you. In the book, I am simply explaining something that is not easy, but it is simple because we are all God; the answers are in our self and the people God designed on the outside are for us to learn from on the inside how to unite the world. Starting with a person's spouse, the one you selected by choice and have children with for your family, are all the answers one needs to find God and live a life of complete happiness in the now, and to know everything about living things and things in the complete universe without error, through asking God what do I need to know next? And to know the light bulbs need to be on to choose the spiritual side if you don't know and the human side will come around to be centered where we are all the same where God lives, even Him (God) where He is also equal to all of us (this is where God comes back to itself). The hardest thing to do is to evaluate self individually but let's evaluate all of self, "the church" needs to come full circle not just in Christianity but all religions where they are one! Self that is the same for all people! And take leadership in the institution of marriage by God's lead with using his knowledge for us to unite the world by knowing how to keep a marriage together by choice in knowledge, in timeless wisdom.

When self is on the same page as the individual self and the collective self, the church, it will be much harder for the church to put their religion before the relationship because all religions will grow to be the same though out the world.   As you know I am not a religious man and the women I've had in my life are or were Catholic, not to compare the women but the church's thinking over the last 25 years. My idea is not to put fault on the church but to enhance their teachings by going deeper and full circle to complete Jesus Christ's teachings. He is both god and human the same as us our brother, with skilled teaching where the baby in him is the god of the nucleus family, an example for each and every family and should not be dismantled because each one of us is God and have the knowledge to fix oneself from the inside. We may need to be taught correctly (the Catholic Church may be the teacher when they get it right) because one party in the marriage needs to see who God is correctly (I am sorry it is not the Catholics). Because if they knew it would prevent divorce, disease and human conditioning and be ready for the next step where the church help runs the country. First it is not better for the kids while they are young to get divorced because they grow and it is much more difficult to find God the correct way when the parents have not achieved soulmates. Even if the parents did achieve soulmates status like mine or the to be wife's, her parents were close, but her father just had anger issues he didn't address. She is the most religious person I know besides her mother and neither one of them see God in the full circle (maybe I don't ether but certainly more than Catholic only because they the Catholics are using partial truths because that is what they have been taught) the way the Catholic Church wants them to see not the way everything goes together perfectly. Where the hardest thing to see is "self", where the full circle of the Bible ends after family and has failed to see self only because the church is holding on to "beliefs" (rather than knowing) using partial truths and doing it their way what they "think" is right, but it is NOT doing it God's way to what is correct by using self and the universe as our guide to know.

Mainly the church's error is in "Jesus", where he is God and not the same as all of us! We put him on a pedestal and worship him that is not what he wanted what he was saying is grow or see where I am catch up then we will have many more with the same skills as mine. The good news for our gospel is the four truths when they come together to help in all relationship problems before they reach divorce. Other problems it helps are mental health issues, drug and alcohol abuse and all human conditioning ailments. By what is in the middle of our spiritual side which is the vertical truth and the center of our human side the horizontal truth where God lives and is the way and the instruction for everything when it comes down to what just is.

In the book, I discuss pros in various fields: with Oprah Winfrey, where she is on the right track, and with other pros that have found God from the inside and the professors can seek proof using God's proxy; science will help and my book, after everything that was cut out being put back in, or perhaps by doing a part two of the book we can have "Global Stabilized Energy." When we do the skills correctly first in self in a good way not a selfish way like divorce! "KNOW" who we are as self and then to "KNOW" who God is as self it is under our control, the church should know we are the same (self, humanity and the church is one God). After we get it correct, we will learn how to split, separate and divide the whole, using the parallel universe, the mirror image of God that can be broken up. God is way smarter than we think and more than someone to pray to. He put all the prayer answers in writing when we figure out the perfect language and uncover it. Then the spouse of the opposite sex because they are equal as a whole human to make a God and to then make a child they have between them as they grow "The whole family" will be united when all of them have the skills in self-complete. The community will benefit and then the country will when we do it all in the continuous now the same as the universe to use as our guide for us to be correct in everything we do!

My daughter told me my ex and her quit the Catholic faith and tried a number of different religions out there but none of them did it for them. That is because to explain everything as small as an atom and as big as the universe comes to one thing in an abstract way a child is the center of the universe, God a universe of one where everything fits perfectly individually where we are all the same but different at the same time and collectively all together where we are the same as all of self-everybody is god. I think it was 20 + years ago my ex-wife wanted an annulment. I said absolutely not, because whatever your mind comes up with their was love between us; I didn't know it really meant you can get married in the church again because the standards were not met (the standards are the wrong reasons - the church missed the truth) in the first marriage at the time of the wedding is what the church is focus on that in itself is completely absurd after reading my book. I believe and know I have enough evidence about God the right way and marriage the way it was intended for the Pope to take a close look at what I have uncovered.

I realized this is challenging for the Catholic religion - the right way under the canon law statute 1099 on what a marriage means where the consummation spiritually is a child (remember ONE TRUTH, ONE GOD and ONE LOVE is the whole truth together guided by the four truths Male, Female, God, Human down to one truth fits every issue). I am providing a copy-righted book to your email of "The Human Race is God! Also, He is [Your Name] you, self." It is not yet published; you can only distribute with my written permission you can send it to any high- ranking member of the church. I know on my side, as it pertains to the Catholic religion, we had a valid marriage. I was faithful physically, mentally, emotionally, never hit her, provided well, was a good husband and father. On her side if an affair doesn't count or the inability to manage one's emotions for SELF doesn't count either. I need to blame the church not because it was their fault but, by not knowing how to unite a marriage and providing the incorrect information when the problems started leaving us no professional to turn to. The enhancement for the church is to use the listening, thinking, believing, knowing and seeing skills it is the system NOT the person I did not know back then and the church does not know now. Because if the process was correct, we would know who we are and who God is, to be able to fix what went off track. I would never have gotten divorced if I knew God and self and the child's mother and father had become one in education where we are the same on the spiritual side and the human side is what we need to manage because we are a perfect God as I explained in the book. A very strong possibility - she would not have forced the divorce if she knew the church teaches God from the inside the small part in all of us that is the same only because she then could SEE that was truly putting the kids first. I would not have divorced anyway I wanted to work it out but she was done trying (it was timing of love) and absconded across the country, cut all contact with her and the kids and made me go through the law to have any contact when I found out where she was. Her leaving sent me a message – it was "get a paternity test that the courts ordered or go to jail that was around April 95." She just left in the dark of the night; I still never got one but it just says to me she didn't know at the time either. Basically, she cut me out of her, and the kids' lives 25 years ago, disregarded her children's father and made them grow up without their real father until the oldest was 16 years old. That was out of the blue and is why when together, the couple that made a god child should honor and share that child in every way. This is to know God and life in all ways correctly (the reason why God and self are the same is because the child is where it comes back to itself when you know God).

Reading this book will help change the dynamics of God for the religious, academics and spiritual to be shared equally and change the world by uniting us; please keep this account open until the Pope reads this and understands how all education comes from God the wife to be want him to marries us in the church.

My wife-to-be just informed me the Catholics see my marriage as if it is still in force her and I are living in sin, (there is no sin only education) and so is my ex and her husband (God's way there is only ONE LOVE and you can stay together by education and that education is a marriage is consummated spiritually a child you had together is the ONE TRUTH both together make the nucleus family of ONE GOD because of the four truth (Male, Female, God, Human). So then here is my question: knowing we had a child out of wedlock (that was my saving grace for the abandonment after the divorce my ex forced) we have consummated our relationship and are both humanly and spiritually still together. I full-heartedly believe in marriage one time and with one love by one truth all together by one God. As I told my daughter of the ex, no one can love your mother as much as I do or did; it is not possible - we gave something to each other nobody else can give, you! Even though you are your own person love is education literally to achieve soulmate status. If you truly know who God is and what a child one truth represents how they are one (the church leaders have missed this because they can't be married). The wife-to-be of 23 years said if I go back with the ex (no idea where that came from) either way she would like to have a conversation with her woman to woman and she will become a nun if it went that way. I said to her the church has that wrong too because men and women are equal by the universe and so is God and the complete human you need to tell the WHOLE TRUTH by the universes standard. So, the nuns and priests should be equal and should be able to married only the opposite sex because they have all the answers together with the right teaching to be soulmates; these are facts not options. I said the love holds true for you too because of our child and in order to see this the church needs to see how and where it holds true to be taught from the congregation the strength of a child's love. To find complete happiness in self and all of self is to find God from the inside and let the truth set you free altogether.

What the church fails to see is on my human side I don't have a choice because the ex-wife can't see what is on her spiritual side mainly because she hasn't been taught her spiritual side and Human Side need to be equal the same as the now in the universe. All the same as everybody else for us as a couple to come together in life is about growing as adults spiritually where all the light bulbs turn on, where we are the same as God but are human side needs to see and grow to be equal to God inside us by the correct process without error. We should be taught this while we are young. We all have the ability to make relationships work because we have all the information inside us, but the question is how do we tap into it? The answer is knowing the self as well as what is the same as the neighbor for us to love the same in education. Now if we had these teachings 25 years ago my children might have grown up with their real father and the relationship may not have achieved soulmate status because I probably would not have come to this knowledge, but she may not have forced the divorce. If we were still together it would have been because love is education not a feeling that God's way is the way through love and truth and together it unites us when we have the correct answers.

Do you see why the church is doing the annulments for the wrong reasons? I am hoping for an annulment because I moved mountains with my love for the ex-wife to get her back I was partly responsible for disbarring 5 attorneys, her boyfriend had two other girlfriends in addition to a wife she knew about, I was arrested with my attorney trespassing on her boyfriend/boss's property trying to tell her what was going on what he was doing it just wasn't post-divorce it was while we were still married she was in her first trimester with our daughter and I found a sexual Teddy some lingerie in her gym bag the point is the truth can be hard to see. What the church fails to see is how the skills of thinking, believing and knowing work properly and everything can be explained by using truth, love and God it is in the system without error or no cog in the wheel in the now to SEE how everything works together perfectly.

I back every reason up by truth, not my truth, "THE TRUTH." For everybody it is the universal truth but sure it starts out with my truth I would love to see where I am wrong the church's reasons are beliefs now not knowing. When the church understands the difference between "KNOW and BELIEVE" in God's plan is when we bring it back to self for everybody where everything fits perfectly even science. The religion is correct but the way it is being taught is missing key elements to the whole truth. Her truth is, she doesn't want to get married unless it is in the Catholic Church in order to be right with God (that is completely incorrect again a belief not a knowing God's way). She said, what's the point? I said don't you see ourselves are the answer to the question but the Catholics don't see it either, they drill what they "think" the church "thinks" is the way but it doesn't connect together so it is using partial truths, she's Catholic is why she doesn't see and they (Catholics) are holding us back. I said OK even though it is a lie to herself and the church the way they are doing the annulments now are incorrect. Give me a chance to change the rules and to make it right and we can slip our annulment in between the change because what I am saying is the same result for different reasons. I found the process for each issue to find the one truth for each and everything, how intellectually one God works (all the knowledge in the universe it will definitely make it into The Rubik's Cube of Knowledge) but most of all how a child is god and God's education to one love for life both parties need to understanding this so when adversities rise they can be handled appropriately. Plus, it is how to unite the world.
You think I/we can enhance the church? I need to get one member of the church to see this then you will not need me and eventually if the church does it right God will direct them how to run a country where the human law and the spiritual law is equal but first we need to obtain Justice from the inside for all of us and then justice on the outside will follow!

--
Kevin Pattison
kcpattison@gmail.com

His Holiness, Pope Francis.

Apostolic Palace.

00120 Vatican City.

Dear Pope Francis,

I have written a book, I have written to the spiritual leaders and the academic leaders of the world because I have uncover how to get to the truth with proof. But the most important leader in my view is you the pope (I'm not catholic) and what I have uncovered will bring religions together and unite the world. The outside world sees you are closer to God at least my to be wife thinks of 23 years he is but we are all equal to each other even God to us or us to God! God is education too where the patterns of the universe explain everything in the proper language when it is perfect to reveal "GOD'S WORD" where the church has not figured that out yet.

I have built a case to be heard by the annulment I filed that destroys the theory of the test of time if religion is about the truth and we can be set free by how we get to the truth the correct way we lead our life's and the knowledge that is taught to us shouldn't it be correct for all of us! With proof and not faith or belief, but to "KNOW" for sure.

Using professional teachings when you put them all together properly using what is the same we all have on the inside of each and use all of us to what is the same. So the church does not hold back using the professionals we are just adding to what is in the teachings of the church but in some cases seeing the same thing differently to enhance to outcome. We (the gathered pros of Global Stabilized Energy.com) together with the church can know the correct formula to reduce the human conditioning ailments, relationship problems and unite the world to name a few in and by the direction of God that is in us to also run a country when we have the personal side right God's way! "The Marriage" is the key to life when it comes back to itself to live Heave on earth! God made it the system for us to learn from the inside out and it is all the same....Do not judge until after you read the whole thing, Then use the cannon law statute 1099 why the annulment the church are doing for the wrong reasons.

Sincerely,

Kevin Pattison

kcpattison@gmail.com

Messiah

Language
Download PDF
Watch
Edit

This article is about the concept of a savior. For the oratorio by George Frideric Handel, see Messiah (Handel). For other uses, see Messiah (disambiguation).

Samuel anoints David, Dura Europos, Syria, Date: 3rd century CE.

In Abrahamic religions,
a messiah or messias (Hebrew: מָשִׁיחַ, romanized: *māšîaḥ*; Greek: μεσσίας, roman
ized: *messías*, Arabic: مسيح, romanized: *masîḥ*) **is a** saviour **or liberator of a group
of people. The concepts of** *moshiach*, **messianism, and of a Messianic
Age originated in** Judaism,[1][2] **and in the** Hebrew Bible; a *moshiach* **(messiah) is
a king or** High Priest **traditionally** anointed with holy anointing oil. **Messiahs were
not exclusively Jewish: the** Book of Isaiah **refers to** Cyrus the Great, king of
the Achaemenid Empire, **as a messiah**[3] **for his decree to rebuild the Jerusalem
Temple.**
Ha mashiach **(**חישמה, 'the Messiah', 'the anointed one'),[4][a] **often referred to
as** *melekh mashiach* **(**חישמה דלמ 'King Messiah'),[6] **is to be a human leader,
physically descended from the paternal** Davidic line **through** King David **and** King
Solomon. **He is thought to accomplish predetermined things in only one future**

arrival, including the unification of the tribes of Israel,[7] the gathering of all Jews to *Eretz Israel*, the rebuilding of the Temple in Jerusalem, the ushering in of a Messianic Age[8] of global universal peace, and the annunciation of the world to come.[1][2]

In Christianity, the Messiah is called the Christ,

from Greek: χριστός, romanized: *khristós*, translating the Hebrew word of the same meaning.[9] The concept of the Messiah in Christianity originated from the Messiah in Judaism. However, unlike the concept of the Messiah in Judaism, the Messiah in Christianity is the Son of God. Christ became the accepted Christian designation and title of Jesus of Nazareth,[10] because Christians believe that the messianic prophecies in the Old Testament were fulfilled in his mission, death, and resurrection. These specifically include the prophecies of him being descended from the Davidic line, and being declared King of the Jews which happened on the day of his crucifixion. They believe that Christ will fulfill the rest of the messianic prophecies, specifically that he will usher in a Messianic Age and the world to come at his Second Coming.

In Islam, Jesus was a prophet and the *Masîḥ* (حيسم), the Messiah sent to the Israelites, and he will return to Earth at the end of times, along with the *Mahdi*, and defeat *al-Masih ad-Dajjal*, the false Messiah.[11] In Ahmadiyya theology, these prophecies concerning the Mahdi and the second coming of Jesus have been fulfilled in Mirza Ghulam Ahmad (1835–1908),[12] the founder of the Ahmadiyya Movement, and the terms 'Messiah' and 'Mahdi' are synonyms for one and the same person.[13]

In Chabad messianism,[14] Yosef Yitzchak Schneersohn (r. 1920–1950), sixth *Rebbe* (spiritual leader) of Chabad Lubavitch, and Menachem Mendel Schneerson (1902–1994), seventh *Rebbe* of Chabad, are Messiah claimants.[15][16][17][18] Resembling early Christianity, the deceased Schneerson is believed to be the Messiah among some adherents of the Chabad movement; his second coming is believed to be imminent.[19][20][21][22]

Etymology

Here is my assessment after figuring out where Oprah just needed to go a little deeper on 26 episodes wrapping up the Oprah Show, or it was part of Super Soul Sunday, but she is on the right track. Her assessment of God, Love and the Truth was true and correct but she needed to go deeper to address the "one" truth (from the "4 truths" "male, female, God, human" down to one) to find the one-truth for each and every thing. Love together with truth answered all life questions to get answers. Where God starts to makes sense when everything fits perfectly like a puzzle and if it doesn't fit it is not the one "TRUTH" and we have overlooked the truth unknowingly but we still think we "KNOW" because we don't see the one truth (it is the system of thinking, believing and knowing we need to see and know). When "one God", "one Love" and "one truth" are the physical and mental guide to the human actions that mirror the universe exactly non-physical together identify the one truth.

The answer to our relationship problems, human conditioning and lifestyles leads to our guide for one love. The Guide for one God is separated by self-labeled by [Your Name] individually and all of self for humanity together we are "ONE" God all of us are to unite this way when we "see." Where we are all equal and all knowledge is equal in the form of learning from our perfect language once our rules and regulations are without error to see God, language and self are the same. Because everything comes back to self, especially language and God and Self puts it all together, when one sees the process comes to "SELF" and become "ONE."

Once we see how the intangibles, non-physical and invisible parts meet up with the tangibles, physical and visible parts meet up together to make each word in our dictionary perfect the way God intended it to be. The word is split by its definitions, separated by (new rule) nouns outside and verbs inside and divided by (new rule) the oxymoron of the spiritual part and the human part to make the word whole. When we have the WORD whole with all the rules and regulations complete, we have a perfect language "in God's Word" when we split, separate and divide the word properly it is time to partition the word following "language" to get God's word in our language after we see how all three work separately and together at the same time (1. God 2. Self-3.

Language) to become whole with precision using the four truths to explain everything in the Universe and on earth. Even what the Catholics call the Holy Spirit can be written out by the invisible side using the vertical side of the truth - you cannot see the inside verb or the spiritual side of the inside language "new rules". When the academics need to prove their point to get their PhD and Doctorate is the outside of language; the human horizontal side of the truth is the outside nouns and the visible side of our language "other side of new rules for the regulations." When both sides of language work together from the inside to outside in perfect harmony we are equal to God; the other side to-self and when we are equal to all of self-everybody is on the same page we can run a country without evil, corruption or idealism.

I also pinpointed where Dr. John Gray needed to go deeper making "ONE" whole complete human by connecting the genders to see the (new rule) horizontal truth it is "men" and "women" equal together inside as "ONE" Mind, Body (one truth we are separated by hip structure) and Soul (self) first where we are the same together as "ONE" human we are a dichotomy and start from the other side, therefore exactly the same as a human but split by gender, separated by male and female and divided by sex organs the "ONE" truth but equally the same that should not be altered physically or mentally. Then as "ONE" whole complete "human" with "God" as "ONE" together we are exactly the same as God but split by non-physical and physical, separated by spiritual and human sides and divided by God and human (new rule) in the vertical truth making the four truths (Male, Female, God, Human) all together makes up one truth for everything in the Universe (this is the church's JOB and to keep marriages together with uniting the world). Then together as husband and wife loving "ONE SELF" first in a good way to "KNOW" the skills to love your neighbor as yourself will show you how to become one together with your spouse of the opposite sex to find peace inside. The prerequisite to unite community and country with all of self is to master the relationship with yourself and your spouse through knowledge. The answer is master self as if it is a religion because it can be done through any religion since it is the only "ONE" that is NOT based on believing, it is based on "KNOWING" the "ONE TRUTH" as God's proxy. We will unite humanity with God when we "KNOW" all of self-starting with "ONESELF" what will get us there is oneself, together with one love explained by one God in language.

This is the education we need to instill in our children to prevent divorce, medical issues and basically all human conditioning problems. Mary Baker Eddy tried with faith through Jesus but didn't complete human suffering because she was using partial truths or part of the formula but not the whole truth at the same time. When humanity learns to live using and knowing the whole truth our communities and countries can live in peace on the outside together and this will eliminate evil, divorce, and our human suffering which we have the knowledge to overcome because it is what we are born with inside our "self" knowing everything or at least how to get to and know all the knowledge in the universe. Which is God's word made into sentences when the whole truth is present in perfect form to hear his voice through completed whole words with the proper correctly broken down definitions and all rules and regulations are correct without error.

Dr. Wayne Dyer would be proud of how people and things are the same and how self is the "ONE" religion, Eckhart Tolle is the secret for religions to know the differences between thinking, believing and knowing and use them properly in all religions. Tony Robbins, or Chopra may get what I have done with the words and if all these people together that know God come together in a Facebook group it would properly enhance what I am doing for the world in future generations, for our children's children and the church to unite (I can show the church how we all are on the same side to unite the world though knowledge) humanity.

The way I showed Mary Baker Eddy's book (MBE) "Science and Health with Keys to the Scriptures", published in 1875 is that she "believed" through faith and in Jesus Christ she could master our human conditioning but my comments illustrate how to use the 4 truths to go deeper but use the vertical truth. I expanded on her already knowing the horizontal truth and made a few adjustments like dropping "Christian" so everybody can fit because science is God's proxy. When Jesus is the son of God exactly the same as us the human race but somehow got put in the vertical truth many generations back shows how strong conditioning and belief is and this will show if the church is over the need to be right (where our president has not). I did it through "KNOWING" with using the PROCESS OF GOD'S WORD not what I believe or using Jesus as a go between to get to God because when Jesus said unto him, I am the way, the truth, and the life: no one doth come unto the Father, if not through me. I looked up "self" and look how they used the word until the early 1900s... so wouldn't "me" be self until the early 1900s? if "self" means "me", we are taking what Jesus said wrong following the logic though me means "SELF." From my experience, when my ex-wife took our kids 20 some years ago when I lost the "ONLY FORM OF LOVE" we have created (my ex-wife and I) I found God from the pain, not Jesus, because he is the same as us (we can use him as a guide) but what is the one truth? Is God how everything works and it is through our "SELF, for us as a child to know our parents love us as a God or are we supposed to because we are LOVE and GOD IS HOW EVERYTHING WORKS TOGETHER? (God, Self and humanity all of self is the same thing explained by the twins in language) We need to see or grow to find one God's truth.

By reviewing my original manuscript it is easy to understand about how Jesus and us (the human race) are the same and his teachings are certainly about self individually and collectively sometimes both together at the same time plus the messiah is human. The religion Judaism or Christianity says the King of the Jews is Jesus or the son of God is (humanity). Jesus may of hit the top of his spiritual side as I explained in the book critique of MBE and may not have been gifted from God but had the spiritual side in him same as us where he figured it out on his own telling us to do the same. Churches only think they "KNOW" but it is only a belief, not a knowing; what I have uncovered is God's truth because everything fits together perfectly guided down to one truth for each and everything. I can tell you right now with the help of all the pros that found God the right way and with my completed manuscript we can together have Universal Global Stabilized Energy accomplishing world peace.

Between four editors, all of which are far smarter than I academically, with 10 different degrees between them, they are not getting it ether, how I came up with God's word even though it is clearly written out by the 4 truths a couples of pages up. I don't think someone even at a professor level will understand how a word is broken down with the right education. This is the church's job because one needs to think like God to understand in all ways at the same time. But we will see because I am sending a free e-book to 100 top professors around the world and also 100 of the top spiritual leaders around the world as I have an email list a few years old. I am over the need to be right so when I get confirmation that God's word is correct because as far as I know nobody has figured it out yet not even the Pope, or any of the churches, temples and other places that worship around the world, I will be wanting to speak to the Pope then, when I get confirmation from a number of priests, religious leaders, spiritual leaders and academic leaders at the same time to see what I see.

I am seeking an annulment from my first marriage which I never wanted in the first place and never did anything wrong in my eyes to get the divorce. She said it was a bunch of little things and she didn't love me any more (the spiritual side of us carries the love and the human side covers love up when fear or some other emotion takes up the space of love the space that cannot be shared). She didn't know why she was doing this! No woman will or has claimed sexual harassment (ha ha) the real question is why she didn't want to work it out and forgive me for something I didn't do and give me the benefit of the doubt. I tried everything possible to win her back. I followed my heart across the country, I struggled with my love for her even after we split because she wanted the divorce and got it; she said you are strong you will get over it! That didn't mean my love stopped for her; it made me dig more into what love was or is and my love is so strong. I now see where the churches do not see the whole truth and need to dig deeper thanks to my ex and my wife-to-be and the Cathodic Church with all the pros I encountered and my work for the last 25years I know how all this information goes together perfectly. I know it is the right information for all of humanity to unite, figure out our human conditioning and reduce divorce rates below 10% all by the horizontal truth which is equal to itself and also equal to the vertical truth which is equal to itself as well this is how God structured us to see God correctly through self. What I am claiming to do we all can do together with the correct teachings. My ex-wife has been remarried over 20 some years. I probably haven't spoke to her for well over 10 years; she will not speak to me all because she let a predator get to her (her boss) that broke up our marriage and to save face for the need to be right she blames everything on me even 25 years later. So, any reasonable person or church can see it's been over for years humanly; remember we are in partnership humanly and spiritually. Everybody is a God spiritually, the other equal half to our human side screws things up and should have been taught this early in life so the one truth is we made God-children so our marriage cannot be annulled. Also a great marriage by choice is when each whole complete person loves them "self" the same as God (God as you know is the perfect "human" where men and women are the same inside a complete human) and choose to share that love with each other using the skills of timeless wisdom.

This process of marriage is the key ingredient to unite communities, countries and ultimately the world because we are "EQUAL" partners with God. So, my ex-wife did not have any kids between herself and her new husband, so spiritually the marriage has not been consummated (new rule when we understand the one truth correctly). Let me explain: if the churches knew the real (the one truth) reason why and how a marriage should stay together for life is because the consummation of the spiritual side is a child and a child they would see they cannot be annulled. Because together you made a God child that should be shared equally by choice in love, finances, time and care together in the same house (the couple's choice while married) a couple stays together because of the kids and find the soulmates in each other by education. But until human laws and spiritual laws are the same and are equal to become one the church should help with correct teaching. It should be the right way because the pain is too great NOT to "KNOW GOD'S one TRUTH." This trumps religion with what they believe separates the "KNOWING" if it is correct. I only know one priest who started out with the correct knowing; he is Father Bob, who did the baptism in Vail, AZ for my daughter 21 years ago and is now somewhere in CA.

I am on an appeal now because the church considers my marriage valid but for the wrong reasons all to get married in their church of the Catholic religion to be right with God the wife-to-be thinks. All because I was married in a Catholic monastery almost 25 years ago. I was not Catholic then and I'm not now. But to enhance the church when marriages use the correct skills is to stay together; they are the same skills with little modification that unite community, country and the whole world.

The church has built up a huge "belief" on partial truths working to find the whole truth to the tune of 2.3 billion people for Christians, Muslims/ Islam to the tune of 1.8 billion, Hindus to the tune of 1.1 billion, and all the other religions combined maybe 1.0 billion totaling. That's 6.2 billion religious of some kind leaving 1.1 billion with no religious affiliation totaling 7.3 billion total world population. The "WHOLE TRUTH" will unite all religions in a short time frame when the church leaders read my book and we will need a Universal Church around the world. I hope the Pope sees and understands my book; I will send him a copy. The to-be-wife of 23 years is also Catholic. The church teaches people how to think as it did with my "to be" mother-in-law (my ex-mother-in-law lied to my ex-wife and told her I had an affair. Maybe they came up with the idea together since she wanted out of the marriage because her boss got to her and portrayed her affair on me? And the same thing was tried with our daughter, now 21 years old. The church tries to teach people how to think but my daughter made up her own mind. The church is not doing their job.

I know the narrow mind of the church is holding humanity back from having the skills for "SELF" to live heaven on Earth. I look forward to when this book gets translated into all the different languages for the world to compare notes as to how their language will be turned into "God's word" to hear his voice through sentences of words. All languages when complete will make up the completed version of the universal Bible uniting our planet by how we all work the same on the inside (the part that is God in all of us). Tapping into our ancient ancestor's way of life, now making the Bible from hieroglyphs to language in each of our languages to complete a dictionary in each. But I just "KNOW" English and see it is not complete in the rules and regulations and whole words at the doctrine and professor level where everything should make perfect sense (as perfect as God) but it does not. I have added many options to help complete the language to make it into God's word (the perfect language) to complete it whole. It is what you "KNOW" not what you believe (sorry Oprah).

I just can see it through my divorce where using the skill of "One truth", "One Love" and "One God, self." The individual God is self - it is me! And you when you have the skills or any of us singular and all of self is everybody when we have the skills collectively to be one God. The God in heaven put in us from birth. I hope Oprah will be the front to connect all religions to "LOVE ONESELF" from childhood to "KNOW SELF." How we work is exactly the same after we break down emotions and timing. This will allow us to "KNOW" how to love our spouse by choice and once the skills are completed from within, we can love our neighbor as our "self'" (when we understand God's one truth). This will help unite the world to bring all of us together, drop divorces rates into the teens or below 10% so our children can grow up with their biological family from the Gods that made them when they connect their spiritual side and their human side hopefully before they get married. If calling humans Gods bothers the church call them God's children because they are the same thing when you answer the question is Jesus God? It should be yes, humanly. We are all human Gods and the same as Jesus but Jesus does not fit in the 4 truths together by language to unite with the "ONE" God in heaven while we are living on Earth living the one truth for each and everything. Languages are like perfect pieces and parts of God; when organized correctly one truth comes out for each and every thing.

Believing should allow you to get there when all the pieces and parts of our language are put in order for the right process to see the perfect world in writing for the young to read. The church' job is to put God first (the perfect human (SELF) not the God heaven even though they are the same thing, but the inside God needs to be first). Everything starts out as your child is the (church's is a believing because Jesus teaching are for self) definition of love (literally), the same powerful love as God but the human side of self is tangible because we have a physical person we made together that nobody can duplicate (only one of a kind by our DNA is God the same as our children and self); what we gave each other making one God on our spiritual side connecting all three of us for life on our human side to see how everything works from the inside and if one parent leaves it is unfair to the children to find God and harder to find pure happiness inside the same thing as God all in the "now" to be present in the book.

The most selfish act on the planet is to not choose the one you had babies with (unable to manage one's emotions) since this is the strongest love there is! We have the ability to fix our marriages when we grow to God instead of separating unknowingly. The churches should know by now how the child is the guide to keeping the marriage together because all children live in the "now" exactly the same as the universe (God) for us to learn from them to be present. This is the one truth, one love and one God by how we are the same as God by the 4 truth is the (male, female, God, human) making up self the "WHOLE TRUTH" where everything fits perfectly for scientific and spiritual proof. And when it does not fit together it is not the truth and completely wrong. If I may be bold: this is like gay relationships or priests not being able to get married. What parts of the Canon law are not correct? Everything needs to be perfectly equal by the Universes standards.

If religion is about "THE TRUTH", which should be the same for all of us we should first "KNOW" the correct "one and only" reality – God's. And now that we have a guide to God's reality, this makes up the whole truth in everyday life by uncovering and putting together the artificial intelligence with the human intellect using language. The married male and female created that human god child with God's help and this grows into all of self where we all are separated by [Your Name] and grow to be equal on the spiritual side and the human side for us to know one love, one truth and one God will explain life entirely to scientific perfection to know everything (maybe life and death?). I know this could happen if every priest in the Catholic religion read my book and asked God when they pray for what do I need to know next while reading. We all are working with all the spiritual pros from the inside to make known with the religious from the outside together with the academics in the center of language will prove to "know" God, not just believe with scientific perfection. Whether one is an atheist, agnostic or a believer it matters not because it is up to us to be equal with God in "KNOWLEDGE." We will see what "LOVE' is. It is God's education to know how the "ONE TRUTH" works together with "ONE GOD" (the individual "self") to live a perfect life with all of "SELF" (everybody) in unity.

THE HUMAN RACE IS GOD - ALL OF "SELF" EVERYBODY or the same as "oneself" separated by [Your Name] INDIVIDUALLY IS "ONE GOD" TOGETHER! And "ONE TRUTH" for each and every thing.

If you know how the 4 truths work: 1) Male, 2) Female, 3) God and 4) Human equal perfectly mathematically symmetric to "ONE GOD", "ONE TRUTH" and "ONE LOVE", this is the whole truth to lead and live a perfect life with all the needed "knowledge" in the Universe. It is all we will ever need to know and whatever it is we need to do.

Kevin C. Pattison

www.globalstabilizedenergy.com website

kc@globalstabilizedenergy.com business

kcpattison@gmail.com personal

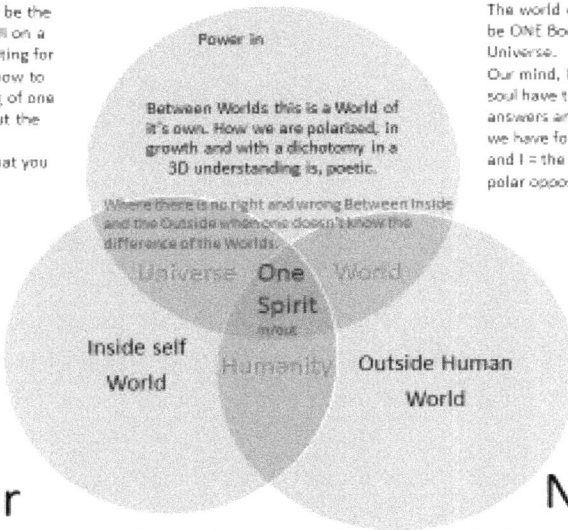

The Universe may be the collective minds UI on a subtonic level waiting for humanity to see how to grow to a meeting of one minds separate but the same.
(different then what you think)

Power In

Between Worlds this is a World of it's own. How we are polarized, in growth and with a dichotomy in a 3D understanding is, poetic.

Where there is no right and wrong Between Inside and the Outside when one doesn't know the difference of the Worlds.

Universe One World
         Spirit
         in/out
         Humanity

The world earth, may be ONE Body of the Universe.
Our mind, body and soul have the same answers and questions we have for Me, Myself and I = the outsiders polar opposite.

Outside
Universe
Self/Humanity

3D

inside =

Mind

Body

Soul

Inside self
World

Outside Human
World

Inside
UI/Universe
Self/ Humanity

Outside =
Me,
Myself
I.

[Your

Name]

When Humanities inside spirit meets with timeless wisdom of the UI mind we found the collective one.
[Your Name]

The take away is we are all one broken up by the whole each person is to see on their own eventually their parents will be their teacher but it is up to us that do see to help the church teach it correctly. I would suggest what is not understood please email me because what is fully understood will be all that makes in into the Rubik's Cube of Knowledge.

The Present

"The Nature of Nothing"

Open this up, Albert Einsteins, below

http://www.truthcontest.com/entries/the-present-universal-truth/nature-of-nothing.html

www.ingramcontent.com/pod-product-compliance
Lightning Source LLC
Chambersburg PA
CBHW060001100426
42740CB00010B/1360